Citizen X

Citizen X

Becoming Undocumented Activists on Both Sides of the Atlantic

THOMAS SWERTS

OXFORD
UNIVERSITY PRESS

OXFORD
UNIVERSITY PRESS

Oxford University Press is a department of the University of Oxford.
It furthers the University's objective of excellence in research, scholarship,
and education by publishing worldwide. Oxford is a registered trade mark of
Oxford University Press in the UK and in certain other countries.

Published in the United States of America by Oxford University Press
198 Madison Avenue, New York, NY 10016, United States of America.

© Thomas Swerts 2026

Library of Congress Cataloging-in-Publication Data

ISBN 9780197844007

ISBN 9780197843994 (hbk.)

DOI: 10.1093/9780197844038.001.0001

Paperback printed by Integrated Books International, United States of America

The manufacturer's authorized representative in the EU for product safety is
Oxford University Press España S.A. of Parque Empresarial San Fernando de Henares,
Avenida de Castilla, 2 – 28830 Madrid (www.oup.es/en or product.safety@oup.com).
OUP España S.A. also acts as importer into Spain of products made by the manufacturer.

Acknowledgments

This book has been many years in the making. The first kernel of an idea for the project developed in graduate school when I was still being immersed in the world of ethnography in the best of American sociological traditions. Enthused by the work of my father-in-law, Erik Swyngedouw, I became fascinated by theoretical work of European philosophers on "the political." Yet I was frustrated by the apparent untranslatability of these theories into empirical sociological research. The exposure to American ethnographies and European theories inspired me to undertake this study of undocumented activism. Taking my cue from Loïc Wacquant's work on urban outcasts, I was convinced this project needed to be a transatlantic ethnography.

From the very first class I took on American soil to the many hours we spent discussing my project, Andreas Glaeser supported me through thick and thin. I relied on Mario Small's insightful and critical advice to make sure the research design and methods were sound. Marco Martiniello represented the voice of European academia to me, questioning things I took for granted and unraveling Belgian migration politics. Lastly, Roberto Gonzales encouraged me to reflect on the ethical aspects of my research and its impact on undocumented communities.

I would like to thank Nancy Foner and Christophe Bertossi for facilitating the transatlantic discussions that served as an inspiration for this book. In addition, I was inspired by the rich discussions I had with leading scholars in the field including Walter Nicholls, Jonathan Darling, and Sébastien Chauvin. At the University of Antwerp, I want to thank Stijn Oosterlynck for allowing me to work on the book as a postdoctoral researcher. At Erasmus University Rotterdam, I want to thank Godfried Engbersen and Peter Scholten for continuing to believe in me throughout the years. I would also like to thank fellow graduate students at the University of Chicago, with special thanks to Jan Doering and Gordon Douglas for sharing tips on how to publish a first book. In addition, I am grateful to former and current colleagues at the University of Liège, the University of Leuven, the University of Antwerp, and Erasmus University Rotterdam as well as to the organizers of the Migration Seminar at UNU-MERI for commenting on earlier versions of the manuscript.

This research would not have been possible without the financial support of the National Science Foundation (Doctoral Dissertation Improvement Grant

#1129651), the Social Science Research Council, the Mellon Foundation, the University of Chicago Human Rights Program, and the University of Chicago Social Sciences Division, as well as the help of research assistants Jonathan Rodrigues and Iliya Gutin and copyeditors Richard Bowles and Anne Lee.

At Oxford University Press, I would like to thank James Cook and Javier Auyero for believing in this book project from the start, supporting me throughout the process and offering the perfect venue for the book in the Global and Comparative Ethnography series. I am also indebted to the anonymous reviewers for their constructive criticism and valuable suggestions. Finally, I am deeply grateful to artist Ninon Mazeaud for agreeing to adapt an existing artwork that emerged from, and was shaped by, the struggle of undocumented activists for the book cover.

As an ethnographer, a lot of the knowledge you think you have quickly fades into the background when you enter the field. Once there, I learned that navigating that field was, above all, a humbling exercise in listening, being patient, and knowing when to speak and when not to speak. I got to know many undocumented activists during my time in Chicago and Brussels. I owe them my sincere gratitude for trusting me as a researcher and for allowing me to—temporarily—be a part of their community. I sincerely hope that the way I portray their struggles over citizenship in this book does them justice.

Many years of contemplation, exhilaration, and frustration lie between the world of conducting ethnography and the world of the written word. In this respect, I would like to thank my family and friends for their unabated support. However, above all, I would like to thank Eva Swyngedouw for her endless patience with me during the writing process, her invaluable advice as a fellow sociologist, and her love and unconditional support as a partner.

In line with the ethical requirements stipulated by the IRB, informed consent was secured from all respondents, and all real names were replaced with pseudonyms.

Contents

Preface

Consider for a moment what your life would be like if you became undocumented. From one day to the next, your life changes drastically. While you still possess the same traits, skills, and competences that characterize you as a human being, not having papers renders your human capital virtually useless. From the viewpoint of the state, you transform from a recognized into an unrecognized resident; an anonymous "citizen X," stripped of legal identity. As a result, you are barred from the rights and privileges you used to enjoy as a citizen. Not only are you deprived of exercising basic human rights, such as the right to work, residence, education, and access to healthcare, but even your very presence on the state's territory—and thereby, your very existence—is deemed "illegal." Whereas the state used to guarantee your rights as a citizen, you now come to fear its power to arrest, detain, and deport you against your will. Branded as a noncitizen, your formal options to hold politicians and state officials accountable are severely limited, if not nonexistent. The same papers that once ensured your institutional visibility now render you invisible; deprived of the opportunity to voice your concerns without risking repercussions.

Imagining life as an undocumented person is not easy for people who have never had to do anything other than be born in the right place at the right time to be considered a citizen. This thought experiment forces citizens, as the undocumented activists I got to know put it, to "check their privilege." In this book, I invite readers to do the same. Doing so will help you to critically question the criminalizing, illegalizing, and dehumanizing discourses on irregular migration that we have grown accustomed to from politicians, political commentators, and much of the media. It will simultaneously reveal that the citizenship many of us take for granted is a flimsy construction, a seemingly stable house of cards that collapses once a single card at the base, named *legal status*, is taken away. This insight is a prerequisite for understanding what it means to become an undocumented activist. The following life stories, which recount the diverging fates of two young men on opposite sides of the Atlantic who do not seem to have much in common except their entanglement with the traffic code of conduct, serve as a case in point.

***

First, consider the case of Fariss.[1] Fariss was a Moroccan citizen in his late twenties when he migrated to Europe. There was nothing left for him to lose back home, only everything left to gain. To the detriment of his parents, his younger sister had tragically been killed in an accident. A few years later, Fariss's father committed suicide. Meanwhile, his brother had built a life as a Belgian citizen in the city of Brussels. When his mother developed a serious form of diabetes, Fariss took care of her as best he could, administering daily insulin injections and taking her to hospitals around Casablanca. However, health insurance was lacking, and his mother became stressed and tired due to the haunting memories of her family's suffering. One day, she decided to leave those memories behind and join her son in Belgium. The procedure for family reunification provided her with the legal tools to do so. Once there, Fariss's brother had a hard time combining work and caring for his mother. For Fariss, who no longer had any family members back in Morocco, it seemed logical to join them. Fariss had not really thought about his legal status when he came to Belgium and figured he would get it sorted out later. As he had done back home, he devoted his time to taking his mother to the hospital, translating during doctor's appointments, and making sure she had everything she needed. The shock he experienced when learning that it was impossible to obtain legal status while already residing in Brussels was tremendous. Optimistic about his odds, he lodged an application for regularization. After months of waiting, his application was rejected and Fariss received an order to leave the territory. At this point, going back was no longer an option, because the legal avenues to rejoin his family would be restricted due to his prior infringement. Although staying enabled him to be with his family, the price to pay was a life in the shadows. Effectively stuck in limbo, Fariss decided to stay put in Brussels and look for ways to contest his legal status. A fellow *sans-papiers* told him about the Collectif des Sans-Papiers Belgique (here, SPBelgique), a collective led by undocumented migrants that fought for regularization. He became a member soon after.

I first met Fariss at the Anchor, a local service center in the working-class Quays neighborhood in Brussels. The Anchor is located just around the corner from the Church of Saint John the Baptist, a seventeenth-century Baroque building that had become a symbolic landmark for the struggle of the sans-papiers in Belgium during multiple occupations in the 1990s. The idea to establish a service center for isolated elderly in the city had sprouted from the mind of the church's head priest, Daniel Alliët. However, the social workers in charge soon found other urban poor, including the homeless and the undocumented, knocking at their door. People from a variety of backgrounds who shared hardly anything but their deprivation would typically meet and exchange a word or two around a hot drink or a shared meal. The décor for these encounters was a sparsely decorated room with a handful of tables, a small stage with theater curtains, a corner with old computers, a closet with donated puzzles and board games, and a kitchen. Once a week after hours, when other regulars had left, the tables and chairs were rearranged into a large circle to accommodate the meetings of SPBelgique.

Depending on the week, anywhere from five to fifty sans-papiers would show up to catch up on circulating rumors about regularization, exchange information about pending demands, and plan actions.

That Thursday, about thirty people had gathered to discuss a recent attempt to gain support from labor unions for the cause of the sans-papiers. Many of the members of SPBelgique were workers who had introduced a demand for regularization based on a labor contract. Fariss was reporting back from the meeting with the unionists. "We have stressed that many of us pay our monthly contributions, but that they are currently not doing anything for the sans-papiers," he explained. During the coffee break, I introduced myself to him. He struck me as an open, sociable guy who seemed up for a laugh and who appeared committed to the cause. Even though he sometimes struggled to clearly express his thoughts during the meetings, you could bet on his presence at demonstrations. We talked about his life in Brussels and how he enjoyed going to the Belgian coast because it reminded him of home. "Did you stay in a hotel at the boardwalk?" I asked. "No," he laughed. "I slept in my car for three nights." He said, "Back in Morocco, it used to be better; I had a cabin, and I often went fishing."

Months after this initial encounter, I got to know Fariss even better, protesting side by side in the European march of the sans-papiers in Strasbourg. The participation of Belgian sans-papiers in the protest abroad was an unprecedented undertaking. A group of allied lawyers was on standby in case things went wrong. A van and a limited budget had been provided by supporters. Three participants who had completed the 1,000-mile marching route had to be brought back to Belgium. This meant that there were three empty seats in the van. The fastest way to cover the roughly 300 miles between Brussels and Strasbourg was to take highways E25 and A4. Fariss had his doubts about this route, since it meant we would have to cross the Luxembourg *and* French borders. However, the others were convinced we should be fine, given the lack of border controls in the Schengen zone. On the day of our departure, everyone was feeling nervous. Abas and Anouar were busy copying lists of contacts to reach in case of emergency when I arrived at the Anchor. They decided that no one should have any documents on them that could possibly ID them in case of arrest. Anouar trusted me to keep his papers safe for the duration of the trip. After a two-hour drive, we approached the first border. Forty minutes later we crossed the second border, not far from the town of Schengen. When we finally arrived in Strasbourg, Fariss told me that this had been a deeply emotional experience for him. Two days later, he urged me to join a circle dance in front of the European Parliament building while a delegation of marchers was meeting with politicians inside. "It is good that you danced with us, but you suck at keeping the rhythm," he joked. In the evening, Fariss asked me why I kept attending SPBelgique's meetings. "We do not know what you think, because you do not say much during the meetings," he said. I told him that I was trying to understand what it is like to be an undocumented activist. "So you are the one who is going to integrate yourself among the sans-papiers?" he asked. "Start by sleeping on cardboard boxes in the Brussels North Station!" Redouan joked, and we all laughed.

A couple of months later, I received a text message informing me of an emergency meeting at the Anchor. When I arrived, everyone was in a state of alarm. Fariss had been arrested during a routine check because he had not been wearing a seat belt in the back of his brother's car. After they paid the fine, he was unable to present an ID. Having spent a night in jail, he was transferred to the Immigration Office's Center for Illegals at Merksplas. Together with supporters and family, SPBelgique set up a campaign called "We are all Fariss" to halt his deportation. Meanwhile, I offered to translate all campaign communications from French to Dutch to maximize outreach.

The campaign was launched the following day. His mother made an emotional call in Arabic on social media platforms to let him stay with her. The first attempt to deport him failed when activists convinced the pilot that deporting him would pose a security threat for the rest of the passengers. Fariss then started a hunger strike from within the detention center. Two weeks later, SPBelgique organized a protest right outside the Immigration Office to demand his release. Activists waved big banners that read "Release Fariss," "We are all Fariss," and "Freedom for Fariss now" while they shouted chants and songs we had picked up at the European march. I approached Zouheir, who had spoken to Fariss earlier. "It is tough for him to hold on right now after the first attempt, because they are physically and mentally intimidating him in the detention center," he told me. Citizen *soutien* (ally) Nathalie had tears in her eyes when she recounted that "Fariss always managed to keep on smiling no matter what." His elderly mother looked visibly distraught at the site of the protest. She briefly thanked everyone who had gathered in support for her son but had to cut her speech short to fight back her tears. Then Anouar took the megaphone to announce that he would join in with Fariss's hunger strike in solidarity for twenty-four hours. In preparation for the protest, we had drafted a joint letter addressed to the authorities, underlining the injustice of his pending deportation. Letters of support were also being written to Fariss, reassuring him that people would be present at the planned action in Brussels to halt his deportation.

As it turned out, his supporters would be unable to keep their promise. The authorities swiftly responded to the demonstrations by rescheduling the flight, advancing it by nine days. The day before his scheduled deportation, Fariss called to say that doctors and social workers were pressuring him to stop resisting. He told his friends and family that he was physically and mentally drained and that he did not have the strength to resist any longer. His mother told him that the time had come to accept defeat. "But the fight will go on," he insisted to his friends, supporters, and family. Fariss was eventually deported to Morocco.

***

Now consider the case of Reyes. Reyes migrated with his parents from the state of Jalisco, Mexico, when he was six years old. In the small village where he grew up, everyone knew each other, and he could stay out late with friends. Being an agricultural state, the local farmers had to compete with American counterparts because NAFTA caused havoc in the region. Reyes's parents lost their jobs and could no longer afford to keep their farm. His grandparents had worked in the United States as seasonal laborers under the Brasero program, and his father had been joining them since the early 1980s, going back and forth. It was not until stricter border enforcement was put in place that his parents realized this was no longer safe, so they made the decision that it would be best to move to the United States. Reyes arrived in Chicago in the summer of 1994. His family settled in a disadvantaged neighborhood in the North Side. Suddenly, Reyes could no longer play outside unaccompanied or stay out late like he used to. Fear became quietly instilled into his everyday routines. His parents would tell him to be careful about who he talked to, and his cousins were the principal kids he was allowed to interact with. Meanwhile, Reyes and his sister were left to fend for themselves, as both of his parents were forced to take up full-time jobs to get by. When he first went to school in Chicago, he struggled to learn the language. He felt miserable and became a quiet kid in class. However, he established close relationships with his teachers and got good grades. School would become a place of sanctuary for Reyes, where he was not being judged for his lack of a green card but merely for his academic merit. Because of his high grades, he was able to attend a charter high school, where he became an honor roll student and student ambassador.

In his sophomore year of high school, Reyes was first confronted with what it means to be undocumented. Like all his classmates, he had been taking driver's education classes, but unlike his peers, he was not able to get a driver's license. When he applied for college, he was accepted by his school of choice right away. However, when the question of financial aid came around, his counselor told him that he would not be able to go there because it was too expensive. Instead, the counselor gave him a short list of scholarships that did not require a social security number. Reyes felt as though he had hit a wall. Everything he had worked for up to then seemed like a lie. He tried to start college without financial aid but had to work full time to be able to afford tuition. He therefore transitioned to community college, where his professors introduced him to Latino studies. Despite the setbacks, Reyes was the first in his family to get a college degree. At college, he started to realize that he wanted to get involved in the immigrant rights movement. His sister had been actively involved in campaigns around the DREAM Act since 2001. Along with many other undocumented youth, he joined the march for immigrant rights in 2006 and participated in some preparatory meetings. Yet he did not feel as though there was a place in the movement for him as a student.

One day, at twenty-one years old, Reyes was driving home after watching a football game with his friends. They had a couple of beers. On his way home, he ignored a stop sign and was pulled over by the police. When they noticed he had been drinking, they asked for his ID. Since he was not able to present a valid identity card, the police took him into custody. Soon Reyes's DUI conviction would be the least of his worries, as they discovered his legal status. While he pleaded guilty to a misdemeanor, Reyes was taken to the county jail to await his pending deportation. Eventually, he received the news that his deportation had been scheduled. Reyes decided to do everything he could to resist it. Friends, family, community organizers, students, church leaders, and politicians gathered in the "Campaign to Save Reyes." Thousands of faxes and letters were sent to the offices of the Department of Homeland Security, US senators, and members of Congress. In the end, the fight for Reyes was no longer just about him but was about the thousands of undocumented youths like him. The Democrat representative from Illinois, Jan Schakowsky, decided to introduce a private bill that would allow Reyes to stay. At the same time, the Chicago City Council passed a resolution that halted his deportation for one year. The public reaction to his deferred deportation was mixed. Representative Schakowsky's statement channeled the response from supporters: "I am thrilled that we won our fight to keep him home. Unfortunately, Reyes's saga illustrates the plight of so many like him who love this country, consider themselves Americans in every way, yet are forced to live in the shadows.... Reyes's ordeal underscores the need to fix the broken immigration system in a comprehensive way."[2] At the other end of the spectrum, Dave Gorak, director of the Midwest Coalition to Reduce Immigration, stated: "It's your basic run-of-the-mill political pandering and it sends a very bad message to others who have no respect for our laws."[3] In the press, Reyes stated:

> Eleven months ago I was told I had no chance to remain here, but I worked very hard and I knew it was unjust and unfair. So I decided to fight to stay in Chicago, because this is my home. I was determined not to give up.... This whole struggle was worth the fight, and I have learned so much about activism and how to create unity in a movement for change and social justice.

The campaign to save Reyes provided the impetus for fellow undocumented youth in Chicago to gather and share their stories. It was during these "shout-it-out meetings" that they realized the need to create a space where they could represent themselves. Not long after that, the Immigrant Youth Justice League (henceforth IYJL) saw the light of day.

****

First, a disclaimer: this book neither claims to explain why certain undocumented activists are more "successful" than others, nor does it suggest that the plight of the sans-papiers is necessarily the same as that experienced by undocumented youth on the other side of the Atlantic. The transatlantic comparison that informs this book reveals contextual differences between the United States and Belgium that led the individual biographies of activists like Fariss and Reyes to diverge in meaningful ways. While Fariss's migration journey resonates with that of many adult men who flee from North Africa in pursuit of a better life, Reyes's journey exemplifies the journey that countless children undertook together with their parents and siblings from Mexico. The exclusion and isolation Fariss experienced when arriving in Brussels stands in contrast with Reyes's educational inclusion and community membership in Chicago. The self-organizations that Fariss and Reyes frequented also differed, since SPBelgique mainly attracted an all-male public of people with a North African background, while IYJL attracted a more mixed public of undocumented youth with a Latin American background. At the national level, the shadow cast by previous regularization campaigns served as a focal point for political action for sans-papiers like Farriss, while the promise of the DREAM Act propelled youth like Reyes into action. When progress for their cause at the national level came to a halt, activists like Fariss tried to further their cause by appealing to EU elected representatives, while activists like Reyes campaigned for incremental changes at the Illinois state level.

Pointing out dissimilarities across societal contexts, immigrant communities and mobilization strategies can be done quite comfortably when observing undocumented activism from afar. However, by carefully comparing the stories of undocumented migrants like Fariss and Reyes side by side, I discovered remarkable *similarities in how undocumented migrants become activists on both sides of the Atlantic.* Thus, the transatlantic ethnographic approach adopted in this book provided a unique lens to better explore the tensions between the precarity that characterizes undocumented life and the activism that aims to reverse its condition. On the one hand, I encountered *stories of precarity*; of homelessness, physical violence, stigmatization, mental illness, forced evictions, people struggling with suicidal thoughts, families being torn apart, racism, abuse by the police, exploitation on the work floor, people being detained and deported against their will, and even public servants taking bribes. On the other hand, I encountered *stories of agency*; of people who resist, who say "enough is enough," who decide to take their life into their own hands, organize themselves collectively, call for solidarity, write letters, stage acts of civil disobedience, demand meetings with policymakers, and put their life on the line to claim their rights. This book introduces a perspective on undocumented activism centered around what I call "precarious agency." This perspective acknowledges that undocumented migrants are creative, resourceful, powerful, and highly visible in the public sphere, yet at the same time they are vulnerable, marginalized, and relatively "invisible." It demonstrates their capacity to collectively contest their illegality, but it also reveals the precariousness of this capacity considering the state's power to strike back. Precarious agency is the running thread throughout this book and connects the trajectories of undocumented activists that unfold themselves more than 4,000 miles apart.

Despite this geographical distance, I studied undocumented activism in Chicago and Brussels *up close and from below*. In order to turn "Citizen X" into a sociological subject of flesh and blood, I had to "dive into the stream of action to the greatest possible depth, rather than watch it from the bank" and "swim along with method and purpose" as Wacquant (2015, 5) has put it. For four years, I immersed myself in the world of the undocumented in Europe and the United States by respectively becoming a "soutien" at SPBelgique and "ally" at IYJL. As a white cis male with a Belgian passport and an American student visa, I entered the field as a privileged researcher. Throughout the years, I learned how to "unlearn" and "check" my privilege by exercising humility and empathy, responding to community needs and putting my access to resources and networks to use for the benefit of both organizations.[4] I gained firsthand experience of some of the challenges that undocumented activists face on both sides of the Atlantic by participating in marches, eating meals together, chanting at rallies, sleeping in gym halls, organizing events, visiting squats, negotiating with the police, and debating about political strategies.

Doing participant observation among undocumented activists comes with great responsibility. In recent years, important undocumented scholarship has emerged that questions the "extractive" knowledge production that characterizes many studies of "the poor, the marginalized, the indigenous, the powerless" (Bejarano et al. 2019, 7) and, by extension, the undocumented. This scholarship makes a passionate plea to decolonize ethnographic research on undocumented communities, which at its worst treats "the lives and experiences of its objects serving as raw materials to fuel the academic engine" (Bejarano et al. 2019, 11). I agree with the argument that academic knowledge production on undocumented communities should be critically scrutinized and ethically justified. Hence, this book develops a methodological and ethical approach that contributes to renegotiating power differentials between privileged citizen researchers and underprivileged undocumented respondents. This implies a constant effort to critically question privileged epistemologies, positionalities, and representations. It also requires a conscious attempt to treat undocumented migrants as research "subjects" rather than "objects" who should have a say in how their stories are represented in ethnographic research (Abrego and Negrón-Gonzales 2020, 12). Finally, it demands ethnographers to intervene into the public debate and reciprocate with undocumented communities by "using their skills to support the advocacy work that they document" (Bejarano et al. 2019, 8). In the Appendix, I elaborate further on the methodological and ethical considerations informing this book.

The book makes three central claims. First, undocumented migrants do not become activists overnight. Living life in irregularity ingrains feelings of fear, shame, and frustration into undocumented people's minds that form obstacles to activism. Existing scholarship that takes the capacity of undocumented activists to act politically as its analytical starting point, bites its own tail. Likewise, structuralist accounts of undocumented activism reduce its emergence to the availability of political opportunities while downplaying immigrant agency. What is needed, then, to better grasp how undocumented migrants overcome the obstacles in the process of becoming activists, is a *sociological take on political subject formation*. The hermeneutic perspective introduced in this book acknowledges that a substantial amount of work needs to be accomplished at the level of immigrants' self-understandings before they can step out of the shadows. It shows that the roots of undocumented activists' precarious agency can be traced back to the vulnerabilities they have lived through before venturing into politics. Undocumented migrants are not passive victims of the "broken immigration system" but embody the core of this system in the most intimate of ways. In their everyday life, undocumented migrants are forced to face the ugly and violent other side of institutions that are generally portrayed as warm and fuzzy, such as citizenship and democracy. This lived reality is rarely acknowledged, let alone experienced by others who benefit from the privileges that citizenship bestows on them. Representing and exposing this reality is therefore a crucial task for which the undocumented are uniquely qualified. Undocumented activism then entails the collective search for an effective and truthful form of political expression that can communicate the plight of Citizen X's alternate reality to the rest of the world.

Second, self-organizations led by and for the undocumented are the privileged sites where undocumented migrants gain precarious agency by collectively turning their vulnerabilities into strengths. This insight contrasts with existing literature that considers all civil society organizations to be "schools" where undocumented migrants can "learn" the rules of the political game. Instead, this book contends that autonomy and self-representation are crucial organizational determinants for nurturing precarious agency. By coming together and bundling their strength, self-organizations function as "activist infrastructures," where undocumented people foster feelings of belonging and community that enable them to collectively speak out in a hostile environment. Denied legal status and the rights and privileges that come with it, noncitizens like the undocumented have to create space for citizenship. The relatively protected environments of "safe spaces" and "solidarity spaces," create opportunities for political recruitment, training, and mobilization of undocumented peers. Creating and maintaining such spaces requires activists to actively claim their autonomy and the right to speak for themselves vis-à-vis other actors. Struggles over representation therefore tend to revolve around the gap between the lived reality of underprivileged subjects and the visions and strategies proposed by privileged subjects. Undocumented activists creatively borrow elements from readily available scripts that dictate how to express themselves in public in their societies of residence, and rewrite these scripts by infusing them with their stories, emotions, and embodied experiences. In the process, they invent new ways to make their voices heard and claim equality in their societies of residence.

On a broader scale, the rise of undocumented activism on both sides of the Atlantic is transforming the meaning of citizenship. The struggle over immigrant rights is a symbol of our time. It is the canary in the coal mine that indicates the current state of core institutions such as democracy and citizenship. Undocumented migrants represent but one historical reincarnation of the figure of the noncitizen—human beings nation-states refuse to recognize as rightfully present within the confines of their bordered territories. The refusal to see and treat human beings as rights-bearing subjects is not an anomaly of an otherwise well-functioning system, but an integral part of the policies Western states have designed to cope with global migration. The liberal values of freedom of speech, mobility, and human rights thereby become a privilege reserved for those who have the proper stamps in their passport. This is a global evolution that connects the undocumented immigrant communities and movement trajectories presented in this book. Despite the differences across societal contexts, the activism of undocumented migrants in North America and Europe exposes the fundamental inequalities and social injustices that result from unevenly distributing citizenship in the world. Regardless of the diverging strategies that undocumented activists deploy, they are all engaged in the search to effectively reveal the gap between undocumented persons' de jure exclusion and their de facto inclusion. Their stories, collective practices, and public performances envision and prefigure a more equal society in which people cross borders rather than being restrained by them, in which democracy means listening to rather than silencing what people have to say, and in which citizenship is no longer a privilege of the few but a right of the many. The face and nature of the struggles for immigrant rights and the people who take the lead in the struggles is ever-changing. But through their enduring actions, undocumented activists around the world continue to give renewed meaning to citizenship from the ground up.

Introduction

Shadow people

Studying undocumented activism is more necessary than ever before. Irregular migration has become a contested issue around the globe. We live in a world in which more than a billion people are migrants.[1] Over 281 million people are international migrants who reside in a country that is not their country of birth, and a record-breaking 103 million people are recognized as forcibly displaced.[2] This represents the highest number of people on the run from persecution, conflict, violence, or human rights violations since the Second World War. The stories of boat refugees who wash up on the Mediterranean shores or families that get caught trying to cross the US-Mexican border can no longer be considered anomalies. Since 2014, more than four thousand people lost their lives at the US-Mexican border and more than twenty-five thousand died while trying to cross the Mediterranean.[3] American and European governments have responded to the migration "crisis" by sending out a populist message of deterrence to future migration candidates. President of the European Council at the time, Donald Tusk, directly addressed them as follows: "I want to appeal to all potential illegal economic migrants wherever you are from: Do not come to Europe. Do not believe the smugglers. Do not risk your lives and your money. It is all for nothing."[4] US President Donald Trump issued similar warnings to undocumented migrants: "We catch them, oh go ahead. Under my administration, anyone who illegally crosses the border will be detained until they are removed out of our country and back to the country from which they came."[5] The tough talk on irregular migration has been accompanied by policy measures aimed at reinforcing border controls, ramping up deportation rates, and curtailing immigrants' rights.

The global undocumented community affected by such dehumanizing discourses and criminalizing policies is substantial. Between thirty and forty million migrants worldwide are considered to be "illegal aliens."[6] As a result of repressive measures, a growing number of people find themselves on the wrong side of the criteria set out by government agencies to authorize their stay. The criteria for (il)legality vary dramatically between places, governments, and time (Ngai 2004). Undocumented status should thus be regarded as a political construction that states rely on to render illegal the presence of unwanted

Citizen X. Thomas Swerts, Oxford University Press. © Thomas Swerts (2026).
DOI: 10.1093/9780197844038.003.0001

populations on their territory. The rules and regulations in North America and Europe at the time of writing have generated an estimated undocumented population of about 11.3 million people in the United States and between 1.9 and 3.8 million in Europe.[7] These shadow populations are often integrated into the informal economy, neighborhood networks, and local schools, but largely excluded from the rights and privileges associated with citizenship. Regardless of their incorporation into the social, cultural, and economic life of their society of residence, their very presence on state territory is criminalized. The constant threat of deportation looms large for these people. The fact that this threat is real is evidenced by the 3.7 million deportations that were carried out between 2003 and 2013 in the United States,[8] and the more than 3.2 million deportations between 2000 and 2014 in the European Union.[9]

Despite this hostile environment, undocumented immigrants have increasingly stepped out of the shadows and organized themselves around the globe to claim their rights. This book traces the process through which undocumented immigrants become political activists. I define *undocumented activism* as the sustained and collective efforts of people who are in a precarious legal position to organize themselves and mobilize support to claim their rights, make their grievances heard, and strive to change their predicament and that of others like them. In the United States, undocumented youth activists, better known as the *DREAMers*, gave a face to the immigrant rights issue by openly declaring their status and sharing their stories (Nicholls 2013). In Western Europe, the sans-papiers gained visibility by occupying churches and engaging in hunger strikes (Siméant 1998). These mobilizations have evoked state responses ranging from local sanctuary policies (for example, in Chicago, LA, and New York) and temporary relief measures (such as the Deferred Action for Childhood Arrivals in the United States) to changes in state-level legislation (for example, the California and Illinois Dream Acts) and large-scale regularizations (such as those in Belgium, France, and Germany). On opposite sides of the Atlantic, noncitizens have thus come knocking on citizenship's door.

The emergence of undocumented activism has challenged sociologists' conceptual toolkits. In migration studies, undocumented immigrants have been regularly portrayed as vulnerable "victims," lacking the necessary social and symbolic capital to participate in political life (Martiniello 2006). Moreover, assimilation and incorporation theories presuppose a willingness on the part of host societies to welcome migrants and assign them a legal status that is virtually absent in the case of the undocumented (Alba and Nee 2003). Cultural sociologists who stress the constraining effects of ideologies and discourses leave little room to maneuver for subjects on the receiving end of uneven power relations (Bourdieu 1998). Social movement theory's focus on the presence of political opportunities and the availability of resources can barely explain how marginalized actors who are illegalized by state authorities can become activists (McAdam et al. 1996; McCarthy and Zald 1977). Lastly, the implicit assumption that the terrain of citizenship is reserved for people who possess legal status has blindsided citizenship scholars for a long time (Bosniak 2006).

In this book, I align with scholars from various disciplinary backgrounds who have tried to move the figure of the undocumented from the periphery to the center of sociological attention in recent years (Bejarano et al. 2019; Abrego and Negrón-Gonzales 2020; Martinez et al. 2020). Key to these attempts is the need to center the experiential knowledge of undocumented migrants themselves. As Abrego and Negrón-Gonzales contend, "the lived experiences of being undocumented inevitably make visible particular kinds of understandings that should be centered in the field" (Abrego and Negrón-Gonzales 2020, 8). Making visible such lived experiences is thus necessary to gain a better understanding of how undocumented immigrants are able take political action despite their precarious legal status. In the appendix, I explain the ethical and political imperatives that come with collecting and representing underprivileged respondents' stories as a privileged researcher.

A transatlantic lens

The local emergence of undocumented activism is a global phenomenon. Hence, sociological research that is confined to within the methodological safe haven of national boundaries is insufficient. In order to avoid falling into the trap of reifying national or local manifestations of this phenomenon, I traced the perils and promises of undocumented activism on both sides of the Atlantic. Terms like "Atlantic" and "transatlantic" immediately evoke the histories of migration between continents. Transatlantic migration from Europe to North America was a defining moment in global migration history that contributed to the image of the United States as a nation of immigrants. The Atlantic also played a crucial role in the history of European colonialism and transatlantic slave trade that forced people from African descent to eventually become part of American society. "Citizen X" takes inspiration from these rich histories when advocating for the importance of adopting a transatlantic lens for two principal ways. On the one hand, these histories point out how states have used and continue to use violence and the law as twin instruments to strip people on the move from their rights and bar them from full citizenship. On the other hand, they show that despite state restrictions on migratory movement, people on the move with various backgrounds and migration motives find ways to circumvent and challenge restrictions to mobility. In this way, the transatlantic comparative approach adopted in this book illuminates how precarious legal status is politically constructed and contested across continents.

"Citizen X" builds on and contributes to scholarship that has made the case for transatlantic comparative research over the years. This literature points out that patterns of immigrant political participation can be accounted for by studying variations in citizenship regimes on both sides of the Atlantic (Hochschild and Mollenkopf 2009). More precisely, this literature points out that European citizenship regimes are historically more reluctant to see their societies as immigrant societies, whereas the American citizenship regime reflects a national immigrant imaginary. European nationhood therefore has ethnic connotations, while immigration is a nation-founding myth in the United States. As a result, several scholars argue that making the case for immigrant rights is more difficult in the former than the latter (Mollenkopf and Hochschild 2010). While "Citizen X" acknowledges the importance of such institutionalized understandings of citizenship to grasp how undocumented activism takes shape (see below), I argue that more attention needs to be paid to immigrants' agency and their capacity to talk back. Furthermore, taking citizenship regimes as an analytical lens for transatlantic comparison risks reifying the political processes whereby noncitizens are illegalized and overlooks the strategic role that cities play as political arenas for undocumented activism.

This insight puts forward the issue of scale in doing transatlantic comparative research. This book does not consider scale to be "out there," but rather adheres to the argument advanced by Neil Smith that scales are socially constructed and contested (Smith 1984). The local, national, and global scale can be considered part of the same globalized world wherein mobility flows are regulated unevenly. For a long time, the hierarchical domination of the national scale was assumed when it came to irregular migration politics. Consequently, for many commentators the "natural" register to contest exclusionary migration politics appeared to be the national scale. However, the erosion and decentering of the power of the nation-state to get to grips with irregular migration flows undercuts this normalcy (Schinkel 2009). Transnational institutions like the European Commission or NAFTA have become crucial instruments in the hand of governments to prevent and control irregular migration (Castles et al. 2012). However, as I explain in Chapter 4, organizing across borders at the transnational scale is far from evident for undocumented migrants. At the same time, cities have regained tremendously in importance as places where undocumented migrants are both policed and politicized (Uitermark and Nicholls 2014). This book mainly focuses on the local scale since most of the organizing by undocumented migrants took place in cities. However, to paraphrase Smith, it is still important to consider the "nested" character of scales despite this emphasis on urban conditions (Smith 1984). Part I of the book demonstrates the necessity to consider the impact of policy developments at the national scale to situate how undocumented movements fare at the local scale. Furthermore, as the in-depth examination of the trajectories of undocumented activists in this part of the book demonstrates, local experiences of immobility can be directly related to experiences of international mobility. By integrating such a "nested perspective" into the analysis, I am thus able to trace how undocumented activists' capacity to contest exclusionary migration policies at the local scale is related to the national and global scales.

Shadow cities

Cities are the primary battlegrounds for undocumented activists' struggles over citizenship (Sassen 2005). The everyday lived reality of undocumented migrants is to a large extent an urban one. Undocumented migrants constitute just one part of what Wacquant (2008) called the "urban outcasts." In cities, undocumented migrants find housing, work, support networks, and civic organizations. Depending on their legal status, they are embedded in informal and formal activities that are part of urban life. The presence of large immigrant communities in cities provides welcome "camouflage" from state authorities (Chauvin and Garcés-Mascareñas 2014). Furthermore, cities offer activists places to meet like-minded people, get organized, and stage protests (Nicholls and Uitermark 2017). However, city governments also try to take local control over irregular migration by putting in place repressive policy measures (Varsanyi et al. 2010). As much as this book paints a picture of the lives of "unwanted subjects" who live, work, and protest among us, it simultaneously offers a glimpse of the shadow cities in which undocumented migrants are embedded (Engbersen 1996). I thereby situate myself in the largely forgotten ethnographic tradition pioneered by Nels Anderson at the margins of the emerging Chicago school (Anderson 1993). This tradition radically adopted the perspective of the outcast, the hobo, or in this case the unknown citizen, to learn more about social changes that manifest in the city. Instead of understanding the position of outcasts within the city as the result of ecological forces, however, I regard urban marginalization to be an outcome of political forces. In other words, undocumented residents do not find themselves at the bottom of the ladder because they have failed to commence their ascent but because the ladder's first rung is deliberately kept out of reach.

Chicago and Brussels are iconic cities with substantial undocumented populations. By the most recent calculations, the city of Chicago houses an estimated 183,000 undocumented residents, or roughly 7 percent of a total population of 2,704,985.[10] Suburban Chicago hosts an additional 307,000 undocumented residents, thereby amounting to more than half a million for the state of Illinois.

More than three-quarters of the Illinois undocumented population is of Mexican origin, and one in four is younger than twenty-four years old. Reliable estimates for the city of Brussels are even harder to come by. In Belgium, the last estimate of the total number of undocumented migrants was around 112,000 (Van Meeteren, Van San, and Engbersen 2007, 17), while the number of sans-papiers in the Brussels region has been estimated at around 52,000—about half of Belgium's undocumented population.[11] In effect, the sans-papiers population in the region, which comprises nineteen autonomous municipalities, has become better known as the "twentieth municipality" of Brussels. Although these numbers remain estimates, they are all we have to get a sense of the magnitude of these shadow cities.

Both cities have a rich history of local migration policies and immigrant rights organizing. The history of Chicago as an immigrant-friendly city dates back to the 1980s, when several places in the United States declared themselves to be "sanctuary cities." These cities vouched to protect undocumented immigrants against the federal government, including not allowing the police to make inquiries about immigration status and withholding funding for the enforcement of deportation policies. Over recent decades, Chicago mayors have expressed their symbolic support for the rights of undocumented residents. Mayor Washington took the initiative in 1985 to declare Chicago a sanctuary city with executive order 85-1, which stipulated that: "The policy of the Office of the Mayor is declared to encourage equal access by persons residing in the City of Chicago, *regardless of nationality or citizenship*, to the full benefits, opportunities and services, including employment and the issuance of licenses, which are provided or administered by the City of Chicago."[12] In response, the Illegal Immigration Reform and Immigrant Responsibility Act tried to curtail the local boycott of the Immigration and Customs Enforcement's (ICE) deportation efforts in 1996. Nevertheless, in 2006, Mayor Daley reinforced Chicago's status as a sanctuary city, with an amendment to the municipal code known as executive order 89-6. This stipulated that "no agent or agency shall request information about or otherwise investigate or assist in the investigation of the citizenship or residency status of any person unless such inquiry or investigation is required by statute, ordinance, federal regulation or court decision." Recent threats by the Trump administration to cut federal funding to sanctuary cities did not deter Mayor Rahm Emanuel from declaring that "the city was not going to move from a set of policies that reflect our values of being a welcoming city."[13]

Chicago is one of the leading cities not only in terms of institutional support for its undocumented residents but also in terms of undocumented activism. It is largely due to pressure from the well-organized Latinx community that local governments were so responsive to immigrant rights issues in the first place. "Mexican Chicago" is a city within a city, comprising a vast network of institutions that work around migration, such as schools, hometown associations, neighborhood councils, community centers, parishes, and labor unions (De Genova 2005). In line with the boom in the Mexican immigrant population since the 1970s, this organizational network expanded in depth and range throughout the city. The existing organizational infrastructure in Chicago in part accounts for the rise of the local immigrant rights movement and its culmination in the mega-marches of 2006, 2007, and 2008 (Pallares and Flores-González 2010). On May 1, 2006, between 400,000 and 750,000 people participated in a march for immigrant rights and against the Sensenbrenner Bill in Chicago. An estimated 26 percent of the marchers were undocumented; 51 percent were aged between fifteen and twenty-eight, and more than 75 percent were Latinx. The rich history and the activist infrastructures would turn out to be assets for the self-organization of undocumented youth in years to come.

Compared with Chicago, institutional support for undocumented residents is relatively limited in Brussels. For years, the approach to undocumented immigrants has been a de facto laissez-faire policy. This allowed sans-papiers activists to undertake political activity, such as occupying buildings, with the tacit approval of mayors in the nineteen different municipalities in the city. Such forms of informal support tended to take place behind closed doors rather than in public view. Brussels can therefore hardly be considered a sanctuary city. Police forces are able to ask for ID at any time, and they are allowed to share this information with the Immigration Office (*Dienst Vreemdelingenzaken*). Security personnel of the city's public transport system have been known to cooperate with police forces when travelers who are caught without a ticket fail to produce an ID. Furthermore, over the last decade, municipalities have opted more regularly for repressive policies toward undocumented activists' squats and camps. Mayors have regularly ordered the expulsion of undocumented activists from their squatted buildings. In 2007, the expulsion of 130 undocumented immigrants was enacted on the orders of Mayor Thielemans, who later commented that "Individuals remain free to put their lives at risk. It's their choice."[14] Similarly, the tents and field kitchen of undocumented activists who were occupying the Maximilian Parc in 2015 were destroyed by police forces and bulldozers on Mayor Mayeur's orders (Depraetere and Oosterlynck 2017; Swerts and Oosterlynck 2021). However, this raid only took place after weeks had passed, during which the federal government had pressured the Brussels mayor to take action in vain. When evaluating a federal project aimed at deporting convicted sans-papiers, Mayor Mayeur stated that "I don't feel like ending up participating in raids…. [I]t is understandable that people who stay here without being given a [legal] status end up serving themselves as they can to survive."[15] The official position of the local government on the matter consequently remains equivocal.

Brussels has historically been the epicenter for undocumented activism in Belgium. Tracing the origins of undocumented activism in Brussels, it all leads back to an event that shocked the public: the death of refused asylum seeker Semira Adamu on October 22, 1998. During an expulsion attempt, officers tried to pacify her by pressing a pillow over her face, which led to her going into a coma and eventually dying from a brain hemorrhage. This event inspired the first church occupations in Brussels. In the subsequent ten years, Brussels became a central hub that helped to initiate and coordinate a national sans-papiers movement. Dozens of churches, public buildings, and university buildings remained occupied from anywhere between a few days to more than a year, and occupiers often resorted to hunger strikes to gain visibility for their cause. Protesters consistently demanded the collective regularization of all the sans-papiers. Their demands were only partially fulfilled when tens of thousands of sans-papiers obtained legal status through two consecutive regularization rounds: first in 1999 and ten years later in 2009. In the Brussels Capital Region alone, 20,500 persons applied for regularization in 2009.[16] However, many did not meet the criteria set out by the government. They typically slipped straight back into the shadows or resorted to activism.

Self-organizations

In search of an appropriate entry point into the world of undocumented activism, I talked to representatives of numerous civic organizations that were or had been involved in the struggle around immigrant rights in Chicago and in Brussels. While the struggle of the undocumented invariably constituted the main topic of conversation, my conversation partners were invariably citizens themselves. Whenever I asked whether undocumented migrants were directly involved in their day-to-day organizing efforts, I was typically referred to actions that had taken place in the past or collaborations that were envisioned for the future. I quickly realized that studying undocumented activism meant turning my gaze away from the usual suspects—the well-established organizations led by citizen professionals who undertake actions in alliance with, in support of, or *in the name of* undocumented migrants. When I managed to do so, I discovered a fascinating microcosm of collectives and initiatives led by and for undocumented migrants. My ethnographic focus therefore lies on what I call *self-organizations* of undocumented activists. The impact and presence of self-organizations in the field of local migration politics is undeniable, yet their actions often remain underrepresented in public accounts, media reporting, and academic work.

It is exactly the relatively unique, yet hidden character of these self-organizations that make them compelling cases for the development of new theoretical insights (Small 2009, 14–17). The case selection logic of this study, whereby highly specific self-organizations in Chicago and Brussels are selected as ethnographic cases, combines insights from the extended case method and multi-sited ethnography (Burawoy 1998, 19). The extended case method argues that case studies can be used to "extract the general from the unique, to move from the micro to the macro, and to connect the present to the past in anticipation for the future" (Burawoy 1998, 5). The primary goal of studying self-organizations is not necessarily to be able to tell us something about a population of similar cases, but rather to tell us something about society as a whole. In this book, I approach the microcosm of these self-organizations and the broader movements that they are embedded in as a unique social milieu that can learn more general lessons about processes of politicization and citizenship transformation. While the book documents the specific period of political self-organizing in the undocumented youth and sans-papiers movements between 2010 and 2014, insights from this period are connected to past, present, and future of the movements.[17] By taking self-organizations as an ethnographic vantage point, the book adopts a "vertical" comparative strategy that traces "the source of small difference" in organizational dynamics to micro processes relating to the lifeworlds of undocumented migrants all the way up to macro processes involving state policies and transnational forces (Burawoy 1998). Furthermore, by adopting a multi-sited case study design, the book aims to enable "horizontal" comparison to help understand how actors are responding locally to global trends like irregular migration and globalization (Marcus 1995; Bartlett and Vavrus 2016).

Ethnographic research is well-placed to help correct the unnoted absence of Citizen X. While most of the undocumented population does not venture into politics, it is precisely the subpopulation of undocumented immigrants who *do* venture into politics that is of main ethnographic interest here. I place at the center of analytical attention the processes through which undocumented immigrants become political subjects. Of all the self-organizations I examined, I found two that met the criterion of being primarily a political organization led by and for undocumented immigrants at the time of observation. I immersed myself as a "citizen ally" at IYJL in Chicago and a *soutien* at SPBelgique in Brussels. This ethnographic perspective allows me to offer an unprecedented inside view into the world of undocumented activism. It reveals how noncitizens, for whom there is no assigned place in the democratic system, carve out a place for themselves by publicly revealing their identity, occupying spaces, sharing stories, and marching through the streets. In Chicago, I studied IYJL. IYJL was a "Chicago-based organization led by undocumented youth working toward full recognition of the rights and contributions of all immigrants through education, leadership development, policy advocacy, resource gathering, and mobilization."[18] The collective originated from the informal group that gathered during the campaign to halt the deportation of Reyes. In 2009, that group became the formal organization IYJL. It is perhaps most well-known for pioneering the "Coming Out of the Shadows" rallies in Chicago, and its ongoing actions contributed to the passing of the Illinois DREAM Act in May 2011. Its membership consisted mainly of undocumented youth between the ages of approximately eighteen and thirty-five, with a majority of women originating from Mexico. SPBelgique was founded in January 2011 in Brussels. Its goal was "to be a collective for all the sans-papiers ... carrying the message of all undocumented immigrants, including those who are in a procedure or have reached the end of the procedure or those who have never submitted a dossier for regularization."[19] SPBelgique was created in response to the perceived failure of the regularization campaign of 2009. In particular, the founding members consisted of undocumented immigrants who tried to be regularized based on a "Permis B," (work permit). At first, the name of the organization included "*en attente*" (waiting), referring to the fact that several members had been waiting to hear the result of their application for several years. Early actions focused on the right to work and the demand to speed up the regularization process. When the majority of the membership finally did receive their (largely negative) results, their actions shifted toward the regularization of all the sans-papiers. SPBelgique's membership mainly comprised Northern African men between the ages of twenty and fifty.

Two things need to be noted about IYJL and SPBelgique as the primary cases around which this book is structured. First, by no means does the book argue that the lived experiences, mobilizing tactics, and organizational dynamics of these specific self-organizations are "representative" for "the" undocumented youth movement or sans-papiers movement. Quite the contrary. I was drawn to both organizations precisely because their mode of operating was clearly different from most other organizations in the local field. As will be explained in Part I of the book where I situate both organizations within the history of the broader movements in the United States and Belgium, self-organizations were often regarded as "radicals" by established civil society organizations. While this positioning initially located them at the margins of the movement, it later propelled them toward a more central position as political innovators and movement leaders (see Nicholls 2013, 2019). The leadership position of specific self-organizations usually fades over time as challengers pop up representing new claims and groups and institutional response (or non-response) to actions impacts the movement. Researchers should therefore recognize and embrace the diversity of experiences and modes of organizing that exists within immigrant rights movements without pretending to be able to paint a photorealistic picture of it (Monico in Abrego and Negrón-Gonzales 2020, 102). Having said that, we need to take the cases of IYJL and SPBelgique for what they are: two rather unique examples of self-organized, undocumented-led collectives that swam against the current and tried to come up with new ways to express themselves politically in two diverging, yet equally hostile contexts.

Note that I use the *past tense* to introduce these collectives. This is not a matter of misguided linguistic romanticism, but instead reflects the reality that both collectives ceased to exist. In the Chicago case, the relative stability awarded by the temporary legal status of DACA (Deferred Action for Childhood Arrivals), launched in 2012 under the Obama administration to provide temporary relief for undocumented youth, caused IYJL's organizing to "grind to a standstill" and reoriented the targets of the activists involved (Mena Robles and Gomberg-Munoz 2016). In the Brussels case, the enduring lack of concessions from the government, activist fatigue, and a change in the legal status of key figures within the organization lay behind the demise of SPBelgique in 2014. The fact that these organizations fell apart a couple of years after they first appeared on the radar underscores the need to theorize the perils and promises of undocumented activism as a collective undertaking. The protracted ethnographic fieldwork I undertook provides a historical snapshot of the state of undocumented activism in circumstances that are particular to the time and locus of observation. This snapshot, however, derives its enduring significance from the theoretical insight it provides into processes of politicization and the citizenship transformation.

Politics as unusual

Undocumented activism does not fit the bill of politics as usual. It requires illegalized people, who are hardly considered to have any claim to rights to begin with, to come out of the shadows, contest their status, and voice their concerns. Correspondingly, it revolves around what Dikeç called "disruptive and inaugurative" politics that "starts or introduces something new and interrupts the established order of things" (Dikec 2017, 50). Such politics are at odds with a commonplace notion of politics that reserves the term for the institutionalized rituals and established practices we call democracy. Within this democracy, undocumented migrants represent one of the most marginalized populations. In a globalized world where legal mobility is a privilege of fully-fledged citizens, the undocumented are frequently cast as societal misfits who appear "out of place." From a state perspective, there is thus no such thing as a legitimate form of undocumented activism, since its very existence lacks an entry in the rulebook of the political game. How then can we start to conceptually consider the possibility of undocumented immigrants becoming political subjects?

Capturing the unusual politics of undocumented activism requires building a flexible theoretical apparatus that allows for the detection of innovative democratic practices and unexpected political actors who are not yet recognized as such. For this purpose, I turn to continental philosopher Jacques Rancière and the many scholars who have taken cues from his work to open up the debate about politics (Rancière 1999, 2010). I embrace a political ontology that locates its primary object not within the sphere of everyday governance, but in the instances and practices that disturb and call into question governance arrangements. This perspective thereby invites "a reflexive withdrawal from the accepted givens, normalized repetitive practices and ordering principles of political communities" (Dikec 2017, 52). The subject of such politics roams the spaces in between de facto inclusion and de jure exclusion from the political community. It epitomizes a subject that not only embodies but also names and unveils the cracks and fissures in the order of things. Becoming political for undocumented migrants thus involves a theatrical appearance on the scene and public denunciation of a wrong that shakes up the way we perceive and interpret things. In the era of globalization, it is hard to find actors who are more engaged in this endeavor than the undocumented.

In order to flesh out the disruptive qualities of undocumented activism, it is worthwhile exploring the distinction Rancière makes between politics and the police.[20] For Rancière, "the police" comprises the sum of all the activities that create order by distributing places, names, and functions. Aesthetics naturalize the policing of subjects by providing an epistemology (also called "partition of the sensible") that encompasses "the manner in which a relation between a shared common and the distribution of exclusive parts is determined in sensory experience" (Rancière 2010, 36). By structuring how we perceive and attribute meaning to the world that surrounds us, policing offers "a delimitation of spaces and times, of the visible and the invisible, of speech and noise, that simultaneously determines the place and the stakes of politics as a form of experience" (Rancière 2010, 36). For unauthorized, unwanted subjects, such as undocumented migrants, no place or voice exists within this order. Undocumented activism subsequently appears as 'noise' from an illegitimate mob to this order to which the only proper response is state repression (Dikeç 2004).

This socially constructed order of things is nevertheless hardly an exhaustive representation of the community. There are always subjects out there who escape the logic of the procedures through which people are policed. By emerging on the scene and demanding equality, unrecognized actors such as undocumented activists politicize themselves as speaking subjects and active participants in the polity, thereby challenging their assigned place in society (Swyngedouw 2011).

Put differently, "politics exist because those who have no right to be counted as speaking beings make themselves of some account" (Rancière 1999, 27). The process of political subject formation disrupts the order of things by making visible the gap between what the order claims to represent and the subjects who have no place or voice within this representation. Politicization then amounts to a disruption of "the visible" and "the sayable" (Rancière 1999, 37). This sets in motion an epistemological shift, transforming "what is seen and what can be said about it, around who has the ability to see and the talent to speak, around the properties of spaces and the possibilities of time" (Rancière 2004, 13). In this way, it exposes "the limits of the governmental regime and its police order, and the new centre that brings to light these very limits" (Simons and Masschelein 2010, 597).

Adopting this heterodox lens to investigate politics enables us to conceive of precarious subjects as being more than victims who lack the ability to contest their assigned status. Undocumented migrants' vulnerable position on the "receiving end" of power relations also entails potential opportunities for political agency. Explaining the sociological roots of this agency, however, falls beyond the scope of this theoretical framework's ambitions. Hence, scholars who try to project Rancièrian politics onto empirical case studies inevitably run into trouble, because they tend to treat the agency of undocumented migrants as the *explanans*, rather than the *explanandum* (Swerts 2021). Opening up the black box of agency therefore requires paying more attention to the "processes in which people develop their sensibilities and perceptions" that in turn guide their political activity (Uitermark and Nicholls 2013, 4). This is precisely the contribution made by the more sociological approach to political subject formation introduced in this book. Despite its limitations, the perspective outlined above underscores that undocumented activists do not simply try to be accepted as insiders but attempt to redraw the lines that demarcate the field of politics and, by extension, citizenship.

Unexpected citizenship

Undocumented migrants are not only unusual political subjects but also unexpected citizens. Yet traditional scholarship on citizenship tends to focus analytical attention on explaining who belongs to citizenship's inner circle, rather than accounting for those who are on the outside looking in. When unrecognized subjects subsequently engage in practices traditionally associated with the behavior of citizens, the theoretical understandings are no longer equipped to grasp their meaning. These theories take the overlap between formal citizenship (referring to legal status) and substantive citizenship (referring to citizenship practices) for granted. They thereby fail to acknowledge the possibility that the institutions distributing and upholding formal citizenship systematically overlook populations that comply with substantive citizenship requirements. It is thus precisely because undocumented immigrants find themselves "betwixt and between" categories that they are not "captured" by these frameworks, which tend to mimic prevailing understandings of who belongs and who does not. The figure of the noncitizen therefore looms as an "absent presence" in theories investigating the migration-citizenship nexus, only sporadically appearing as the citizen's shadow.

In recent years, a new critical school of citizenship studies has emerged that tries to fill in the analytical blanks. Citizenship is traditionally associated with participation, legal status, rights, and belonging. The focus on the stability and endurance of citizenship regimes tends to reify what is essentially a dynamic social and political construction. However, the historical development of citizenship is characterized by expanded inclusions. The demands of outsiders are important drivers of these inclusions. Or, as Sassen put it, "citizenship is partly produced by the practices of the excluded" (Sassen 2005, 84). Critical citizenship scholars therefore point to an insurgent citizenship, in which outsiders are reclaiming their rights by creating new public spheres of participation (Holsten 2021). Commonplace understandings of citizenship are abandoned in favor of a re-appropriation of the term in relation to what noncitizens are doing on the ground. The influential theory of "acts of citizenship" usefully proposes looking beyond citizenship as a legal status, toward the events through which subjects constitute themselves as citizens (Isin and Nielsen 2008). In this way, undocumented migrants are no longer conceived of as "immanent others" but as citizens in the making (Isin 2002). Acts of citizenship are defined as "those acts that transform forms (orientations, strategies, technologies) and modes (citizens, strangers, outsiders, aliens) of being political by bringing into being new actors as activist citizens (claimants of rights and responsibilities) through creating new sites and scales of struggle" (Isin 2002, 39). According to Isin, "acts rupture or break given orders, practices and habitus" associated with citizenship. In this context, Isin argued that "it is hard to imagine sans-papiers acting out of an already written script" (Isin 2009, 380). This perspective is thus remarkably compatible with the Rancièrian theory of disruptive politics presented above.

In the current book, I follow this school's lead to place the political practices of noncitizens at the center of analytical attention. Moreover, I purposefully evoke the term citizenship to describe the new forms of community and political belonging that undocumented activists are enacting from below. At the same time, the framework laid out here tries to overcome what I perceive to be several shortcomings. The empirical work on migrant activism that has sprung from this school has mapped the proliferation of immigrants' protest events and activist practices in different countries. Yet the focus on the episodic "ruptures" of citizenship obscures the minor acts and incremental politics involved in undocumented activism (Darling 2014). Exactly how or what these ruptures entail is barely specified, since the act in itself is presented as the beginning and the end point of analysis. The cumulative analytical effect of labeling and filing protest events under the conceptual umbrella of acts of citizenship only takes us so far in analyzing the contextual factors that shape political agency (Swerts 2021). Moreover, the capacity of undocumented activists to "write new political scripts" seems to fall out of thin air. In order to better capture the seemingly contradictory phenomenon of undocumented activism, it is therefore necessary to descend from the theoretical high grounds to the treacherous valleys of real-world activism.

Precarious agency

The mere thought of undocumented migrants becoming political activists defies the sociological odds. Why would people who lack the right to participate in public life and risk being arrested—or even worse, deported—engage in the seemingly unrealistic and improbable pursuit of demanding betterment of their situation? No matter how unlikely, it is the pursuit of this impossible demand that drives and motivates undocumented activists. Despite the repressive climate, the sans-papiers in Brussels have never relinquished their demand for regularization *for all*, as exemplified by the well-known chant *"Papiers pour tous ou tous sans papiers!"* Likewise, the Education Not Deportation (END) campaigns pioneered by youth activists in Chicago to stop the deportation of undocumented students was expanded to the #Not1More campaign, aimed at halting deportations *for all*. Since there are hardly any quick wins or easy victories in the field of irregular migration politics, a crucial task for undocumented activism is learning how to cope with and persist within a hostile political environment. It is no coincidence that SPBelgique leader Abas evoked the imagery of a flickering flame to symbolize the need to "keep hope alive" in difficult times. This is because undocumented activists rely on hope and imagination to make the present bearable and the future thinkable. Based on a collaborative study on stories of resistance, Loredo alludes to the ability of undocumented activists to resist as a "mystical power that rises from our insides" during "moments where giving up is expected" (Anderson and Laredo 2021, 16). Rather than designating this capacity as a "mystical," however, this book traces the sociological conditions that enable undocumented migrants to become activists.

Undocumented activists' powerful, albeit vulnerable, capacity to disrupt the order of things and prefigure and imagine an alternate order is what I designate by the term *precarious agency*. Read out loud, the term sounds like a contradiction in terms. Remarkably, so do most attempts at theorizing and conceptualizing the ambiguous figure of the noncitizen. This is because Citizen X is a slippery subject that proves hard to capture in clear-cut, circumscribed categories. Many authors revert to familiar conceptual grounds by taking a theoretical route describing the lack of a place within, the relative distance to, or the cracks in existing social structures. Examples include concepts such as liminal legality, abjectivity, deportability, denizenship, and noncitizenship (Menjívar 2006; De Genova 2002; Goldring and Landolt 2013). Such concepts have advanced the theorization of illegalization and, arguably, our understanding of the constraining and often destructive impact that legal status has on the lives of undocumented migrants. What is missing in these accounts, however, is a perspective that acknowledges the collective ability of undocumented activists to take the initiative, resist, and be creative—both *in spite of* and *because of* their vulnerability. The framework I lay out in this book argues that precarity and agency are not antithetical to each other.

The term "precarious" is meant to evoke the subjection that undocumented migrants experience in relation to forms of exclusion and violence that are inflicted on them by the state. To return to Fariss's story, he suffered from feelings of anxiety, helplessness, and despair while trying to legalize his status. The time Fariss spent living in uncertainty came to an end when he was arrested for not being able to present a valid ID card. His efforts to contest his arrest were dwarfed by the state's power to deport him against his will. Precariousness thus concerns the conditionality that surrounds legal presence on state territory and the uncertainty about access to rights that is largely "established externally, beyond the control" of migrants (Goldring and Landolt 2013, 19). It is a condition that is directly related to the political and legal construction of illegality by the state. The very existence of "illegal aliens" is not so much a testament to changes in migration patterns, but more the ways in which states historically decided to label and treat migrant populations differently. The official negation of the presence of undocumented migrants erases their legal personhood and renders them "legally non-existent" (Coutin 2000). Due to the many ambiguities, inconsistencies, and flat-out arbitrariness involved in the bureaucratic ordering of migrant desirability, many migrants hover in a precarious temporary state of "liminal legality" (Menjívar 2006). The threat of being subjected to detention or deportation against one's will permeates the lived experience of illegality (De Genova 2002). This situation of perpetual uncertainty instills fear, trauma, anxiety, and shame within the minds of undocumented migrants, amounting to what some observers call "legal violence" (Menjiva and Abrego 2012).

Precariousness also exposes the inherent vulnerability that characterizes the figure of the noncitizen.[21] Noncitizens are nominally precluded from what Bosniak has called the "soft inside" of citizenship and confronted with its "hard outside," referring to the often-violent means by which states try to block access to or remove unwanted populations from their territories (Bosniak 2006). There is growing consensus that alienage and citizenship presuppose one another, since the bounded community of citizenship remains devoid of content if it cannot be defined against "immanent others" (Isin 2002). "Illegal aliens" have been historically preceded by slaves, African Americans, women, and other marginalized populations deemed less than worthy of citizenship in the long lineage of noncitizenship. The subjects of noncitizenship are denied the "right to have rights," stripped of their humanity, and reduced to their "bare life" (Agamben 1998). Noncitizenship is therefore associated with "limits in terms of voice, membership, and rights in a political community, and with social exclusion and vulnerability" (Goldring and Landolt 2013, 3). Ethnographic accounts of the everyday lived experiences of illegality have documented in great empirical detail this precariousness and vulnerability in the spheres of the family, coming of age, education, work, healthcare, and housing (Dreby 2015; Gonzales 2015; Gomberg-Munoz 2010; Ticktin 2011; Chavez 1998). The picture that emerges from these accounts confirms the image of undocumented migrants as a vulnerable population that falls victim to social inequalities and injustice.

The danger of overstressing vulnerability is that "Citizen X" becomes portrayed as an apolitical, quiescent subject. As a consequence, the very possibility of political agency becomes unthinkable. For instance, several authors have argued that Agamben's notion of the powerless homo sacer does not hold up under empirical scrutiny (Isin 2009; McNevin 2013; Darling 2014). In fact, there has been a wealth of research on everyday practices of resistance and outright activist struggles of undocumented migrants that defy the vulnerability thesis (Nicholls 2013; Swerts and Nicholls 2021; Escudero 2021; Abrams 2022). In order to break the deadlock between romanticizing and trivializing undocumented activism, a perspective centered on *precarious agency* unites the lived realities of vulnerability with the equally precarious collective undertaking to overturn these realities in a single perspective. Judith Butler has argued that we have to rethink the relationship between vulnerability and resistance (Butler et al. 2016). Talking about the vulnerability to police violence that ensues from engaging in activism, she points to the precarity that *precedes* agency as follows (Butler et al. 2016, 12):

> First you resist, and then you are confronted with your vulnerability either in relation to police power or those who show up to oppose your political stance. Yet vulnerability emerges earlier, prior to any gathering, and this becomes especially true when people demonstrate to oppose the precarious conditions in which they live.... If we also say that the vulnerability to dispossession, poverty, insecurity, and harm that constitutes a precarious position in the world itself

leads to resistance, then it seems we reverse the sequence: we are first vulnerable and then overcome that vulnerability, at least provisionally, through acts of resistance.

Recalling the story of Fariss at the beginning of this chapter, his vulnerability to being arrested and deported by the state was not engendered by activism but instigated his activist engagement to begin with. By overcoming his fear and putting his body on the line during the European march and later during his hunger strike in detention, he found agency through publicly displaying his vulnerability. Butler insisted that agency is always performative and never a one-way street, or as she put it, "we are invariably acted on and acting" (Butler et al. 2016, 24). In the case of the undocumented, being "acted on" takes the form of being subjected to illegalizing, criminalizing, and dehumanizing practices that seek to transform agentic migrants into docile, vulnerable bodies that are ready, willing, and able to self-deport. Nevertheless, this vulnerability does not erase the potential for undocumented migrants to engage in politics, but instead offers them ways of "being exposed and agentic at the same time" (Butler et al. 2016, 24). Put differently, there is an agency that stems from precarity.

The work of McNevin offers additional insights into how a precarious position can, under certain circumstances, contain seeds of agency (McNevin 2011, 2013). McNevin pointed out the inherent "ambivalence" of the political claims of irregular migrants, "whose substance and effects cannot be captured on a register of subjection-agency that corresponds to an inside-outside relation with respect to sovereign power" (McNevin 2013). Structurally speaking, undocumented migrants are outsiders who are de facto incorporated in social, cultural, and economic life but are denied the status of insiders. They are hence always simultaneously inside and outside the political community, or as Balibar called it, "excluded insiders" (Balibar 2004). This ambiguous positioning entails both a particular vulnerability and potential. According to McNevin, it is precisely the inherent vulnerability to state violence that makes undocumented activists intrinsically challenging to prevailing understandings of citizenship. Yet according to McNevin, the claim-making activities of undocumented activists remain ambiguous because they are "wedged between cultural resonance and the aspiration toward what is culturally unrecognizable" on the one hand and striving to express "what cannot yet be thought or spoken" on the other hand (McNevin 2013, 195). The latter statement corroborates a Rancièrian reading of undocumented activism as a prefiguration of the new order of things. The reference made to cultural resonance nevertheless simultaneously entails a warning that their search for recognition can reinforce existing power relations.

In a similar vein, Nicholls (2013) pointed out that there is potential for agency to be discovered in undocumented migrants' societal inclusion. Legal, economic, and moral ambiguities combine to create "niche openings" for immigrants who fit a specific profile to "be considered deserving of some form of legal residency status" (Nicholls 2013, 10). Such openings provide necessary room to maneuver for undocumented activists to create a legitimate public voice. Nicholls conceived of "voice" as the pursuit to "craft representations that counter stigmatizing arguments of their adversaries and build a sympathetic public portrait of their group" (Nicholls 2013, 11). His analysis of the transformation of the dispersed, stigmatized group of undocumented youth into the political group of the DREAMers stressed the importance of networking and organizational labor to build alliances, gain public traction, and discipline movement members. Compared with previous authors, these insights point to the collective nature of undocumented activism as a social phenomenon. Because activists are in search of recognition, however, Nicholls detected a bias within the movement to produce representations that "demonstrate both conformity to national values and the ways they stand to make an important contribution to the country" (Nicholls 2013, 12). This led him to conclude that the assimilationist strategies of undocumented activists reinforce rather than challenge prevailing understandings of citizenship (Nicholls 2013, 171–172).

More recent work by emerging undocumented scholars partly challenges academic attempts to theorize undocumented activism. Stemming mostly from a US context, this literature not only provides an eyewitness source of the rise of the undocumented youth movement but also formulates what Bejarano et al. call an "undocumented activist theory" (2019, 90). Undocumented scholars thereby try to "restore agency to people for whom self-determination is denied, both by the state ... and by those academics who would subscribe to an overly structural perspective on the immigrant condition" (Bejarano et al. 2019, 95). There are several important insights in such theory that this book builds on and contributes to. First, this line of scholarship adopts a critical stance toward the assimilationist tendencies within the undocumented youth movement by explicitly rejecting and resisting the DREAMer narrative (Abrego and Negrón-Gonzales 2020, 10; Martinez et al. 2020). Although many undocumented scholars recognize the pragmatic reasons for framing undocumented youth experiences in line with prevailing understandings of deservingness, they point out how they "further marginalized undocumented immigrants who do not fit the mold" (Sati 2020, 39). Second, undocumented scholars have been at the forefront of moving away from demands based on the deservingness of undocumented migrants to demands that reject measures of deservingness at all. This involves a shift in analytical attention toward the articulation of and experimentation with new forms of claims-making rooted in, for example, indigeneity or border abolitionism (Monico 2020, 101). In this sense, undocumented scholarship reflects broader developments within undocumented movements, like the rise of more radical anti-deportation activism like the #Not1More campaign.[22]

The previously cited scholarship is onto something when it points out that political subject formation requires strenuous work in crafting compelling messages and representations. Furthermore, all authors pinpoint the difficulty of undocumented activists having to navigate the treacherous waters between expressing themselves politically in ways that align with existing narratives and attempting to move beyond such narratives. However, I disagree with the rather pessimistic structuralist reading that undocumented activists do little more than repoint the crumbling walls of citizenship as we know it when they resort to existing political tropes. I simultaneously argue that we need to resist the temptation to be overly optimistic when interpreting the disruptive nature of undocumented activism. Instead, this book takes cues from undocumented activist theory, which perhaps acknowledges the messiness, inherent tensions, and ambiguities that are prevalent in undocumented activism in the most intimate of ways. In line with this insight, the framework I develop in this book centered around precarious agency neither readily assumes the transformative potential of undocumented activism nor precludes the possibility of state co-optation, assimilation, or subjection. Rather, it hints at the fact that, under certain conditions, undocumented activists can step out of line and act collectively in ways that potentially unsettle citizenship as we know it. In order to grasp how undocumented migrants gain the courage to speak out and step up, what provides them with a moral compass, and what ultimately drives them to become activists, we thus need to turn Citizen X into a sociological subject made of flesh and blood.

A sociological take on political subject formation

Sociology brings much to the table when it comes to grasping how people in precarious circumstances become political subjects. From its inception, sociology has tried to get to grips with how people understand the world around them. *Verstehen*, or the attempt to form an "interpretative understanding of social action," as Weber (2021) put it, is at the core of the hermeneutic methodology that informs the bulk of sociological research. Yet understandings are not just a methodological or epistemological device. For Weber, an action can only be considered social "insofar as by virtue of the *subjective meaning* attached to it by the acting individual it takes account of the behaviour of others and thereby oriented in its course" (Weber 1921, 4). Applied to the case here, the collective actions that undocumented activists undertake are informed by the subjective meanings they attribute to them. Conceived in this way, precarious agency becomes a product of undocumented migrants' ability to transform their understandings (or self-understandings) in such a way that they come to support, orient, and legitimize taking a stance against the order of things. What is needed then, in order to untangle the knot of undocumented activism, is a theoretical toolbox that substantiates the relationship between political understandings and precarious agency.

To be fair, existing sociological research on *political* understandings is thinly spread between scholarship that emphasizes the chokehold of ideology over civil society, rationalizes political activity as calculated attempts at "framing," or explains away differences between political adversaries with catchall concepts such as "identity." A major exception is the seminal work of Andreas Glaeser (2011), who has made a compelling case for considering political epistemology as a proper field of inquiry. Political epistemology is concerned with "how, in an effort to orient themselves into the world, historically, socially and culturally situated people actually form and interrogate what to them appears as valid understanding" (Glaeser 2011, xxv). By talking about *formation*, Glaeser made the crucial point that political understandings do not simply present themselves as a given to political actors but that these actors are equally involved in producing them. Likewise, the verb *interrogate* signals people's capacity for the critical reflection that is a prerequisite for any resistance to emerge. Understandings are the condition sine qua non for agency, because they "orient, direct, coordinate, explain, and legitimate or justify" political activity (Glaeser 2011, 37). They stipulate what Glaeser called "a practical ontology" that "orders relevant aspects of the world by simultaneously differentiating and integrating it" (Glaeser 2011, 11).

This concept of understandings does not stray far from Bourdieu's theory of habitus, which argues that people become socialized into an inner-worldly "structuring structure" that directs practice (Bourdieu 1998). This structuring structure is in turn shaped by the social location of an actor in the hierarchical ordering of society, which becomes deeply engrained in people's self-understanding. While for Bourdieu, understandings thus make agency possible, they inevitably pave the way for the social reproduction of unequal class relations. Trapped between the legal and the illegal, the social position of undocumented migrants is far more complex than class-based accounts of reality can give credit for. There is no denying that the precarious status of undocumented migrants affects how they come to perceive themselves and the world that surrounds them (see Chapters 5 and 6). However, I argue that undocumented migrants have significantly more leeway than the mimetic model of habitus allows for, to break away from prevailing understandings (see Chapters 7 and 8).

Prevailing understandings are institutionalized understandings that orient, direct, and coordinate actions aimed at the perpetual effort to (re-)establish the order of things and legitimize and justify the status quo. They amount to a taken-for-granted political imaginary; a set of shared "background understand-ings" that allows for actions to proceed with minimal coordination, deliberation, or communication (Glaeser 2011, 43). It is fair to say that the all-too-familiar mantra "illegals are illegal" has gained the status of such a background under-standing, which informs how the state, as well as institutions and organizations affiliated with it, distinguish between "asylum seekers," "economic migrants," "political refugees," and "welfare profiteers." They provide the practical ontol-ogy for state technologies such as border controls, deportations, and security screening, also similarly for organizational technologies designed to separate "deserving migrants" from "undeserving illegals." These epistemic procedures either assign noncitizens a place within the order of things or expel them to the abyss of illegality. In this way, prevailing understandings of citizenship set out the epistemological borders and boundaries of a political playing field that is off limits for undocumented activists.

This book is nevertheless involved in exploring how, against all odds, precari-ous actors such as undocumented immigrants can break into the caged political playing field. Foucault's work on the care of the self offers pointers. It shows that understandings not only come about through subjection to the order of things but also by a more active part-taking of the subject in the construction of the self, in which "people are invited or incited to recognize their moral obligations" (Foucault 1983, 264). The capacity to resist and reject prevailing understand-ings thus stems from the necessity for subjects to position themselves vis-à-vis those understandings. Relating this insight back to Rancière's theory of political subjectivation, resistance emerges when "unqualified" people intervene, thereby demonstrating that they are "intellectually equal in the very act of interven-tion, and competent in view of the common from which they are nevertheless excluded" (Simons and Masschelein 2010, 596–97). Translated into the world of irregular migration politics, the goal for undocumented activists is therefore "not to discover what we are but to refuse what we are" (Foucault 1982, 785). Through their activism, undocumented immigrants reject the label of "illegal alien" that they are assigned by state actors and redefine how they understand themselves as members of the political community. It is in response to and in dialogue with prevailing understandings of citizenship that undocumented immigrants form their political understandings. For noncitizens, becoming a political subject thus always involves strategies of dis-identification and re-identification (Rancière 1999).

Political hermeneutics provides undocumented activists with the tools to dis-identify themselves from their assigned status and appear on the scene as activists. Precarious agency presupposes the ability to creatively reinterpret and appropriate existing political understandings and corresponding modes of action. Undocumented migrants are liminal subjects who occupy the social, political, and moral interstices. The fact that they are neither "here" nor "there"—in parts considered "illegal" but in other parts "legal"—means that they are uniquely placed to *innovate political repertoires* (Tilly 2010). In this respect, Sewell defined agency as an "actor's capacity to reinterpret and mobilize an array of resources in terms of cultural schemas other than those that initially constituted the array" (Sewell 1992, 18). Schemas refer here to the assembly of cultural symbols, narratives, and practices that make up a specific domain of action. In this case, the domain of action is irregular migration politics, and the schemas involved pertain to understandings of citizenship. I argue that when new actors, such as the undocumented, creatively (re)interpret and redeploy elements from existing political repertoires and tropes for new claim-making purposes, this can transform the very understandings that they appeal to. Undocumented immigrants can thus frame their claims by inscribing themselves as characters in meta-narratives about the nation, civil rights, or labor rights, thereby opening up symbolic spaces for future recognition. In this way, existing political scripts and repertoires provide the colors, shapes, and tools that undocumented activists can use to paint a whole new picture.

How undocumented activists decide to pick and choose elements from the local political culture to innovate these scripts and repertoires is mediated by the means through which they come to "know" their society of residence. Building on Glaeser, I focus on the *discursive, embodied, and emotional understandings* that emerge through the personal and collective trajectories of undocumented immigrants (Glaeser 2011, 11). In doing so, I align myself with the argument advanced by Abrego and Negrón-Gonzales that "the lived experiences of being undocumented inevitably make visible particular kinds of understandings that should be centered in the field" (Abrego and Negrón-Gonzales 2020, 8). Stigmatizing discourses are internalized by undocumented immigrants. Emotions such as fear of deportation, shame, and low self-esteem encourage a life in the shadows. The embodied experiences of being subjected to police brutality, restricted in mobility, and trying to avoid detection in public add to this experience. I subsequently argue that lived experiences of illegality become "politicized" when they start to inform and guide the organizing practices of undocumented activists. Because undocumented migrants feel and embody the "wrong" of the current order, this shapes and informs the collective undertaking to challenge that very order. At this point, the work of social movement and feminist scholars on narratives, emotions, and embodiment helps to explain how precarious subjects who have little more resources available to them than their own stories, emotions, and bodies turn these resources into political tools (Polletta 2006; Jasper 1997; Gould 2009; Butler 1990).

Plan of the book

In the remainder of the book, I rely on a transatlantic ethnography to trace the processes through which undocumented migrants transformed themselves into full-blown activists in Chicago and Brussels. Throughout, I show that undocumented activists gain precarious agency by organizing themselves collectively, creating political understandings that run counter to the order of things, and putting these understandings to the test. The structure of the book corresponds with the effort to map political subject formation as the combined outcome of interactions, reflections, and actions at multiple levels.

The first part of the book analyzes how undocumented movements took shape on both sides of the Atlantic. I specifically focus on *interactions between organizations* to investigate how undocumented migrants emerged on the scene as political subjects in the United States and Belgium. Chapters 1 and 2 independently reveal the political understandings that lie at the basis of conflicts over representation between undocumented-led and citizen-led organizations. I argue that immigrant rights advocates with legal status who work in well-established civil society organizations (CSOs) tend to have a different understanding of what needs to be done than undocumented migrants who experience a life in the shadows on a daily basis. In Chapters 3 and 4, I argue that undocumented activists relied on creating spaces where they took matters into their own hands to become political subjects in their own right. Self-organizations operate as spaces of political expression, experimentation, and innovation for undocumented migrants. The organizational histories of IYJL and SPBelgique are presented to show how undocumented activists slowly start to see themselves as more than poster-girls and boys for policy reforms or woeful victims of labor exploitation. I demonstrate that the strategies, discourses, and actions that they developed in self-organizations were radically different from those propagated by well-established CSOs.

The second part of the book outlines the personal and collective *activist trajectories* of undocumented migrants in Brussels and Chicago. In Chapters 5 and 6, I present the embodied, emotional, and discursive lived experiences of illegality that affected undocumented migrants' political (self)-understandings. First, I show how youth activists at IYJL struggled with their legal status while growing up. I identify that it was in the relatively supportive environment of schools that these young people learned organizing skills, connected with other undocumented youth, and gained a general understanding of the American political culture. Second, I show how undocumented workers and rejected asylum seekers at SPBelgique made the decision to migrate themselves, albeit for diverging reasons. Compared with undocumented youth activists in Chicago, access to education or other institutions is a lot more thinly distributed for the sans-papiers in Brussels. This creates significant obstacles for political participation in terms of skills, know-how, and resources.

In Chapters 7 and 8, I zoom in on the *intra-organizational level* to show how self-organizations function as activist infrastructures that enable undocumented activists to collectively turn their precarity into agency. I present how the undocumented youth at IYJL overcame barriers to participation by politicizing storytelling. I argue that storytelling functioned as a powerful political tool to build communities, mobilize supporters, and legitimize demands. Moreover, I reveal how undocumented youth relied on discursive and embodied strategies borrowed from the civil and gay rights movements. In this way, undocumented youth mobilized and transformed widespread notions of what it means to be an American citizen to demonstrate their belonging. Turning to SPBelgique, I describe how the sans-papiers' search for recognition was exacerbated by the hostile political context in which they had to operate. Hence, gaining public visibility became the primary aim for these activists. The sans-papiers relied on the politicization of one of the few resources at their disposal, namely their bodies. I show how different physical techniques were used as a political tool to publicly "perform" their suffering, presence, mobility, and civic engagement. I argue that the sans-papiers strategically borrowed discursive and embodied strategies from the local labor and squatters' movements to present themselves and their cause to the broader public.

I conclude the book by contrasting and comparing the lessons learned from the two case studies. I argue that both cases demonstrate how the emerging forms of political expression exercised by unanticipated actors potentially change the face and meaning of citizenship. Against all odds, these "excluded insiders" are stretching the boundaries and defying the borders of citizenship as we know it. Regardless of the circumstances, undocumented activists contest prevailing understandings of (non)citizenship and (il)legality by creatively inventing new ways of being political. While undocumented activism differs depending on the social context, it points toward a reconfiguration of state-citizen relations in the twenty-first century.

PART I

UNDOCUMENTED MOVEMENTS

In the first part of this book, I analyze and compare how the rise and fall of undocumented movements has unfolded on both sides of the Atlantic. When I talk about "undocumented movements," I have in mind the occasional coming together of civic organizations and networks between these organizations around the common goal of contesting, disrupting, and transforming the illegalizing immigration order. By using the terms "undocumented" and "movement" in a single expression, I do not in any way wish to suggest that all immigrant rights movements are necessarily led by undocumented activists or that the presence of immigrant rights organizations in a given setting automatically provides evidence of the existence of movements. However, given this book's ambition to disentangle the processes and mechanisms through which undocumented migrants gain precarious agency, I pay specific attention to the times when movements served as vehicles for the political demands of the undocumented.

There are three main arguments made in the following chapters.

First, I argue that in both cases, the politicization of migrant illegality[1] and immigrant rights as a public issue at the national scale was initially in the hands of well-established CSOs in the field of civil society. These organizations used their accumulated expertise and professional knowledge in the field of immigrant "integration" to underscore and legitimize the social problems and injustices relating to the illegalization of immigrant communities. The networks, resources, and know-how they built up over the years allowed them to draw the attention of the media and political elites to the issue of migrant illegality. Members of the "target community" were carefully chosen by these organizations to "give a face" to the issue and represent the grassroots during public spectacles. However, both in Belgium and in the United States, undocumented immigrants failed to gain a seat at the negotiation table. Instead, privileged subjects regularly claimed to speak in the name of underprivileged subjects who were said to be "too vulnerable" to represent their own interests. As a result, prevailing understandings of citizenship and deservingness tended to be reinforced by the external representations and political compromises made by privileged subjects.

Second, I argue that the monopoly that well-established actors had over representing the issue of migrant illegality in the national debate invariably fueled internal struggles over representation within undocumented movements. Of course, struggles over representation are present in any social movement. They are an essential part of the process through which actors try to make sense of the political situation. Undocumented movements are a particularly interesting case because of the unequal distribution of political, social, and cultural capital between privileged subjects and underprivileged subjects. Whereas struggles over representation are equally pertinent in the case of other populations in a precarious situation—such as the homeless, battered women, or the unemployed—they are often formally recognized as citizens by the state. Undocumented migrants, however, try to influence political institutions from which they are fundamentally excluded. Moreover, they have to do so in a political climate that is extremely hostile. This significantly affected the power dynamics at play in both the undocumented youth movement in the United States and the sans-papiers movement in Belgium.

Lastly, I argue that for undocumented migrants to become political subjects with an equal right to being and speaking, they need to create autonomous and relatively protected spaces that help to facilitate the development of new and—potentially—disruptive political understandings. The creation of such spaces, which is described in more ethnographic detail in Chapters 7 and 8, primarily takes place at the local scale. Such spaces typically rely on material resources and physical spaces of urban institutions like schools, local community centers, churches, and squats. In that sense, autonomy pertains less to material than to non-material or symbolic self-sufficiency. Even when "safe spaces" rely on the material resources of such established institutions, they only start to function as activist infrastructures if and when undocumented migrants claim leadership and ownership over the production and representation of political understandings. Such understandings are, as will be shown in Part II of the book, essentially rooted in underprivileged subjects' lived experiences of illegality.

1

Chasing the dream

The politicization of migrant illegality in the United States

In August 2001, a US senator from Illinois, Richard Durbin, introduced the Development, Relief, and Education for Alien Minors (DREAM) Act in the 107th Congress, with bipartisan support from Chuck Hagel and Richard Lugar. The DREAM Act foresaw a path to citizenship for the undocumented youth who had been brought to the United States at a young age, provided they pursued higher education or carried out military service. When addressing the 108th Congress, Senator Durbin told the stories of the "original" DREAMers, Diana and Tereza, who inspired him to take action:[1]

Why is the DREAM Act so important? Because of the extraordinary young people it would help. Let me tell you about two of them, whom I have had the pleasure of meeting. … Tereza was … raised in Illinois; her Korean parents brought her to the U.S. when she was two. Tereza began playing piano when she was eight. She became a musical prodigy, winning the Chicago Symphony Orchestra Youth Auditions, which enabled her to perform with the Orchestra. I first learned about Tereza when her family called to ask for my help. Tereza first discovered that she was undocumented when she was preparing to apply to colleges. The top music schools in the country had recruited Tereza, but when they learned about her immigration status, most would not permit her to apply. I called the INS to ask for their help and they told me that Tereza should go back to Korea. Tereza now attends one of the top music schools in the country. … Due to support from their communities, Diana and Tereza are among the lucky ones who have been able to attend college. However, their futures are uncertain—they could be deported at any time. Diana and Tereza are not alone—thousands of other young people are prevented from pursuing their dreams by our immigration laws. They are honor-roll students, star athletes, talented artists, homecoming queens, and aspiring teachers and doctors. Their parents brought them to the United States when they were young children. They have lived in this country for most of their lives. It is the only home they know. They have followed the rules and worked hard in school. The

DREAM Act would ... permit them to become permanent residents if they are long-term U.S. residents, have good moral character, and attend college or enlist in the military for at least two years.

Tereza's story proved to be far from unique. In fact, the campaign to garner support for the DREAM Act would heavily rely on the recruitment of exemplary undocumented students whose stories resonated with the American Dream in years to come (Nicholls 2013; Swerts 2015; Escudero 2021). Well-established CSOs such as ICIRR actively reached out to undocumented students like Tereza in order to "give a face" to the issue. Tamara, who would become one of the central leaders of IYJL, was one of the young people who had been approached by Senator Durbin's entourage to give a testimony at a congressional hearing. At this point in her life, Tamara had applied to universities as an international student. In order to obtain her visa, she had to return to Mexico and then come back to the United States. The media picked up her story, and her parents got in touch with ICIRR, who in turn contacted Senator Durbin. In the interview I did with Tamara a decade after these events, she recounted how she was preparing to testify before the commission when September 11 happened:

> I feel like it was a complete coincidence, like the year that Senator Durbin discovered undocumented students. ... So it was in the same year he was planning to introduce the DREAM Act, ... and my parents' work, and people's advocacy made it so that he paid attention to my case and kind of used it as like, um, "look this is what undocumented students have to do to go to school." ... I was doing a lot of press conferences with Senator Durbin ... talking about my story. ... And I prepared a testimony to go in front of Congress and tell my story and [I had] tickets to fly to Washington, DC, on September 11, 2001. And so I got a call that morning from Senator Durbin's office, like, I don't think we're going to Washington, DC, and that's where a lot of the DREAM Act stopped. Any talk of immigration reform stopped, everything became about national security and that's it. ... At that point I went back into the shadows.

Tereza's story demonstrates how this campaign model proved to be a successful strategy. However, the initial enthusiasm for the DREAM Act quickly dwindled after the September 11 attacks. Professional organizers had been setting the stage for Tamara to come out of the shadows and step into the limelight. However, as already shines through from her statement, she felt as though her story was being instrumentalized by others to further their political agenda. When her champions no longer considered the time to be "right," she subsequently retreated into the shadows.

****

Both Tereza's and Tamara's stories highlight that the politicization of migrant illegality as a public issue was initially firmly in the hands of established civil society organizations. When undocumented immigrants enter the political arena of their society of residence, they are confronted with established actors who are already advocating immigrant rights, such as community organizations, nongovernmental organizations, labor unions, and elected officials. It may seem self-evident that those directly concerned are best placed to communicate their grievances to policymakers and the broader audience. However, the increasing professionalization of advocacy work has left many social workers, policy directors, and politicians convinced that their long-standing involvement makes them, rather than the "target audience," the real experts. The expertise that professionals accumulate through years of experience in gathering material resources, establishing good relations with policymakers, and building coalitions thereby becomes pitted against the lived experience of undocumented migrants. What is at stake here is the question of who should represent undocumented immigrants, how they should be represented, which discourses should be used vis-à-vis the government, and which strategies are most suitable given the context.

Academic discussions about the role civic organizations play for immigrant political representation are unbalanced. On the one hand, civic organizations are said to operate as "political schools," where immigrants can acquire the necessary skills to make their voices heard and represent themselves in the public debate (Ramakrishnan and Bloemraad 2008). Since established civic organizations are well-incorporated in the political fabric, they are claimed to facilitate the representation of immigrants' interests. This reasoning is applied even more so in the case of those who are excluded from electoral participation, such as undocumented immigrants, since they are supposed to "need" civic organizations to engage in representational politics in their name. On the other hand, recent work has taken a more critical stance concerning the capacity of civic organizations to engage in representational politics. Most notably, Nicholls showed that becoming "representational brokers" during policy negotiations can force well-established CSOs to reproduce the exclusionary practices that the movement is trying to change (Nicholls 2013). Furthermore, he showed that the voice of the undocumented youth in the immigrant rights debate is not necessarily crafted by undocumented immigrants themselves (Nicholls 2013, 13–15). The discipline and struggle needed to create a legitimate voice therefore exposes disagreements between actors within the immigrant rights movement.

In the case of the undocumented youth movement, these disputes and disagreements over representation are deeply rooted in the unequal distribution of legal status. Citizenship is "both a system of privilege and a source of social identity" (Gee et al. 2016). Psychologists have convincingly shown that patterns of psychological distress vary by citizenship status within the same immigrant community. These discrepancies in the extent of distress are the combined outcome of "objective" markers of social disadvantage, such as poverty and discrimination, and "subjective" markers, such as perceptions of success and of stigma. The point here is not to reduce the differences between the documented and the undocumented to their state of mind, but to fully acknowledge the extent to which citizenship permeates, structures, and saturates the ways of "doing, seeing, and speaking" politics. If we accept the importance of legal status in determining how people come to experience and interpret themselves and the political environment they are immersed in, then we can also start to understand its impact on how people act politically. I therefore choose to use the terms *privileged subjects* and *underprivileged subjects* to talk, respectively, about citizen-led and undocumented-led organizations. Returning to the opening scene of this chapter, I argue that privileged subjects tend to rely on *prevailing understandings* of the political game to guide their strategic action. Struggles over representation are intensified because of the unequal distribution of political, economic, social, and cultural capital between privileged and underprivileged subjects.

In the remainder of this chapter, I review how well-established CSOs built momentum by moving from class-action lawsuits to mass mobilization in the period from the 1970s to 2006. Second, I investigate how these organizations facilitated entry into the political arena for the undocumented youth. Lastly, I focus on how the strategic debate between proponents of Comprehensive Immigration Reform (CIR) and a stand-alone Dream Act bill in the 2007–11 period unmasked a fundamental gap in political understandings between undocumented migrants and their supporters. I argue that this gap is essentially rooted in the lack of lived experience of illegality that citizen supporters display vis-à-vis their undocumented counterparts.

Building momentum: From case-by-case lawsuits to legislative recognition

The presence of the undocumented youth in US territory became a contested issue for the first time in the 1970s (Seif 2004). Anti-immigrant coalitions started to emerge that lobbied at the state and local levels to deny undocumented youth access to public education. Five years later, the Texan government translated these lobbying efforts into the Alien Children Education (ACE) law, which stipulated that state funds for the education of undocumented youth would be withheld and schools would have the ability to deny them enrollment. In the absence of a strongly organized immigrant rights movement, the response from civil society was restricted to the filing of class-action lawsuits by actors such as the Mexican American Legal Defense and Education Fund (MALDEF).[2] In October 1980, the 5th US Circuit Court of Appeals ruled that "all aliens—even those illegally within the territorial bounds of the US—are entitled to protection of the laws" (*Telegraph*, December 1, 1981). The high watermark of class-action lawsuits was the *Plyler v. Doe* case, which sought to revoke the Texan ACE law. In 1982, the Supreme Court declared that excluding undocumented youths from primary and secondary education in Texas violated the Equal Protection Clause of the Fourteenth Amendment. Justice Brennan, who delivered the Supreme Court's majority opinion (the case was approved by a narrow five to four vote), explained the rationale behind this opinion as follows:[3]

> [T]he Texas statute imposes a lifetime hardship on a discrete class of children not accountable for their disabling status. These children can neither affect their parents' conduct nor their own undocumented status. The deprivation of public education is not like the deprivation of some other governmental benefit. Public education has a pivotal role in maintaining the fabric of our society and in sustaining our political and cultural heritage; the deprivation of education takes an inestimable toll on the social, economic, intellectual, and psychological well-being of the individual, and poses an obstacle to individual achievement.

As this excerpt shows, the Supreme Court took into consideration that undocumented youths could not be held accountable for their legal status in the same way as their parents. Using this legal status against them to deny them access to public education could thus not be justified in light of their potential future contribution to American society. Justice Brennan thereby actively appealed to the conflict between how the undocumented youth were being treated and the principles underlying American citizenship. Moreover, the court stressed the importance of public education in order to become integrated into the cultural, social, and political fabric of the society of residence. Being denied access to these institutions not only risks the exclusion of the undocumented youth from American society but also exacerbates the growth of "shadow populations," as Justice Brennan put it:[4]

> This situation raises the specter of a permanent caste of undocumented resident aliens, encouraged by some to remain here as a source of cheap labor, but nevertheless denied the benefits that our society makes available to citizens and lawful residents. The existence of such an underclass presents most difficult problems for a Nation that prides itself on adherence to principles of equality under law.

Plyler v. Doe thus established the unprecedented symbolic and legal recognition of undocumented youth as a population.

In the same year, the Supreme Court decided in the *Toll v. Moreno* case that a 1973 University of Maryland policy limiting access to in-state tuition for undocumented youth was unconstitutional. Justice Brennan's reasoning was that the University of Maryland policy violated the Supremacy Clause, which delineates the supremacy of the federal government in immigration policy by denying undocumented youth reduced in-state tuition (Olivas 1984). The Supreme Court's ruling created a precedent for struggles over college attendance for undocumented youth that was particularly fierce in California. The struggle mainly revolved around a 1983 California state bill that could be interpreted as providing the right to in-state tuition for undocumented youth at public colleges and universities. The state attorney general succumbed to pressure from the Republicans by denouncing this interpretation, which led to a lawsuit against California colleges and universities by individual students with the help of MALDEF. In 1985, the *Leticia A. et al. v. The Board of Regents of the University of California et al.* case tested the application of the Plyler ruling at the college level. In the previous year, five undocumented students who had been admitted to the University of California were charged the non-resident tuition fees rates (Olivas 1984, 33). While these students, who had been brought to the United States by their parents, had lived and resided in California for between three and eleven years, they did not qualify for legal residence. The University of California's argument that these youths should therefore be considered non-residents was dismissed by the Supreme Court, which stipulated that the university should treat them "in the same manner and on the same terms as US citizens."[5] At that time, advocacy efforts were still being led by university officials and legal experts, which resulted in the participation of undocumented students in the ad hoc Leticia A. network.

Due to the increased visibility of undocumented immigrants and mounting pressure from civil society, several political actors at the federal level became convinced of the need for more sweeping measures in response to irregular migration. In 1986, a compromise was reached in the form of the Immigration Reform and Control Act (IRCA), which on the one hand provided sanctions for employers who hired undocumented workers, and on the other hand, the regularization of about three million undocumented immigrants (Bloemraad et al. 2011, 14). In order to qualify, undocumented immigrants had to have entered the United States prior to January 1, 1982, and had to be able to prove uninterrupted residence. While IRCA was a major victory for immigrant rights advocacy, there were nevertheless three main reasons to have mixed feelings about the compromise (Flores-Gonzalez and Gutierrez 2010). First, many undocumented immigrants remained ineligible under the set criteria. Second, undocumented workers were criminalized. Third, IRCA provided increased funds for border control and immigration enforcement. As an unintended consequence of IRCA, organizations that would play an important role in the movement later on, such as the Illinois Coalition for Immigrant and Refugee Rights (ICIRR) in Chicago, were founded at this time to assist undocumented immigrants with the paperwork involved in the application process. While the main task of these organizations revolved around amnesty assistance, this shifted toward other forms of support, services, advocacy, and even mobilization into the 1990s (Flores-Gonzalez and Gutierrez 2010).

The 1990s were characterized by an anti-immigrant backlash in the United States (Voss and Bloemraad 2011). Researchers gathered evidence that IRCA had not eliminated irregular migration and the immigrant population was rapidly growing (Voss and Bloemraad 2011, 14–15). Public discourses about irregular migration became permeated by associations with the "flooding" of the border, crime waves, the "stealing" of jobs, the "profiting" from social services like healthcare and education, the devaluating of English as the *lingua franca*, and the threat to American norms and values. Such anti-immigrant sentiments gained popular legitimacy because of their endorsement by policymakers on both sides of the political spectrum, public intellectuals such as (among others) Samuel Huntington, and restrictionist groups including the Federation of American Immigration Reform (FAIR). Some of the first translations of these sentiments into policy practices were Operation Hold, Operation Gatekeeper, and Operation Safeguard—three programs instituted by the Border Control Agency to prevent the unauthorized influx of undocumented immigrants (Flores-Gonzalez and Gutierrez 2010, 9). At the federal level, anti-immigrant policies were introduced by the Clinton administration in 1996, aimed at restricting social benefits for undocumented immigrants (the Personal Responsibility and Work Opportunity Reconciliation Act: PRWORA) and expanding border enforcement (the Illegal Immigration Reform and Immigrant Responsibility Act: IIRIRA). The IIRIRA in particular had a substantial impact on the undocumented community, since it established a relationship between the federal government and undocumented immigrants based on law enforcement, policing, and deportation. In response to these restrictive measures, immigrant rights organizations joined forces in the national coalition organization Coordinara '96, which organized the first national march for immigrant rights in Washington, DC, drawing a crowd of about twenty-five thousand people. The effect of these mobilizations nevertheless remained largely symbolic. Hence, the hostile and restrictive political environment of the 1990s offered little opportunity for undocumented activism.

At the beginning of the new millennium, the political environment slowly started to change, and the restrictionists of the 1990s seemed to become replaced by expansionists. The idea of initiating regularization similar to that implemented in 1986 gained more and more ground, and even President Bush appeared to be open to discussing such measures. The immigrant rights movement increased their coherence and coordination in 1999, by creating the National Coalition for Dignity and Amnesty for Undocumented Immigrants. It was in this context that the case of undocumented youth reappeared on the political agenda. In 1999, CHIRLA[6] (an organization with a history dating back to 1986) had already created a network comprising students from ten high schools, aimed at developing "immigrant youth leadership" and called Wise-Up! It was this group of youths that under the leadership of CHIRLA's senior organizers was put into contact with Assemblyman Marco Firebaugh, who was working on a California state bill to improve the access to education of undocumented students. CHIRLA recognized that this was the right time to put the undocumented youth gathered in Wise Up! into the spotlight. In the spring of 2001, a group of thirty high school students traveled to Sacramento by bus, accompanied by their parents. Rose and Martin,[7] two members of Wise Up!, testified before the Senate Higher Education Committee in Sacramento that day. Undocumented high school student Martin stated the following in his testimony: "After I have worked so hard, after my parents have sacrificed so much, after I believed I could be someone, I now face with tremendous fear the possibility of not having a future."[8] Sitting next to Assemblyman Firebaugh, who had to comfort her during her emotional testimony, Rose stressed the importance of education: "As we all know, in this society, the key to success is education. I have known this all my life. That's why I have challenged myself with the most rigorous courses available."[9] Her testimony continued as she listed her Grade Point Average (GPA), the honors she had received during her education, and her extracurricular engagement. The undocumented youths CHIRLA had mobilized to speak before the committee represented a well-crafted image of the perfect student who is denied further opportunities to continue their education. In a retrospective report reflecting on the success of the campaign, a CHIRLA policy coordinator explained how she viewed this: "The students were all academically excellent. They went to legislators and said, 'I am the future. I am the first one in my family who will graduate from high school, the first who has the opportunity to attend college.'"[10] In October 2001, Governor Davis signed AB 540, permitting undocumented students to pay the less-expensive in-state tuition at California state universities and community colleges. At the time, this was seen as a victory for the immigrant rights movement and the first step to "giving a voice" to youth within the movement. Undocumented youth were put into the public spotlight, and AB 540 fueled the emergence of initiatives in schools across the state to support the right to education.

In August 2001, the first version of the federal DREAM Act was introduced. As the story of Tereza at the beginning of this chapter shows, several elected officials, together with well-established CSOs, explored ways to involve undocumented youth in their advocacy campaigns. However, the terrorist attacks of September 11 caused the issue of immigrant rights to be put on hold—as McKenzie put it, changing America from a "nation of immigrants" to a "nation of suspects" (McKenzie 2004). Claiming immigrant rights at the federal level thus became an increasingly difficult task. Yet at the same time, significant progress was being made at the state level. AB 540 came into effect in October 2001, thereby waiving out-of-state tuition fees for undocumented youth in California attending higher education institutions. Other bills ensued in Texas (HB 1402), Utah (HB 144), New York (SB 7784), Washington (HB 1079), Oklahoma (HB 1559), Illinois (HB 60), Kansas (HB 2145), New Mexico (SB 582), and Minnesota (HF 1063) (Seif 2004). By 2010, an estimated forty thousand AB 540 students were enrolled in colleges and universities in California (Patler and Appelbaum 2011), but the importance of AB 540 extends beyond the fact that it made college more accessible to undocumented youth (Abrego 2008). This label proved to outsiders as well to as to the youths themselves that they were more than "illegal aliens"—they had the right to rights. AB 540 thus unintentionally legitimized a disenfranchised group. The term "DREAMer"—generally referring to undocumented youth who would be eligible to a path to citizenship under the DREAM Act—gradually became a ready-made identity for undocumented youth (Nicholls 2013, 47–59). In July 2003, the DREAM Act was introduced in Congress once more, spurring campaigns by pro-immigrant advocacy organizations. Despite these evolutions, the political climate nevertheless remained unfavorable to advance legislative measures on their behalf.

A first taste of politics: The March 10 mega-marches

Up to that time, the impetus for immigrant rights organizing had largely come from the West Coast rather than the Midwest. This all changed in 2006 when the struggle for immigrant rights reached a historic turning point with some of the largest mass marches the United States has ever witnessed. The protests were sparked by the introduction of the Border, Protection, Antiterrorism, and Illegal Immigration Control Act, better known as the Sensenbrenner Bill, in 2005. This federal act would charge undocumented immigrants residing in the United States with a felony for their presence and make them ineligible to regularize their legal status in the future. The purpose of the bill, which was proposed by the Republican James Sensenbrenner, was to increase enforcement and simultaneously criminalize undocumented immigrants as such. The prospect of this immediate and nationwide threat evoked a sense of anxiety and urgency in immigrant rights organizations across the country that fueled immigrant organizing in the South and Midwest in places like Dallas, Phoenix, Detroit, and Chicago (Voss and Bloemraad 2011, 8).

Immigrant rights organizations in Chicago were at the forefront of organizing the collective response to the bill. On March 10, 2006, some one hundred thousand people marched in what the *Chicago Tribune* dubbed "one of the biggest pro-immigrant rallies in U.S. history."[11] Waving American and Mexican flags side by side and chanting slogans such as "We are America" and "*Sí se puede*" (Yes, it can be done), the protesters tried to express their right to citizenship. The marchers' discourses referred extensively to the importance of undocumented workers to the American economy. As one of the many youths present told a reporter, they were "supporting our parents and our parents' parents, who came here and worked hard. A lot of classrooms are empty today." Democratic Representative Luis Gutierrez addressed the crowd by expressing his pride about this historic undertaking: "We have brought together the true fabric of what Chicago is, of what our country is." The Chicago "fabric" that had made this unprecedented turnout possible involved the long-standing cooperative efforts and networks of well-established CSOs that had taken root in the city (Cordero-Guzman et al. 2008). The bar set by the March 10 rally was quickly raised by historically high turnouts in follow-up protests later that month in Los Angeles (650,000), Dallas (350,000), Washington, DC (180,000), and New York (100,000) (Voss and Bloemraad 2011, 8). In the aftermath of the protests, the first of May—better known as International Workers Day—was proclaimed to be a "Day without immigrants." That day, classrooms were half empty, factories had to shut down, and shops and restaurants remained closed. In the end, the Sensenbrenner Bill was revoked. However, the cry for immigration reform went unanswered.

Most of the undocumented youth I would come to know later were still too young at the time to really register what was going on, let alone be actively involved in the movement. Yet, for later-to-be undocumented youth organizers who were present, the significance of the mega-marches was that an unprecedented number of peers had "stepped out of the shadows." The visual presence of youth during the march was undeniable, with groups of students marching on the frontlines. Based on a survey of 410 marchers, it was estimated that about 25 percent of the marchers in Chicago were undocumented youth (Pallares and Flores-Gonzales 2010, xvi). In the interviews I did with IYJL organizers in Chicago five years after the marches, it became apparent that the emotional and kinesthetic experience of marching alongside thousands demanding their rights was crucial to conceive of themselves as subjects capable of claiming their rights.

For example, Yolanda recounts how participating in the march in Chicago was the first "political" event she attended:

> The very first time that I found anything when people were mobilizing or something was when I was twelve. And that's when the 2006 marches were happening. And they were huge and—my mom always puts the radio on in Spanish and … they always talk about immigrant stuff. And they were talking about the marches and how people were going to come out and like, we're going to show them how big of a community we are and all that. And I went with my mom, like I missed school and I know a lot of kids in my school also went—it was a Mexican school. When I was at the march I felt really powerful, like, I've never seen so many undocumented people come and say, "I'm undocumented!" and like, actually mobilizing, I guess. I didn't know at the time what it took to do that, but it was a big moment.

For Yolanda, the march represented her first encounter with immigrant rights mobilization. The participation of her family explains her presence that day, because she was too young at the time to participate in organizing. The experience of Jobito was slightly different in that he was more "aware" of what was going on.

> The first time I attended an event was the 2006 marches in downtown Chicago. Those were huge. I went with a high school teacher and a couple of other students who weren't undocumented, but were just supportive, because they had parents who had just immigrated. And … that march, it kind of seemed more like I'm going to support immigrants, instead of being because like I'm undocumented and I need to work and do this for myself. And I think it was partly because I was so young and I just wasn't at that point where I was like, yes, I need to fight for my rights. And I think it was partly because there weren't a lot of youth speakers, like I never saw someone who was young speak. … I mean I'm an immigrant, but they're not really speaking about me or for me, I felt like.

In the above interview excerpt, Jobito reflected on the fact that he had a hard time identifying with the cause of the march because of the relative absence of young speakers. This demonstrates a more general sentiment among undocumented youth that well-established CSOs were speaking "for" them. Through student networks, schools, and local community organizations, undocumented youth had been crucial in terms of grassroots organizing. Yet strategic decisions were being made by adult organizers, supposedly to guarantee the public safety of "vulnerable" undocumented youth.

As an older youth, Tamara, who had become more involved in the movement since her involvement in the 2001 DREAM Act campaign, participated in the actual organizing of the marches. In an interview, she recounted how young people were underrepresented and how she felt as though it was hard to match her personal understandings with the understandings of older immigrant organizers:

> I remember for example in the 2006 marches ... it was me and someone else at a meeting, and like two people in the room out of thirty were under twenty-five. ... In that meeting, for example, most of them were citizens. But most of them were older immigrants from other countries, but undocumented immigrants of some kind. And so ... *I didn't find a personal connection* with them beyond the politics. ... A lot of them are scared from my experience. ... *And I think there aren't a lot of shared experiences* that we've had between me and older immigrants. ... I think we have a lot of the same frustrations when it comes to work etc., but ... they don't see themselves as having a legitimate right to things. Like they, as opposed to us who grew up undocumented, like I feel, like I have the right to work, to travel and to be in school, and to all of those things, I feel like there's no reason why I can't have that right. ... I don't think they feel any entitlement, and those of us who have grown up here do.

As Tamara explained, the limited involvement of undocumented youth within the organization of the 2006 marches was problematic because of the absence of shared lived experiences of illegality. In response to a need on the ground for a virtual "safe space"[12] for undocumented youth to connect and share experiences as underprivileged subjects, the forum DREAM Act Portal (DAP) was launched in March 2006. The emerging undocumented youth movement heavily relied on the use of online venues to create nationwide networks, raise awareness, and organize the local community (Corrunker 2012, 162–63). A forum like the DAP functioned as a tool to break the pattern of isolation that characterizes life for many undocumented youths. For example, in an interview, Damian told me how he felt isolated throughout college. However, it was by getting in touch with people online and learning about the actions around the DREAM Act that he started to become involved in the movement. Damian eventually became one of the portal's moderators, an IYJL member, and the founder of an on-campus student organization. Anita also testified to the importance of these online spaces to make sense of her own situation:

> When I was in high school and doing all this—like trying to figure out what it was to be undocumented or what I was to do, most of the things that I would come across were the blogs, like it wasn't really talked about in a newspaper

or online or another website ... It was so important, I think, for me personally, right, coming to terms with what I was going through, so I think it also helps to share that information with other youth who might be going through the same thing now that I was going through six years ago.

The DAP fulfilled the need within the undocumented community to exchange views on the political situation and fuel increasing dissent against their so-called allies. Social media such as Facebook, YouTube, Twitter, Tumblr, and blogs gradually became important tools for the undocumented youth movement to break away from their parent organizations and voice their concerns. They equally allowed for the experimentation of undocumented youth with sharing stories and "coming out" to one another long before this would become a strategy to gain public visibility (Corrunker 2012, 162–63)

Increasing dissent: The generalists vs. the particularists

On October 24, 2007, the DREAM Act was stranded once more with a vote of fifty-two to forty-four in the senate. While the Bush administration had supported measures for undocumented youth as part of the CIR bills, it opposed the DREAM Act, stating that it would create a "preferential path to citizenship for a special class of illegal aliens":[13]

The Administration is sympathetic to the position of young people who were brought here illegally as children and have come to know the United States as home. Any resolution of their status, however, must be careful not to provide *incentives for recurrence of the illegal conduct* that has brought the Nation to this point. By creating a special path to citizenship that is unavailable to other prospective immigrants ... S. 2205 [The DREAM Act Bill] falls short. ... The path to citizenship remains open for decades, thus creating a strong temptation for future illegal aliens to purchase fraudulent documents on a burgeoning black market. Moreover, the bill's confidentiality provisions are drawn straight from the 1986 amnesty law and will provide the same haven for fraud and criminality as that law did.

As this excerpt shows, criminalizing and illegalizing discourses were mobilized by the Bush administration to undermine the bill's legitimacy. The DREAM Act was dismissed by its opposers as a piece of legislation that, if passed, could potentially undermine the institution of citizenship in the United States.

The failure of the DREAM Act was a massive defeat for those who had advocated focusing on piecemeal legislation rather than a comprehensive approach.

The defeat was interpreted in diverging ways, depending on which standpoint actors had on the CIR versus DREAM Act strategy. From 2007 to 2010, the movement became polarized between *generalists* and *particularists*. The *generalists*, who were led by the well-established organizations that had taken the lead in arranging the marches, were reaffirmed in their view that the piecemeal demand for the DREAM Act should be made subordinate to the more sweeping demand for Comprehensive Immigration Reform (CIR). They responded in January 2008 by founding Reform Immigration for America (RIFA), an ambitious coalition comprising the largest and most powerful pro-immigrant organizations in the United States. RIFA's strategy was to push for an all-encompassing CIR bill that would include the measures proposed under the DREAM Act. Central to the strategic efforts to make the DREAM Act part of the struggle for CIR was setting up new networks that could foster undocumented youth leadership. This was the United We Dream (UWD) coalition (Zimmerman 2011, 16), which would become the largest undocumented youth network in the United States. The *particularists*, mainly comprising up-and-coming, youth-centered organizations that wanted to focus on passing the DREAM Act, in turn interpreted the defeat of the DREAM Act as a signal that a radical shift in strategy was necessary (Amador 2011). Undocumented youth who were already connected through the DAP took the initiative to set up a new militant website called Dream Activist. Particularists would become centered on a novel style of youth organizing, the political self-presentation of which would increasingly drift away from the DREAMer template that had been created for them.

The coming of age of a new generation of undocumented youth activists ready to speak out about what they wanted and to take up an active leadership role inadvertently led to conflicts over strategy and representation within the movement (Nicholls 2013). Even though UWD had started as a way for RIFA to establish a strong youth chapter, it nevertheless strived to become more autonomous. In 2008, UWD joined up with Dream Activist members to organize a national field meeting with students from more than fifteen states. In contrast to RIFA's approach, the main goal was to design a strategy that would allow for the passing of the DREAM Act. The conference paid testament to a growing number of youth-led initiatives, including but not limited to the IYJL, ONE Michigan, the Kansas Missouri Dream Alliance (KM/DA), and the New York Student Youth Leadership Council (NYSYLC).

Organizations such as IYJL launched Education Not Deportation (END) campaigns across the country. Through heavily mediatized and personal public campaigns, they were able to halt the deportation of dozens of undocumented students (Patler and Gonzales 2015). Reyes, whose story was mentioned in the book's introduction, was one of the first and most prominent of the undocumented youth in Chicago whose deportation was successfully halted.

The pioneering campaign that had been jointly launched by ICIRR and IYJL would become a model of sorts for the campaigns that ensued. In a guide drafted by NIYA and Dream Activist, Reyes provided a personal testimony to urge people to "go public":

Four days before my scheduled deportation, I had been forced to purchase a one-way ticket to Mexico. Not knowing where I would live or who I would stay with, I knew that I had no choice but to fight. In doing so, I had to prove that I deserved to remain in this country. Although uncommon now, the fight to stop my deportation would last a whole year. In the beginning, attorney after attorney told me that they would not pick up my case, because my case was simple: there was nothing they could do, and my best option was to go back. … It would not be until I met other undocumented youth like myself, that I found the support that I had been looking for. Unlike the lawyers, they agreed that I deserved to remain in this country, that this was my home. Shortly thereafter, we came together to formalize a campaign. The message was simple: I had been a contributing member to my community, and someone that would benefit the United States. It would take 25,000 faxes sent to the Department of Homeland Security (DHS), over 1,000 faculty members signing a petition, thousands of calls to DHS, five congress people, two city resolutions (City of Chicago, Berwyn), one private bill, and several rallies to stop my deportation. The halting of my deportation came with the realization that I owed it to myself, to all the people that contributed to my campaign, and to the immigrant rights movement to continue to fight. *We therefore must all come to the self-realization that we are the only ones that can change our situation and living in the shadows is no longer an option.*

Meanwhile, the presidential election of Barack Obama spurred enthusiasm and hope for change among many undocumented youth. During a debate in California in January 2008, Obama expressed how he had supported the Illinois Dream Act, which provided access to college to undocumented youth, "because we actually want well-educated kids in our country who are able to succeed and become part of this economy and part of the American dream."[14] Furthermore, when asked for his opinion about the DREAM Act during a debate in February, Obama replied as follows:[15]

Something that we can do immediately that I think is very important is to pass the DREAM Act, which allows children who through no fault of their own are here but have essentially grown up as Americans, allow them the opportunity for higher education. … I do not want two classes of citizens in this country. I want everybody to prosper.

In view of these remarks, it should not be surprising that undocumented youth participated heavily in Get-Out-The-Vote drives in support of Obama during the presidential elections. When Obama was elected in November 2008, it was generally expected that immigration reform—and by extension, the DREAM Act—would be a top priority, as he had promised. On January 20, 2009, Barack Obama was inaugurated as the 44th President of the United States. The 2009–10 period that followed was characterized by mounting intra-movement disputes, youth empowerment, and increased public visibility. Over time, it would become more and more apparent that what well-established CSOs wanted and what undocumented youth organizations wanted were not one and the same thing. RIFA responded to the new president's inauguration by launching a massive nationwide campaign to pass CIR before the congressional elections in the fall of 2010 (Nicholls 2013, 77). Millions of dollars were invested by coalition members into mobilizing more than one hundred thousand people for a march on Washington on March 21, 2010.

During my fieldwork at ICIRR, I participated in preparatory meetings for that march. The main issue revolved around getting the community to fill buses to go to DC. At a grassroots leaders training event sponsored by ICIRR, I first encountered the undocumented youth organizers from IYJL. The training began by explaining the goals that would have to be met by the local grassroots leaders to make the march happen. What struck me during the training and the preparatory events that followed was the way ICIRR put youth into the spotlight to gain support from the local community. After the initial presentation, a "call to action" by IYJL member Reyes was scheduled.

> I have been in the US for fifteen years. I was undocumented in high school, did everything I was expected to do. But then, in 2009, ICE came looking for me. Everyone told me that I had two options: either live in the shadows and not go to school or go back to Mexico. Then the immigrant rights movement came looking for me; they wanted to put a face to the movement. … We can no longer live in the shadows: just like the immigrant rights movement came looking for me, I'm looking for you!

As Reyes explained, the immigrant rights movement had come "looking for him" once more to display youth support for CIR. This example demonstrates how ICIRR co-opted undocumented youth to support the call for CIR through the RIFA campaign.

While RIFA-affiliated organizations had been gearing up since the beginning of 2009 to organize nationally, youth-led organizations such as IYJL, DREAM Activist, and NYLSYNC autonomously started to mobilize locally. Frustrated with the generalists' course, they increasingly tried to spread a different type of public message based on their personal, emotional experiences rather than on calculated professionalism. The DREAM Act and the American Dream Act were re-introduced in Congress and in the senate, respectively, by bipartisan supporters in March 2009. In June 2009, the United We Dream network, supported by Dream Activist members, organized its first National Dream Act Graduation in Washington, DC, with acts of solidarity taking place locally in Arizona, California, Florida, Illinois, Indiana, Kentucky, Massachusetts, Montana, New Jersey, New York, North Carolina, and Texas. More than four hundred undocumented youth participated in the events.[16] The youth wore caps and gowns as a symbolic way to demand their right to education—and citizenship—through the DREAM Act. Speakers shared their stories of hardship with the crowd, stating their full names. Some of them were in proceedings to be deported, and END campaigns had been launched to halt their deportations. Lizzie, one of the student speakers, urged others to come out as undocumented: "Share your story with close friends. ... Wherever you are, choose to fight. Be more than a dreamer. Be a leader." Those last words expressed a general sentiment among undocumented youth activists: it was the right time to supersede the imposed stereotypical image of the testifying DREAMer by becoming leaders. What this leadership would look like, is what I will turn to in the next chapter.

Conclusion

This chapter shows that the politicization of migrant illegality as a public issue and undocumented youths' entry into the political field were facilitated by well-established CSOs. These organizations employed their accumulated know-how, resources, and networks to place the issue of rights to education and a path to citizenship for undocumented youth on the political agenda. Obtaining limited forms of legal recognition was central to the movement's strategy in the start-up phase. Rights-claiming strategies ranged from class-action lawsuits to school walkouts and mass marches. The monopoly over the framing of actions remained largely in the hands of well-established CSOs. This power imbalance within the field affected the conditions under which undocumented youth could gain precarious agency. Undocumented youth gradually became incorporated into campaigns set up by these organizations. The template for the ideal-typical DREAMer was created by citizen organizers as a ready-made public identity for undocumented youth to represent the student voice within the movement. This image was put into practice by directing the undocumented youths to give public testimonies. Despite the youths' involvement, their participation in the everyday working of these organizations was limited, if not nonexistent. Decisions were made by a small group of experienced immigrant rights leaders, and "stakeholders," such as undocumented youth, were invited to follow their lead. Political activity and strategies were typically nonconfrontational in nature in this phase, as was the case with the class-action lawsuits aimed at securing educational rights for undocumented youth.

At the same time, however, the involvement of undocumented youth in these campaigns played an important part in their future activist trajectories (see Part II). Partial legal recognition and incorporation into the educational system fostered feelings of entitlement among undocumented youth, as these aspects are normally associated with full-blown citizenship. A positive and empowering self-understanding was created as an unintended by-product of the legal recognition of undocumented students' educational rights at the local level. In the wake of this recognition, student support networks were created in many schools across the country, and these groups quickly became spaces for youth to develop their own political (self-)understandings. Virtual spaces such as the DAP fulfilled a similar role in the online world. At this point, these "safe spaces" were still informal meeting places for young people who were struggling with similar issues related to their legal status. Nevertheless, within the immigrant rights movement, these spaces gradually became sites of contestation against the hierarchical structure. Despite their participation in the campaign for CIR, undocumented youth started to feel as if this was not "their struggle," and they grew increasingly uncomfortable and frustrated with the fact that others claimed to represent their interests. Well-established CSOs were accused of co-opting DREAMers, and the image of the "perfect DREAMer" that had been forced on undocumented youth by the spin-doctors of these organizations no longer resonated with their own understandings. What once functioned well for immigrant rights organizations as a clever way to "put a face to the issue" now felt like yet another straitjacket imposed on undocumented youth.

2

Undocumented, unafraid, unapologetic

The rise of undocumented youth activism in Chicago

*"People are starting to see that undocumented people are finally tak-
ing the lead and that they're deciding what's right for them and their
communities rather than having these executive directors of really
well-known national organizations decide on … the future and legislation that will not affect them at all." (Cynthia, IYJL member,
interview)*

In August 2011, IYJL members Claudia, Jobito, Ilene, and three other undocumented youth organizers were arrested during an act of civil disobedience in
Chicago. I had become acquainted with the "Chicago Six," as they became better known in the press, especially since I joined the group the year before. As
one of the first undocumented youths who had participated in an act of civil disobedience, Tamara had overseen preparing and training them. The action was a
response to a public hearing about Secure Communities, a federal program set
up in 2008 to ensure that local law enforcement shared identifying information
with Immigration Customs and Enforcement (ICE), implying that minor violations could lead to deportation. The program was voluntary by nature, meaning
that states had the ability to opt out. By the time the action took place, an estimated one hundred thousand people had already been deported through the
program. After months of protests, Illinois Governor Quinn decided to terminate
the agreement with ICE, thereby opting out of the program. However, in August
2011, ICE announced that Secure Communities was mandatory, and a Secure
Communities Task Force was put in place and scheduled its first public hearing
on August 17. That day, hundreds of people gathered at the Haymarket Memo-
rial in Chicago to listen to the stories of families who were "torn apart" by Secure
Communities. The crowd then walked to the place of the public hearing. After
part of the crowd had entered the room, the police decided to shut the door, to
which the crowd responded by chanting "Let them in! Let them in!" In the end,
everybody was allowed to enter the room and the hearing began. After the usual
introductory remarks were made, IYJL member Ara took the floor. Ara introduced herself as "undocumented" and talked about the devastating effect of the

Citizen X. Thomas Swerts, Oxford University Press. © Thomas Swerts (2026).
DOI: 10.1093/9780197844038.003.0003

program on her family and the community. Next, she called on those gathered to collectively leave the hearing as a way of protest:[17]

> Enough! Enough with the lies to us and to yourselves that somehow you will fix something that is designed to deport our families. I can't in good conscience stay at a hearing that's a front for something so irreparable and insecure. Sometimes words are not enough, hearings are not enough, press conferences and speeches are not enough. I am here today with my undocumented friends, because there comes a time when we need to take greater action. We are tired of fear, and today, today we will break that fear from Secure Communities. I and five others are going to walk outside of this building right now. We are going to intentionally block traffic and put ourselves under arrest, knowing full well that under Secure Communities, this act of protest, this minor offence, will mean that we could get placed in deportation. This is the risk that immigrants all across the country take every day. We ask the community to follow us outside, and we ask the people on the task force to have courage for your communities and do the right thing.... *We will walk out because we are undocumented, unafraid, and unapologetic. Join us!*

When the six IYJL organizers left the room, over three hundred people followed them. Next, the six sat down and blocked an exit of the 90/94 Highway, wearing their "Undocumented, Unafraid" T-shirts. A press statement was released, containing the stories of the arrested youth. Fundraising efforts were held to pay their $1,500 bail. In September, the Chicago Six appeared in court facing a mob action charge. While a deal was offered by the prosecutor, they rejected it because they "refused to be labeled as criminals." These youth were no longer merely enlisted by well-established organizations to prove their point. The image of the bold community leader engaging in civil disobedience did not resemble the perfect image of the DREAMer. As Claudia would later put it, "Taking risks is one of the biggest things IYJL stands for, because you can't like, move, you can't like *progress* as a movement without people taking risks." These youths had taken matters into their own hands, determining what they wanted to state about themselves and putting their existence on the line by being arrested for civil disobedience. In other words, they relied on their precarious agency to step out of the shadows, reborn as activists who are "undocumented, unafraid, and unapologetic."

***

This ethnographic vignette serves to underscore the epistemological shift that took place within the immigrant rights movement when undocumented youth broke free from well-established CSOs. Existing accounts of immigrants' political participation tend to focus on the myriad ways in which well-established

CSOs provide opportunities for the integration and incorporation of undocumented immigrants. The previous chapter has shown, however, that accounts which emphasize the importance of political representation by well-established CSOs are harder to rhyme with the rise of autonomous forms of undocumented activism. More specifically, such accounts ignore the question of why undocumented migrants feel the urge to develop autonomous spaces for political participation and how they are able to develop their distinctive style of political being and speaking in the first place. In order to formulate answers to these types of questions, we need to turn attention away from overly structuralist and rationalist accounts of immigrant political representation, toward the hermeneutic mechanisms at play. Doing so will allow us to investigate how differences in political understandings and corresponding ideas about tactics drive conflicts over representation. In this regard, representation can be seen as a *process* that involves disputes over understandings, morality, and truth that in turn affect strategy, tactics, and political activity.

In the previous chapter, I showed that privileged subjects tend to rely on *prevailing understandings* of the political game to guide their strategic action. By contrast, underprivileged subjects tend to rely on understandings that are rooted in the discursive, embodied, and emotional experience of being radically excluded from that very order to inform their strategic outlook. Undocumented activists use the lived experiences of illegality as their clay to mold new and more radical political understandings. This does not mean, however, that the understandings of underprivileged subjects are not citing from existing repertoires and discourses. Such understandings nevertheless often do have a prefigurative quality to them, in that they try to actively imagine a more just and egalitarian alternative to the status quo. While the former understandings are generally regarded as "suitable" or "constructive" by established political elites, the latter understandings are often deemed "unsuitable" or "unconstructive." Struggles over representation are intensified because of the unequal distribution of political, economic, social, and cultural capital between citizens and non-citizens. However, these struggles do not just occur on the fault lines between citizens and noncitizens. Since struggles over citizenship necessarily entail the drawing of boundaries, they also precipitate conflicts *among* undocumented immigrants according to diverging levels of deservingness (Chauvin and Garcés-Mascareñas 2014).

Anticipating what will be demonstrated in further detail in Part II of the book, the "safe spaces" of undocumented-led organizations represent the studios or ateliers where the process of crafting, experimenting, and fine-tuning of political understandings takes place. After working hours, classrooms, the backrooms of churches, or online discussion fora are transformed into what Polletta has called "free spaces," or "small-scale settings within a community or movement that are removed from the direct control of dominant groups, are voluntarily participated in, and generate the cultural challenge that precedes or accompanies political mobilization" (Polletta 1999). Through open dialogue and the exchange of deeply personal experiences, undocumented activists were able to erect activist infrastructures that created a milieu suitable for the innovation of existing political repertoires.[18] As Nicholls recently argued, the geography of such activist infrastructures is unevenly distributed and deeply urbanized (Nicholls 2021). In fact, as I have argued elsewhere, urban space offers undocumented activists opportunities to become political by creating, using, and appropriating in-between spaces (Swerts 2017). The erecting and maintaining of safe spaces that can support marginalized groups like the undocumented requires continuous relational work (The Roestone Collective 2014). Safe spaces can start to function as a "backstage" where undocumented migrants can conquer their fears, (re)imagine themselves as political subjects, and develop political scripts. As will be explained in further ethnographic detail in Chapter 7, the functioning of self-organizations as safe spaces is therefore a crucial factor that helps to explain the rise of the undocumented youth activism (The Roestone Collective 2014, 383).

In the remainder of this chapter, I situate this remarkable rise within the broader history of the immigrant rights movement. First, I show how undocumented youth relied on autonomous "safe spaces" to develop their own ideas about how they should be represented, thereby motivating their emancipation from well-established CSOs within the movement. Next, I study the implications of the self-representation and radicalization of undocumented youth activists in the 2011–13 period. Lastly, I argue that the political understandings that undocumented youth come up with and act out in self-organizations are radically different from the prevailing understandings propagated by citizens in well-established CSOs.

Coming out of the shadows: Storytelling acts

In the previous chapter, I argued that what appeared to be purely strategic conflicts between proponents of CIR and the DREAM Act hid a deeper hermeneutic conflict over insurmountable political understandings between citizens and noncitizens. These tensions eventually culminated in a seminal event: the National Coming out of the Shadows Day on March 10, 2010. I deliberately use the word "seminal" here, as this rally exemplifies an epistemological break that undocumented youth felt as though they needed to make to become political subjects with equal rights to being and speaking.

The IYJL in Chicago pioneered this first "coming out" event. IYJL closely cooperated with other youth-led organizations within the United We Dream network to set up the National Coming Out of the Shadows action week between March 15 and March 21. In their press release, IYJL member Ilene expressed the sense of urgency that was in the air:[19]

> We cannot wait any more. Not while our parents are getting deported and our youths' dreams fall apart due to an obsolete immigration system that has failed us and the country. I have supported Senator Durbin and President Obama, and now we need them to act. This country cannot wait any more, we will not wait any longer.

In a reversal of roles, a letter of invitation was sent out to President Obama, Senator Durbin, and Janet Napolitano to come and sit down at IYJL's negotiating table. In the following press release, IYJL described how they refused to be shut out of policy negotiations any longer. The makeshift stage where they would perform their "coming out" speeches would be their symbolic "table":[20]

> Having been negated to sit at the table from the various countries from where our parents brought us, having been negated to sit at the table by our politicians who make of us undocumented suspects, criminals and, at times, lesser than human, we undocumented youth have opened our own table, and this March 10th we have formally invited President Obama, Senator Durbin, and Director of Homeland Security Janet Napolitano and their respective family members to join us. At our table they are welcomed. At our table they are not negated a place. At our table we will be able to break bread, at our table President Obama, Senator Durbin, and Mrs. Napolitano will be able to see us face to face and not as an amorphous group which statistics and reports have distorted from time to time.

On March 10, about one thousand undocumented youths gathered in Union Park to march to Federal Plaza in downtown Chicago. Eight IYJL members "came out" that day within footsteps of the local ICE headquarters. Solidarity actions simultaneously took place in New York, Seattle, and various cities in California. The speech by IYJL member Raquel reflected on the political moment then:

> Last week several people asked me: "What are you going to do if nothing happens?" What they really meant is: "What are you going to do if everything that has been put into this is not enough?" Where would all the energy go? Where would all the stories of frustration and sadness go? Where would the hopelessness go? And I decided not to answer that question. I refuse to think of what another ten years of frustration, sadness, and fear would feel like.

My name is Raquel and I am undocumented. I refuse to think of what another ten years of not knowing if I will be able to come home to my mother and brother will feel like. I refuse to think of what another ten years of dreams shut down will feel like. Dreams of a good education, dreams of a normal life without fear. I am undocumented; I am not afraid and I will not answer that question; I refuse to answer that question and I don't want anyone to answer that question.

We are here today for a reason; I am doing this for you, for all my friends, for my family. I will not hide any longer; I will come out of the shadows every day if I have to; I am a human being; I deserve to be happy!

Compared with the ideal-typical representation of the DREAMer that had been developed as a template by well-established CSOs, this story clearly strikes a different tone: it communicates emotions such as anger, fear, and frustration, and it evokes a certain urgency aimed at empowering others like them. It is, in other words, a highly personal and emotional account that is not so much directed at gaining the approval of the mainstream through highlighting educational achievements, but instead at motivating and mobilizing other undocumented youths to come out, join the movement, and be vocal about their political demands. A few weeks after the "coming out" rally, IYJL members organized four buses full of Chicago youth to join RIFA's March for America national demonstration in Washington, DC. Yet this did not mean that they would give up on their newly discovered autonomy.

Undocumented, unafraid: Acts of civil disobedience

In the spring of 2010, undocumented youth declared themselves "Undocumented and Unafraid" in "coming out" rallies around the nation. The expression referred to a widely circulated op-ed (see Nicholls 2013, 74–75) written by a handful of undocumented youth leaders that urged others like them to "refuse to be silent any longer."[21] The tone of this piece communicated the feelings of frustration that had built up among undocumented youth with regard to issues of strategy and representation. The generalists who had been leading the efforts to push for CIR were denounced as part of the "nonprofit industrial complex"—a "social justice elite" portrayed as having blocked the DREAM Act from being introduced and as profiting from co-opting the case of undocumented youth for their own purposes. The message of this op-ed piece was loud and clear concerning the issue of representation:

Our so-called allies need to realize that they are not undocumented and, as such, do not have the right to say what undocumented youth need or want.

Our progressive allies insist in imposing their paternalistic stand to oppose the DREAM Act and tell us that this is not the "right" choice for us to acquire "legal" status in this country. We wonder: Who are they to decide for us? And by what criteria do they deem the DREAM Act not to be the "right" legislation for undocumented youth to become "legal" in this country?... WE DO NOT WANT IMMIGRATION RIGHTS "ADVOCATES" SPEAKING FOR US ANY LONGER. WE DEMAND THE RIGHT TO REPRESENT OURSELVES!

These undocumented youths argued that privileged subjects could not possibly claim to be legitimate representatives of underprivileged subjects like themselves. From then on, allies who wanted to support undocumented youth in their organizing efforts would be invited to "check their privilege," as well as to "step back" to enable others to "step up."

In the months preceding the coming out rallies, undocumented youth actions had become more radical in nature. The success of the national Coming Out of the Shadows week had led to enthusiasm, renewed confidence, and empowerment among the undocumented youth movement's rank and file. The symbolic impact of the groundbreaking coming out actions was further enhanced by countless reposting, liking, and self-analyzing in videos, slide montages, personal accounts, and opinion pieces—all serving to highlight the dawn of a new era. There was widespread agreement at the time that the representation *of* undocumented youth *by* undocumented youth had to rely on novel strategies and techniques that were rooted in, and more closely aligned with, their shared lived experiences. The campaign against Arizona's anti-immigration Support Our Law Enforcement and Safe Neighborhoods Act (SB 1070) put these new political understandings and their tactics to the test. The passage of SB 1070 meant that the police could stop immigrants and demand identification, thereby resulting in racial profiling. Similar laws ensued in Pennsylvania, Rhode Island, Michigan, Minnesota, and South Carolina.

It was in this increasingly anti-immigrant climate that five prominent undocumented youth leaders, better known as "the DREAM Act 5," staged an act of civil disobedience at Senator McCain's office in Tucson on May 17, 2010. Enthused by the March 10 event that she had helped to organize in Chicago weeks before, Tamara traveled all the way from Chicago to participate in the action. In what would later be called a watershed event in the history of the movement, undocumented youth tried to pressure Senator McCain into supporting the DREAM Act as he had done in previous years (Galindo 2012). When police officers came that day to arrest them for trespassing, Tamara decided to leave the room. In a blog post, she reflected on this moment:

That day we walked into the office wearing our blue caps and gowns, said that we would not leave until McCain co-sponsored the DREAM Act, and sat on the floor in a circle. We linked arms with our backs to each other, and began to chant. The police were called, and we spent the day talking to the press, negotiating with the police, and listening to our friends chant outside. Almost seven hours later the police gave us an ultimatum, and said that if we did not leave we would be arrested. Our lawyer turned to me and said "You're coming with me. I don't want to hear otherwise." I froze. I had thought this whole time that I was going to get arrested. Lara and Leticia also told me that I should leave because they could not feel good if I was going to have to fight from inside detention. Mohammad said that we needed a person outside to tell the story of those on the inside, someone from our project who was also undocumented and could speak to the press. And so when the police asked if we were staying or leaving, I stood up and walked out. The moment that I walked out of the office, I knew it meant I was going to push myself to be fearless, just like my friends had just been.... I walked up to the rally, asked for the megaphone, and began: "My name is Tamara and I'm undocumented."... A few minutes after we saw the police vans pull up to Senator McCain's office, and managed to see Lara and Leticia wave to us as they were carried off to jail.

The DREAM Act 5 represented undocumented youth organizations from California, Michigan, Kansas, Illinois, and Arizona. Risking arrest and deportation was indicative of the strategic public display of the embodied vulnerability these undocumented youths experienced due to their precarious legal status. Immediately after the act of civil disobedience, members from youth organizations IYJL, Dream Team LA, ONE Michigan, Kansas Missouri Dream Alliance, and DREAM Activist announced the launch of the "Dream is Coming" campaign. Similar sit-in protests led to arrests in LA, St. Louis, and Washington, DC, later that month. In June, ten undocumented students held a hunger strike in Senator Schumer's office in DC. Another hunger strike followed in North Carolina. Once more, youth activists were putting themselves on the line to gain visibility for their cause. Between July 19 and 21, the second National Dream Act Mobilization took place in DC, repeating the staging of a mass mock graduation ceremony. This time around, the mobilization was accompanied by a large-scale sit-in at the congressional offices of several senators on Capitol Hill that led to the arrest of twenty-one undocumented youth activists. Eight of them were IYJL members, who were charged with "illegal entry," meaning that they could face up to a year in prison and $1,000 in fines. In a press release, IYJL stated that they would "represent ourselves in US court, in the heart of the country, making our arrest, our actions, and our immigration status central to our defense," an act through which they said they "may be making some kind of history."[22] Their decision to represent themselves in court was motivated as follows:

When we were arrested for the civil disobedience, we decided as a group that we wanted to make sure to have a voice in our trial. With the encouragement and support of our attorneys, we have been preparing for the last few months to present our own defense. We will be presenting the testimonies, interrogating the witnesses, making the concluding arguments, and in general trying to convince the judge that we have the right to lobby our representatives and urge them with all of our strategies, to understand that we are indeed fighting for our lives when we talk about the DREAM Act.

The increased public visibility of undocumented youth activists forced the generalists, including RIFA, to change their position in the summer of 2010. Whereas many well-established CSOs had frowned on undocumented youths' radical actions and had even publicly denounced the particularists' call for a stand-alone DREAM Act bill, they had to reconsider their position in the face of mounting public and partisan support. In a blog post, IYJL organizer Tamara reflected on the "political fight in the trenches" between well-established CSOs and undocumented youth organizations:[23]

While there were some RIFA organizations that were supportive, particularly in Illinois, there were others that accused DREAM Act advocates of being selfish, petulant, and politically naive, and actively blocked our access to legislators and policy-makers. There were others who asked us to "wait" for continuously moving deadlines, because soon there would be a CIR bill.

Despite RIFA's lack of support, the acts of civil disobedience that had taken place in 2010 led senate majority leader Harry Reid to introduce the DREAM Act as a stand-alone bill. It was estimated that at this point, about 1.9 million undocumented youth in the United States would be eligible for legal status under the DREAM Act.[24] When it was finally reintroduced, first in September and later in December of 2010, the DREAM Act passed the House of Representatives but failed to advance in the senate. Many IYJL members recounted later what an emotional and disappointing event this had been for them personally. Ulises, for example, reflected on this moment as follows:

When I was watching C-SPAN [the Cable-Satellite Public Affairs Network], I think when it finally got to the vote, there was like excitement, happiness, but only so much excitement and happiness because it was like surreal, because now the senate has to pass it.... Especially when Nancy Pelosi read out the votes, and you could hear the cheers in the background, I mean that was just great. And so, that gave me some hope.... And then when it came down to um, I kind of was expecting it, I mean there weren't enough votes,... that was just really disappointing, and it made me really angry. Because I knew that it was all just politics, that they didn't really care about the issue.

Ulises' personal account shows the general disappointment undocumented youth felt toward the political elite who were supposed to do "the right thing," but whose inaction he explained by a lack of passion and caring about the issue.

Despite the DREAM Act defeat, the undocumented youth movement did not collapse. On the contrary, the defeat made many youth activists more determined while simultaneously convincing certain factions within the movement of the need for further radicalization and the escalation of political tactics. This collective sentiment is exemplified by Luna's speech on the second Coming out of the Shadows rally on March 10, 2011. In the speech, Luna talked about the disappointment of the DREAM Act failure and the need for civil disobedience:

Last week I spoke to four undocumented high school students. Unlike other speaking opportunities I've had, this was the first time I was able to talk one on one with youth who were exactly where I was two years ago. I was asked a question I had asked myself countless nights. "Do you ever think it's not worth it?" As I looked back at her I saw the disappointment that came after the DREAM Act failed in the senate, I saw years of hard work, fear and uncertainty. I saw hope. I saw my friends, my brother, I saw myself....

Last year I was one of twenty undocumented students who staged a civil disobedience that resulted with arrest and a risk of deportation. The night before I had a conversation with my parents and brother, and I struggled to convince my mom not to worry. But I knew there was a chance I would not be coming home. I knew there was a chance I might not be there to hug and kiss my little brother after he graduated from high school. I knew that this risk I was taking might determine the next ten years of my life in an unfamiliar country.

I am standing here today because one year ago when my friends came out of the shadows on this stage I was still waiting. I was still afraid, afraid that graduating from college would be an impossible task, afraid that coming out and risking our future in this country would not be enough, afraid that the lives my parents had left behind would be in vain.

I am standing here today because I want to tell that scared girl who did not know what would come next after high school that she is worth it. That the sacrifices she and her parents made are worth it. That the fact that she is now standing on this stage is a sign that a future without fear is possible. I am standing here right now because I want to tell those four girls that they can be up here too, that they are the reasons why I am up here.

DREAMing local: Legislative wins and their aftermath

Infused with renewed confidence and experience, IYJL helped to found the National Immigrant Youth Alliance (NIYA) in April 2011. From the beginning, NIYA emphasized that they stood for a grassroots, undocumented youth–led model of organizing. In their own words, they "believe that only a grassroots movement led by undocumented immigrant youth can properly address the inequities and seemingly insurmountable obstacles facing our communities."[25] The operational philosophy of NIYA is captured by three core values, namely, "Empower, Educate, and Escalate":

Empower: We are undocumented and unafraid. We realize that our greatest power comes from accepting ourselves and realizing that we, as the people most affected, are the ones that need to be at the forefront of our movement. We are committed to making sure that all undocumented youth realize the potential and power they have as undocumented youth, to embrace their identity and to demand nothing less than equality.

Educate: The core of our work not only relies in our methods but also our stories and pedagogy that are embedded in the history of social movements. While we understand the "how" and the "what" of our work, we also need to be aware of the "why." An essential aspect of NIYA is to learn from past social movements successes and be able to incorporate and innovate that wisdom into today's pursuit of justice.

Escalate: Throughout the years of restless organizing across this country, undocumented youth have claimed a place within the historical immigrant rights movement we must now take the lead. We have reached a point where lobbying alone is not adequate to accomplish our mission. We strongly believe that our movement needs to escalate, and we will use mindful and intentional strategic acts of civil disobedience to be effective.

These core values built on the earlier philosophies of "coming out" and civil disobedience as advocated by the group The DREAM is Coming. At the same time, this mission statement reflects how these new political understandings were institutionalized so as to facilitate their spread and reproduction among organizers.

One of the major shifts in strategy propagated by NIYA was a renewed focus on local mobilization. As making progress at the federal level seemed increasingly unfeasible, NIYA-affiliated groups strategically jumped scales by focusing on local versions of the DREAM Act (Seif 2011, 72). While these local DREAM Act bills would be unable to provide undocumented youth with a pathway to citizenship, they could still provide relief for everyday concerns, such as paying tuition fees for higher education and obtaining a driver's license. Moreover, waging a local struggle against policymakers at the city and state levels in Chicago and Illinois was closer to home for most activists than lobbying for change at the federal level in Washington. In Chicago, as in other states, a campaign to push for the Illinois DREAM Act was set up as a collaborative effort between IYJL and ICIRR. The Illinois DREAM Act was important because it demonstrated that when the interests of well-established CSOs and self-organizations overlapped, the former could benefit from the grassroots community support and direct action performed by the latter, while the latter could profit from the resources, networks, and institutional access of the former. In my interview with the director of organizing at ICIRR, he explained how this process worked:

> In this room that we're sitting in [ICIRR headquarters meeting room] we had seventy-five people, on like three days' notice, because we got word that there might be an opening to do some sort of Illinois DREAM Act, right. And so, it was amazing. It was like half undocumented students and half community allies. The best in the state, most experienced leaders, and seventeen-year-olds sitting next to each other and "so what should this be? What should this Illinois DREAM Act bill be?" And we sat in teams and discussed and brainstormed and voted and haggled. And when it came time for all of us collectively to decide, we need to put 1,300 people in, in St. Nicholas of Tolentine Church, it wasn't us saying, "you need to do this, you need to do this! Mobilize, mobilize, mobilize!" It was all of us collectively because we had all created the thing collectively.... *We also, intentionally, on issues that affect undocumented people, are very conscientious to make sure that undocumented people are within the volunteer leadership of those issues.*

IYJL had been actively participating in drafting the bill together with ICIRR and Senate President John Cullerton, the chief sponsor of the bill, from the very start. For the first time, the undocumented youth at IYJL were an intrinsic part of how a piece of legislation came into being over the course of an intensive five-month period filled with meetings, phone calls, press conferences, and lobby days in Springfield. Buses of undocumented youth were sent to the Illinois state capital at regular intervals to make sure that the bill remained a priority on politicians' agendas. ICIRR and IYJL co-organized a "New Americans Rally" with over 1,200 attendees, where Senate President Cullerton and Speaker of the House Madigan expressed their support for the Illinois DREAM Act. In a personal blog, Claudia described how she experienced IYJL's "first legislative victory":[26]

> Our group headed to the House Chamber to witness the vote. I literally sat at the edge of my seat, leaning as far forward as I could without falling from the balcony onto the floor. THIS WAS IT. With my fingers clutching my

phone, ready to tweet out the most-to-date news, I saw those beside me, high school students and parents, holding hands in anticipation.... I couldn't blink. I couldn't swallow. Not until the bell dinged and voting began. We needed sixty votes to pass it, and when the counter lingered on fifty-nine, I thought I was having an aneurysm. The two longest seconds of my life. Then BAM! Green light, sixty-one votes! Bipartisan support! We won! There's hope here in this state and light in the horizon.

The Illinois DREAM Act (known as SB 2185) made scholarships, college savings, and prepaid tuition programs available to undocumented students who graduated from Illinois high schools. Moreover, the governor appointed a nine-member Illinois DREAM Commission that included IYJL member Reyes with senate consent. The Illinois DREAM Act represented the unprecedented institutional and legal recognition of undocumented youth. The local DREAM Act victory in Illinois was a beacon of hope that showed undocumented youth that change was in fact possible. In the following two years, thirteen other states would approve their version of the DREAM Act, including Texas, California, Utah, Nebraska, Kansas, New Mexico, New Jersey, New York, Washington, Wisconsin, Massachusetts, Maryland, and Minnesota.

Regardless of this local victory, anti-immigrant measures remained popular in the April–June 2011 period. Seven NIYA members, including two IYJL representatives, participated in an act of civil disobedience in Georgia after a board of regents' decision banned undocumented students from access to public colleges and universities. This action was the first of its kind by undocumented youth in the South. In November 2011, the father of IYJL members Tamara and Ilene was arrested during an act of civil disobedience alongside three other undocumented workers and ten undocumented youth protesting the anti-immigrant law HB 56 in Alabama. Never before had a parent been implicated in a similar youth-led act of civil disobedience. The father of two justified his participation as follows: "I am risking deportation because I'm tired of seeing the suffering of our children, tired of the lies of Immigration and Customs Enforcement. We do civil disobedience because we are not afraid of those who persecute us."[27] The father's involvement in the action reflects the fluctuating importance of strategically playing out "the family" in immigrant rights struggles (Pallares 2015).

DACA and beyond

IYJL's participation in outer state actions was an opportunity for them to help start up youth-led organizations in the South, while transferring knowledge and tactics to local activists. However, the intensity of undocumented youth acts of civil disobedience also did not go unnoticed at the federal level. In August 2011, the Obama administration announced that undocumented immigrants who did not have criminal records would no longer be a priority for deportations and that it would review all existing deportation cases involving noncriminal immigrants on a case-by-case basis. The announcement was the direct consequence of a week in which undocumented activists had staged sit-in protests in Obama's campaign offices in Denver, Cincinnati, Dearborn, Oakland, and Los Angeles. The decision was hailed by long-time immigrant rights proponents, such as Representative Luis Gutierrez from Illinois: "This is the Barack Obama I have been waiting for and that Latino and immigrant voters helped put in office to fight for sensible immigration policies."[28] Nevertheless, NIYA was less optimistic, as they released a statement revealing distrust based on earlier experiences of "empty promises":[29]

> We are pleased to see this administration make progress, but we will not accept the announcement at its word. Prosecutorial discretion turned out to be ineffectual, and essentially a broken promise. We will review the announcement and will not back down until we are certain the commitment is firm.

While this decision created temporary relief for undocumented youth from deportation after being arrested, it was still a far cry from the moratorium on deportations that they demanded from the Obama administration. For example, IYJL had organized several acts of civil disobedience at the secure detention center in Broadview, where groups of youth prevented buses with deportees from leaving by blocking the exit roads. By creating "human chains," these youths used their bodies to put a spoke in the wheel of the deportation machine. Moreover, NIYA-affiliated organizations kept on resisting pending deportations of undocumented youth through END campaigns. There was also a dark side to the Obama administration's decision to deprioritize the deportation of noncriminal offenders—namely, the increasing emphasis on locating, arresting, and deporting supposedly criminal undocumented offenders. The Secure Communities program designed by the Bush administration was the hallmark legislation in this regard. As explained in the introductory remarks in this chapter, IYJL members staged a "community walk-out" and an act of civil disobedience, during which the Chicago Six were arrested. Despite these actions, Secure Communities was enforced in Illinois.

NIYA-affiliated organizations kept on mobilizing undocumented youth across the country in 2012. Skills-sharing workshops and training events were organized where more-experienced youth organizers transferred their know-how to less-experienced organizers. New initiatives were taken to explore the "intersectional identities" of undocumented youth to put a check on the unrealistic image of the "ideal DREAMer" that had been painted in the past

(Nicholls 2013, 125–33). IYJL took up a leading role in this regard, helping to set up UndocuQueer and UndocuHealth projects; the former focusing on "coming out" as undocumented and queer, and the latter on the mental health problems that many undocumented youth face due to their legal status.[30] The third installment of the Coming Out of the Shadows event was held in Chicago, with supporting actions all over the state of Illinois. The term "Unapologetic" was added to the previous slogan of "Undocumented, Unafraid," and an additional slogan was launched emphasizing the importance of self-representation: "I define myself." In June 2012, IYJL also mobilized fifty Chicago-area youths to attend the third installment of the "Dream Graduation" in Washington, DC. In the same period, NIYA-affiliated undocumented youth staged sit-ins and hunger strikes in four key "Obama for America" campaign offices. One of the coordinators of UWD issued the following statement to the press:[31]

> The President has clear legal authority to give our community relief, yet he continues to say he doesn't have the power. Rest assured, we will take our voices to the White House and to his campaign offices until we see Obama exercise leadership.... Obama has offered fixes in the past, but these changes are not working. We need something more concrete.

In the wake of the upcoming November 2012 elections, the Obama administration did offer something "concrete," by announcing the Deferred Action for Childhood Arrivals (DACA) program. The program directed ICE to apply prosecutorial discretion toward undocumented youth who had come to the United States as children. In his June 15 speech in the Rose Garden of the White House, Obama justified this decision as follows:[32]

> Put yourself in their shoes. Imagine you've done everything right your entire life—studied hard, worked hard, maybe even graduated at the top of your class—only to suddenly face the threat of deportation to a country that you know nothing about, with a language that you may not even speak.... [I]t makes no sense to expel talented young people, who, for all intents and purposes, are Americans.... Now, let's be clear—this is not amnesty, this is not immunity. This is not a path to citizenship. It's not a permanent fix. This is a temporary stopgap measure that lets us focus our resources wisely while giving a degree of relief and hope to talented, driven, patriotic young people. It is... the right thing to do.

While President Obama was making his final statement, a member of the audience interrupted him by shouting "Foreigners over American workers!" This illustrates that even when undocumented youth had been able to gain recognition from the man occupying the highest political office, namely the president of the United States, there was still a lot of work to be done to win over the hearts and minds of the American public. Following the announcement, a list of DACA qualifications was posted, including requirements regarding age, residence, migration history, and educational and criminal record criteria. About nine hundred thousand youth were estimated to be immediately eligible to apply for deferred action. A few months later, in October 2012, IYJL left NIYA, the coalition organization it had helped to found. At the basis of this decision were conflicts over strategy, as well as personal feuds between some of the undocumented youth leaders. Meanwhile, several core IYJL members applied for DACA. In a blog post, Cynthia shared her experience as follows:

> I arrived at Navy Pier at 5:00 p.m. the day before and already two families from Elgin were at the front of the line eager to start the process. I returned at 11:00 p.m. that night and dozens of undocumented youth and their families were lined up outside the gate. By 5:00 a.m. on August 15th [2012], hundreds of young immigrants were waiting for the opportunity of a lifetime: protection from deportation and the opportunity to legally work in the United States. Estimates show that more than 11,000 people came to Navy Pier that day seeking assistance in applying for DACA. I, like many of the estimated 1.8 million potential DACA beneficiaries, was excited. It was the day that I was waiting for since my college graduation in 2011. I would finally be able to legally work in the United States and no longer be afraid of being deported.

Cynthia's story exemplifies the impact DACA status had on the personal lives of these undocumented activists. While becoming "DACAmented" still fell short of being documented, this temporary status forced activists to "work against deportations and for the rights of undocumented immigrants, including those who do not qualify for DACA" (IYJL website). Robles and Gomberg-Munoz have argued that the conditional immigration status of DACA is a mechanism of state repression that removed the sense of urgency for immigration reform, while bringing activists under state surveillance (Robles and Gomberg-Munoz 2016). In fact, DACA dampened the very reason for IYJL existing as an organization. Nevertheless, this neither meant the end of the road for the small group of what had by now become seasoned undocumented activists nor limited the influence of their past efforts on future mobilizations. As undocumented scholarship has documented extensively by now, undocumented activists continue to radically push the boundaries by increasingly focusing on anti-deportation campaigns and broadening the narrative to include intersectional identities like UndocQueer (Ramirez 2020; Kocher and Stuesse 2021). Both dynamics guided the continuing efforts of undocumented youth activists to organize after IYJL's demise (see the Epilogue). As the links between the practices initiated by IYJL and future incarnations like Organized Communities Against Deportations (OCAD) make clear, the historical legacy of this particular episode in the undocumented youth movement's history continues to inspire undocumented activism to this very day.

Conclusion

In this chapter, I have demonstrated that the politicization of undocumented youth necessarily involves struggles over representation. These struggles concern gaining visibility within the public debate over immigration and securing the right to speak within the very movement that is supposed to represent their interests. Political understandings are crucial to explain why undocumented youth felt the need to create activist infrastructures where they could invent and experiment with new modes of political expression. In the previous chapter, I argued that privileged subjects such as well-established CSOs mainly tend to cite and reinforce prevailing understandings of citizenship. By contrast, underprivileged subjects like self-organizations are more inclined to rely on lived experiences of illegality to challenge and think beyond such understandings. If your very existence hangs on a thin thread called legal status, and you risk being arrested and deported at any point, this changes decisions about priorities, strategies, and demands. Representational cleavages can therefore neither be reduced to rationalist calculations of actors trying to maximize their self-interest nor to the structural opening and closing of political opportunities. A hermeneutic approach reveals that what appears as valid, just, and truthful for undocumented activists is regulated by the political understandings that these youths develop over time in interaction with others.

The chapter also shows that undocumented youth were able to develop the necessary political skills and know-how to express the need for self-representation. What started in the back rooms of online forums, in the "safe spaces" of on-campus groups, and on the stage of "coming out" actions eventually led to a reprogramming of youth's political understandings. As will be demonstrated in further ethnographic detail in the second part of the book (Chapters 7 and 8), the importance of these safe spaces is that they functioned as activist infrastructures, in which a new style of organizing, networking, chanting, communicating, and outright "being political" was developed *by* and *for* undocumented youth. In order to decide for themselves how they wanted to be represented, undocumented youth forced an epistemological break from their "parent organizations." The break with well-established CSOs was communicated as an inevitable consequence of a divide that ran deeper than purely strategic differences. At the core of the divide lies the insurmountable gap between political understandings that are formed through underprivileged subjects' discursive, emotional, and embodied lived experiences of illegality (see Chapters 3 and 4) versus privileged subjects' rationalistic and professional understandings.

Translated into action, these understandings lead undocumented activists to strategically deploy their vulnerability as what Scott (2008) has called a "weapon of the weak." Unlike Scott, however, these youths did not content themselves with subtly interrupting everyday routines. In a highly spectacular and dramatic fashion, they forged new forms of action, exemplified by the "coming out" strategy and acts of civil disobedience, which respectively put their stories, bodies, and emotions into public space. The modes of action used by underprivileged subjects, represented a radical departure from the more moderate and traditional political repertoire exercised by privileged subjects. What began as collective experiments in the fringes of the movement supported by a handful of brave undocumented youths was rapidly picked up and amplified by traditional and social media. Despite their legal status, undocumented youths have thus been able to become political subjects who can speak for themselves in the public arena. Nevertheless, as the post-DACA experiences of undocumented youth activists demonstrate, this precarious agency can come under pressure in the face of changes in citizenship status and state repression.

3

Behind the white mask

The politicization of migrant illegality in Belgium

"Nobody speaks to the sans-papiers, but everyone thinks they are an expert on the sans-papiers." (Abas, SPBelgique member)

Located in the heart of Brussels in the Quays[1] neighborhood, the Beguinage Church is a well-known landmark with its typical seventeenth-century Flemish Baroque architecture. Yet ever since priest Daniel Alliët first opened its doors to a group of Congolese sans-papiers in October 1998, the church has become better known among undocumented migrants as the go-to "safe space" in Brussels. At the time, the occupation was orchestrated by the well-established CSO Coordination and Initiatives for Refugees and Strangers (CIRÉ) as part of a broader sensibilization campaign intended to "give a face" to the sans-papiers. White masks symbolized the invisibility and lack of recognition that "faceless" undocumented migrants experienced in the public debate. However, it was not until Semira Adamu, a twenty-year-old Nigerian whose application for asylum had been rejected, died on September 22, 1998, during the sixth attempt to deport her that the sans-papiers issue really hit the national spotlight. One year after her death, the Belgian government succumbed to mounting pressure from civil society by issuing a regularization campaign that gave legal status to forty-two thousand people. Despite this legislative win, strategic disagreements would lead the coalition between the sans-papiers and their *soutiens* (allies) to disintegrate amidst accusations of manipulation and paternalism.

In this chapter, I trace the process through which migrant illegality became a public issue in the Belgian context. The opening scene reveals important analogies with the rise of undocumented youth activism in the United States. Firstly, as was the case with the DREAMers, becoming political entailed struggles over representation for the sans-papiers. As discussed in the previous chapters, I argue that the main driver of these struggles was the disparity between understandings of the political situation advocated by privileged and underprivileged subjects. Legal status leads to what Gonzales and Chavez called a "state of abjectivity," which is a permanent way of "being in the world" (Gonzales and Chavez 2012).

Citizen X. Thomas Swerts, Oxford University Press. © Thomas Swerts (2026).
DOI: 10.1093/9780197844038.003.0004

Extending this insight into the sphere of politics, this abjectivity causes undocumented immigrants to discursively, kinesthetically, and emotionally interpret the political world around them in ways that are diametrically opposed to fully-fledged citizens. Or, as an undocumented leader once put it, the associations speak "the language of the elite," whereas the sans-papiers speak "the language of the heart." However, these diverging political hermeneutics are not just a matter of different "styles" or "cultures" of representation. This became painfully clear in the run-up and immediate aftermath of the regularizations of 1999 and 2008, where deals were struck with the government that left many undocumented activists feeling betrayed.

Despite these similarities, there are also important differences that can be discerned between the two cases. Compared with the US federal government, the Belgian federal government has adopted far more drastic policy measures, as exemplified by the collective regularizations cited above, in their attempt to "end illegal migration once and for all." Furthermore, as I will show below, the Belgian government has proactively tried to disempower the sans-papiers movement by making targeted concessions to specific groups and by arresting and deporting movement leaders. Lastly, as explained in the introductory chapter, the support from local governments is somewhat limited compared with the sanctuary and DREAM Act policies that are in place in Chicago. In the remainder of this chapter, I demonstrate how conflicting political understandings fuel conflicts over representation in Brussels.

Putting regularization on the political agenda

On March 22, 1974, a group of undocumented workers went on a hunger strike in the Saint-Jean Church in Schaarbeek. The undocumented protesters were arrested and deported to their home countries, Morocco and Tunisia, on April 1 of that year. When civil society actors protested this course of events, the Belgian government issued the first regularization of undocumented workers. Out of 8,420 applications, 7,448 sans-papiers received papers (Ciré 2006). The first regularization was presented in official discourse as a one-time-only emergency measure that would permanently "solve" the problem of irregular migration. It was part of a broader legislative initiative taken by the Council of Ministers in 1974 that installed a "zero-immigration" doctrine as the touchstone for future immigration policy in Belgium (Martiniello 2003). Over six decades prior to this, Belgium had been regularly recruiting migrant workers; this recruitment was then officially halted. The official ban on immigration was announced in an economic climate characterized by rising unemployment rates and struggling industries that had traditionally employed foreign laborers.

Officially declaring a "migration stop" meant little in practice, in terms of halting the flow of migration. In fact, immigration to Belgium continued through family reunifications, irregular migration, and the free movement of EU citizens, foreign students, refugees, and asylum seekers. Yet because of the installment of the zero-immigration doctrine, no proactive migration policy measures were taken in Belgium. Nonetheless, it never ceased to be an immigration country.

In response to increasing migration flows in the second half of the 1970s, more restrictive policies were put in place. The law of 1980 on access to the territory, residence, establishment, and expulsion of aliens became the reference point for Belgium's immigration policy in the decades to come. According to the law, foreigners who wanted to stay in Belgium for a period longer than three years needed to obtain an official authorization of admission from the Belgian embassy in their home country unless extraordinary circumstances applied. Yet the law did not stipulate what these extraordinary circumstances entailed. Over the years, medical reasons, a long asylum procedure, non-removability, and humanitarian reasons would be invoked successfully, albeit on a case-by-case basis. The absence of systematic criteria was especially problematic in view of the large incoming streams of refugees during the mid-1980s and 1990s. Between 1988 and 1999, more than 180,000 immigrants applied for asylum in Belgium (Martiniello 2003, 228). Many of these immigrants were not recognized as refugees, as the acceptance rate was relatively low at approximately 5–10 percent. This problem was aggravated by the fact that the examination of applications in this period was very slow, with waiting periods that could extend anywhere from two to seven years, during which applicants developed sustainable social ties in Belgium. As a combined outcome of the lack of clear criteria and the slow examination procedures, the population of immigrants with precarious legal status grew significantly in the eighties and nineties.

In the meantime, immigrants had become popular scapegoats for unemployment and other social issues in politicians' electoral discourses in the mid-1980s. Nevertheless, policies based around encouraging "voluntary return" were still preferred over those rooted in forced deportation. It was not until the extreme-right Flemish party Vlaams Blok gained electoral success that the government turned toward more repressive policy measures. The 1996 law *Vande Lanotte* represented a turning point in that it reinforced the removal and length of detention of "illegal aliens" and made it a criminal offense to help immigrants enter the country without authorization. This law even foresaw an unlimited length of detention, which was eventually diminished to eight months (and later, in 1999, to five months) due to its unconstitutional character. Nevertheless, the tone of the more repressive immigration policies of the 1990s was set. Undocumented immigrants whose application for regularization had been turned down increasingly risked arrest and deportation. In order to facilitate the deportation process, the first detention centers, called "closed centers," were built in Zaventem, Steenokkerzeel, and Merksplas between 1988 and 1995. These restrictive migration policies fueled discontent within civil society.

It is in this context of increasing state repression that we need to situate the death of refused asylum seeker Semira Adamu[2] on September 22, 1998 (Martiniello 2003). Adamu was a twenty-year-old woman who had fled from Nigeria because she was about to be married involuntarily to a sixty-five-year-old man. The Collective against Deportations (CCLE) had supported her in her resistance against deportation at the detention center of Steenokkerzeel 127bis. During the sixth deportation attempt, officers tried to calm her down by pushing a pillow over her face, the so-called cushion technique. This eventually resulted in her falling into a coma, and she subsequently died in the hospital from a brain hemorrhage. The tragic event shocked the public, and Minister of Internal Affairs Louis Tobback, who was also responsible for asylum and migration policy, offered his resignation. It was the "moral shock" of this asylum seeker's death that provided the momentum to draw attention to the cause of the sans-papiers (see Jasper 1997).

In the months before Adamu's death, CIRÉ had already tried to put the issue of regularization on the political agenda. CIRÉ was originally established in 1954 in order to accommodate political and economic refugees, and over the years, it had become a powerful coalition organization of twenty-three associations working around migration issues. In 1998, they organized a debate called "Sans-papiers: In Search of Constructive Solutions." As an outcome of this initiative, the National Movement for the Regularization of the Sans-papiers and Refugees (MNRSPR) was created (Kagné 2000, 19–20). The MNRSPR consisted of a coalition of thirty-two Flemish and Walloon organizations that launched the "Let's Give a Face to the Sans-papiers" campaign. As part of the campaign, CIRÉ orchestrated the first major church occupation in Brussels. Around the same time, about a thousand Congolese refugees had received the news that they had to return to their country, since the death of Mobutu supposedly removed the threat justifying their right to asylum. These Congolese immigrants, many of whom had been in Belgium for several years, subsequently organized a protest. Because of the imminent threat of deportation, this community was ready to be mobilized. As a spokesperson of the occupiers recalled, it was the president of CIRÉ who took the initiative to occupy the Beguinage Church in response to Adamu's death (Bouchoukh 2002, 240):

> The occupation of churches, which we thought to be done by surprise, and which we thought was a spontaneous movement, was done in October 1998. An African friend of mine told me: "We're going to come together to occupy churches." There had been two meetings with Mario Gotto; a small group of

eight persons.... [On] the 26th, we occupied the Beguinage church in Brussels.
I became the spokesperson.

A group of twenty-six sans-papiers were granted church asylum in dialogue
with priest Daniel Alliët. The occupation would last until November 2000, when
the building was struck by lightning. Catholic churches in Belgium had a tradition of offering protection to refugees whose request for asylum had been turned
down, based on customs related to canon law. By November 1998, three hundred undocumented immigrants were occupying churches in Brussels, Antwerp,
Mons, Verviers, Charleroi, and Liège.[3]

The Belgian media reported the sans-papiers' actions as if they were sponta-
neous outbursts of discontent. In fact, these actions were well planned by the
intricate network of well-established CSOs in Brussels. Long before the occupations, these organizations had been confronted with the issues and everyday
struggles of undocumented immigrants in their daily work. When they deemed
the time was right, they mobilized support from CSOs across sectors, including universities and labor unions. Because CIRÉ had a great deal of experience
with campaigns, outreach, and policy negotiations, they were able to launch the
cause of the sans-papiers in the public debate. By relying on their pre-established
networks and social capital, they facilitated the initial political entry of undocumented immigrants. However, the leadership role that CIRÉ took within the
movement quickly became the subject of internal criticism. Recalling the first
meeting with CIRÉ, a spokesperson of the occupiers said he "had the impression
of being manipulated from that very moment onward" (Bouchoukh 2002, 240).
MNRSPR, the official national movement, tried to reach a compromise with the
government concerning limited regularization of sans-papiers. Three months
after the beginning of the occupation, it became clear that the government was
willing to regularize the Congolese immigrants. In December 1998, the Van
Den Bossche circular was released, pretending to respond to the MNRSPR's
demands by establishing a commission for regularizations. However, the movement's principal demand, namely, collective regularization for all sans-papiers,
was denied in favor of the existing system of case-by-case regularizations.

Internal disagreements within MNRSPR about how to respond led some support organizations to leave the network, refusing to negotiate over measures
that would divide the sans-papiers into "regularizable" and "non-regularizable"
candidates. In Brussels, the occupants of the Beguinage Church, the majority
of whom were non-Congolese, took their fate in their own hands by insisting on their demand for regularization for all. By now, tensions had started to
arise between the undocumented activists and the organizations that claimed to
represent them in the MNRSPR. Another undocumented spokesperson of the
occupiers acknowledged the importance of the support they received from civic

organizations. At the same time, he critically assessed the impact of that support for the sans-papiers themselves (Kalubi 2002, 250):

> There has been real support within civil society.... In the associative environment, even if there have been associations, closer to the government, who thought that what we were doing was too much, and advocated to await governmental decisions ... and others who led themselves to be instrumentalized, and who did not want the sans-papiers to express themselves ... there have also been a lot of people who have really come to realize this problem that reigned in Belgium since 1974, the date of the last regularization.

Direct actions continued, with the number of participants in occupations growing to 650 in 1999. Increasingly, the sans-papiers were also given support by universities, as shown by the occupation of a building of the University of Liège in March 1999. On April 25, after more than 140 days of occupations, a national protest was organized to demand the regularization of all sans-papiers, the closure of detention centers, and a halt to deportations. However, by June 1999, media attention was declining in the wake of the upcoming federal elections, and the Beguinage Church became the only place where the occupation continued. After the elections, a "rainbow coalition" government was installed, comprising French and Flemish liberals (PRL, VLD), ecologists (ECOLO, AGALEV), and socialists (PS, SP), who introduced a proposed law for regularization in parliament.

It was the moral shock of Yaguine Koita and Fode Tounkara's tragic death that provided political openings for the sans-papiers once more. On August 2, 1999, the frozen corpses of these two children from Guinea were found in an airplane's wheel bay at Brussels airport. They carried a letter with them stating that they needed the help of European officials to escape poverty, analphabetism, and war (Pickels 2002, 10). Pressure mounted on politicians to respond to the sans-papiers' demands. On December 22, 1999, a law was enacted that entailed a second collective regularization of undocumented immigrants who had been present on Belgian territory before October 1, 1999 (Martiniello 2003, 229). Four criteria were used to determine eligibility: an asylum procedure of longer than four years without a definitive answer, a serious illness, non-removability, and humanitarian reasons. However, the criteria for collective regularization were not permanent, but "once only." There was a three-week window in which applications were accepted. In response to this call, 32,776 files were collected, representing close to sixty thousand people. About 140 nationalities were counted among the applications, of which 15.2 percent were Congolese and 14.5 percent were Moroccan (Ciré 2006).[4] By 2002, some 23,000 of the files had resulted in regularizations, while about 5,000 were denied (Van Meeteren et al. 2007, 32). The regularization campaign represented an attempt by the Belgian government to end "migrant illegality" with a big gesture. After the three-week window, the Federal Alien Law of 1980 and its case-by-case methodology came into effect once more.

Despite this legislative success, only a restricted part of the undocumented population had eligibility for regularization. Most undocumented workers remained ineligible. The compromise that had been negotiated between the MNRSPR and the government deepened the divide within the movement. A spokesperson of the occupiers put it like this (Kalubi 2002, 249):

> We have never been the standard-bearers of the doctrine carried by the associative world. *They considered us to be like children, and they believed that we didn't understand what was going on.* But the church remained occupied after the law had been passed. Even when the "file had been closed" for policy, the movement continued.... The associations on one side, the state security services and the political parties, they have all reached an agreement, without reflecting about the fact that it might not lead to giving papers to the sans-papiers, expect for a minority.

Kalil, an undocumented participant in the occupation of the Beguinage Church, explained the division within the movement:[5]

> We have had great difficulties with associations that constitute in principle the National Movement for the Regularization of Undocumented Migrants and Refugees (MNRSPR). If you look closely, you realize that they are themselves somewhat divided on questions of strategy. We saw this situation too late because we had already been carried away by this movement's logic. So we found ourselves in a situation that led to controversy and division among us.

The Collective against Deportations (CCLE) voiced similar concerns about the role of the MNRSPR led by CIRÉ. They accused the national movement organization of dividing undocumented immigrants into "good" and "bad" sans-papiers according to their "regularizability." This demonstrates the paradox that characterizes the sans-papiers movement: as soon as actors respond to political openings for certain groups within the undocumented population, they tend to reproduce the exclusions that they try to challenge. The general sentiment among the undocumented leadership was that they had been misrepresented by their *soutiens*. SOS Sans-papiers withdrew their support from the MNRSPR, claiming that "responsible and realist" organizations like CIRÉ were negotiating with the government in the name of the sans-papiers in an undemocratic way. Or, as a spokesperson for the collective put it, quoting an undocumented leader in France: "*Rentrez chez vous, on s'occupe de tout*" (Go home, we'll take care of everything).[6]

Increasing dissent and representational autonomy

While the regularization campaign of 2000 was considered a victory for the movement, the issue of permanent regularization criteria remained unsolved. Especially among the sans-papiers who did not qualify for regularization, there was a sense that they had been forgotten. Increasingly, the sans-papiers started to organize themselves collectively. In January 2001, a group of sans-papiers who had also been involved in the occupation of the Beguinage Church squatted in the abandoned embassy of Somalia. After a while, this building became known as the "Universal Embassy." While the embassy was initially mainly a place where sans-papiers could sleep, it was gradually transformed into a "safe space" in which undocumented immigrants could organize themselves. In this space, the sans-papiers arranged language courses, tutoring for children, cultural activities, and juridical support.[7] As undocumented spokesperson Mohammed put it, their activities were "neither humanitarian nor assistance, but political." This was a deliberate strategy behind the Universal Embassy from the beginning, as Mohammed describes:[8]

> The day that the undocumented will take their struggle in their own hands, then things will only be able to progress. I often make the comparison with the struggle against slavery, which had become abolished when the slaves themselves took their destiny in their own hands. *They are the ones who are the most involved; they must carry the fight....* People from the outside will never be able to tell them which issues they need to address any more. It is the people themselves who need to find solutions to their problems.

It was not only the sans-papiers but also the larger civic organizations that made attempts to reorganize themselves after the 2000 regularization campaign. In the autumn of 2002, the former protagonists of the MNRSPR founded the Forum for Asylum and Migrations (FAM) (Laureys 2013, 20). While twenty organizations took the initiative, there were about 120 organizations from the two linguistic communities of Belgium that were involved in FAM. The forum was spearheaded by CIRÉ on the Walloon side and Refugee Work Flanders (VWV) on the Flemish side. Powerful organizations, such as the main Belgian syndicates, were represented from the beginning and FAM would continuously attempt to integrate undocumented leaders in its operations. The forum's actions revolved around four main policy demands: expansion of who could apply for asylum, regularization for everyone who had been in Belgium for longer than three years, basic rights for undocumented immigrants, and the abolition of secure detention centers.

In the aftermath of the regularization, measures were taken by the government to speed up the asylum procedure. However, since a lot of political capital had been spent on the collective regularization, additional reforms stalled. Due to this deadlock, the sans-papiers' protests became more radical. In the summer of 2003, some three hundred Afghans occupied the Holy Cross Church in Elsene. A council of neighbors gathered regularly in support of these rejected asylum seekers. Out of these efforts, the organization CRER (Coordination against Raids, Deportations and for Regularization) emerged. In September 2003, around five hundred rejected asylum seekers from Iran started an occupation at the Free University of Brussels, supported by a student organization. What these examples show is that self-organizations actively looked for support from local actors such as neighborhood councils, artists, church communities, cultural centers, and student organizations to gain representational autonomy.

It was in this spirit of autonomy that the sans-papiers reached out to participate in a European march for undocumented immigrants in May 2004. The march, which was led by French organizations, aimed to denounce recent measures taken at the level of the European Union concerning member states' asylum procedures and the status of refugees. During the preparations for the event, the idea for a nationwide self-organization of sans-papiers started to gain support (Laureys 2013, 21). The sans-papiers' emancipation from the "paternalism" of well-established CSOs had its institutional translation in the foundation of the Union for the Defense of Sans-Papiers (UDEP) in Liège. UDEP adopted "regularization for all, without exceptions" as its main goal. From the very start, the issue of self-representation was critical, as Tarik, one of the founders, explained:[9]

> After three months of meetings, at the end of the summer of 2004, the idea of creating some kind of association, movement, or group for undocumented immigrants started to take inception. *We were seven, and we wanted to launch a struggle for and by the sans-papiers. From the beginning, we were very concerned about this "by" and "for."* In this regard, our goal was clear from the start: we wanted the undocumented to leave their fear and inertia behind, get together and fight for their rights.

There were many associations at the time that were fighting for the rights of undocumented immigrants, but almost none of them included the sans-papiers among their ranks. It was this lack of self-representation that UDEP wanted to address. They were given funds by the organization Bruxelles Laïque to secure their existence. These funds came with a mission: to set up local UDEP branches in Brussels, Charleroi, Antwerp, Gent, and Leuven.

After UDEP organized a protest in Brussels in September 2005, one of the main spokespeople was arrested. Due to UDEP's fierce actions, he was released by the end of the month. The kinesthetic experience of one of their leaders being arrested and locked up led UDEP to decide that the time was right for action. However, the sans-papiers would soon be faced with internal strategic disagreements. At the national coordination meeting, UDEP decided to organize a large event in February 2006. The plan was that each of the five local committees would prepare to occupy a church in their respective cities by February. These occupations would then be announced a couple of days beforehand to gain political momentum. All the local committees seemed to be on board, and they started to look for churches and universities that would be receptive to their plans. However, there had been disagreement before between leaders from UDEP Bruxelles and UDEP Liège about questions of strategy. This explains why, four months earlier than planned, UDEP Bruxelles decided to go ahead with their church occupation as soon as they found a willing partner.

On October 19, 2005, eighty UDEP activists occupied the Saint-Bonifacius Church in Elsene. Kaba, an undocumented leader, explained the action as follows:[10]

> With the occupation, we want to come out of the shadows. And because the Minister of Interior Affairs considers a hunger strike to be a form of blackmail, we chose this action. We did not want the population to pity us by holding a hunger strike. We only demand the enforcement of the *rights of refugees*. We also want to demonstrate that *refugees* make a positive contribution.

From the start, UDEP's general strategy had been to demand the regularization of all sans-papiers. UDEP Bruxelles, which consisted mainly of rejected asylum seekers, presented themselves as fighting for the rights of refugees. In contrast to previous actions, they also pledged to refrain from using hunger strikes as a political tool. Together with an ad hoc committee of neighbors, they organized the photo exhibition *Gueules d'amers*. Portraits of sans-papiers were displayed in shops in the neighborhood to raise awareness. These collaborative initiatives with local shop owners, parishes, and neighborhood residents point to the fact that self-organizations such as UDEP Bruxelles depend much more on grassroots organizing and the involvement of *soutiens*.

The support of the Catholic Church proved to be crucial during these moments of escalation. In an October 19, 2005, open letter to the ministry, the priest of Saint-Bonifacius Church, Norbert Maréchal, explained his reasons for allowing the sans-papiers to occupy the church:

> I allowed these sans-papiers to find shelter in the church at a time when anxiety is growing.... I take no pleasure in feeling invaded, but ... can you still close the door? Having lived abroad myself for many years (admittedly with papers), I know how painful it can be not to be recognized, accepted. How much more so if you no longer legally exist. That is why I respect them and their approach.

Furthermore, the Church's support was formally recognized in May 2006 with the following declaration by Cardinal Danneels, the Belgian Primate and Archbishop of Brussels:[11]

> The bishops understand that some of these people [sans-papiers] take recourse to a "church occupation" in order to give voice to their distress and in that way, continue to attract the attention of the public. The bishops therefore accept that this happens, in agreement with local priests.

Monsignor Karl-Josef Rauber, the Papal Nuncio, even gave his support to the actions of undocumented immigrants in name of the Vatican, stating that "[t]he Church has always chosen the side of the weakest."[12] The church would remain an important safe space for the sans-papiers.

Despite the sans-papiers' actions, politicians refrained from responding with the federal elections of 2007 in sight. After months of silence by the government, the occupiers withdrew from their earlier pledge and decided that a hunger strike was the only way to move forward. Aqib of UDEP Bruxelles explained this shift in strategy as follows:[13]

> When you're with your back against the wall and you have nothing left, one can do extreme things.... The Immigration Office and the Ministry of Interior Affairs regularize those who go on hunger strike. In contrast, if you try to negotiate, to apply for citizenship, to make proposals, using the values of democracy and European citizenship, your application is refused. This amounts to saying, in a very schematic way, that we must not be intelligent but that one has to sacrifice one's life to be regularized. We want to be the voice of the voiceless.

This example illustrates how the government's refusal to sit around the table with the sans-papiers spurred the radicalization of tactics. Allies heard the sans-papiers' cry for recognition. Pol Van Camp, a sixty-four-year-old citizen syndicalist, joined the hunger strike in a highly publicized manner. A month after the start of the hunger strike, the Minister of Interior Affairs regularized the 130 occupiers after an action that had lasted twenty-five days. While this was far from the collective regularization that UDEP had demanded, it was nevertheless a victory for the organizers in Brussels. At the end of the hunger strike,

UDEP Bruxelles communicated the following message in a March 3, 2006, press release:

> All the members of the government that we have met in our occupied church; all the associations have explained to us that it was not the time to demand regularization. Their strategy, their program is this, or that the political power relationships are not favorable for regularization…. And so we waited…. And we have endured…. And we have won: almost all occupants of the church (130) were regularized! The door is wide open to all undocumented migrants in Belgium thanks to the church occupation and the mobilization of undocumented immigrants by UDEP since one year. *Struggle is the only means to obtain what we want.*

When information about the deal was leaked to the press, it triggered a series of protests and church occupations across the country. By June 2006, there had been twelve occupations by sans-papiers in the Brussels Capital Region. Altogether, occupations had been organized in churches, mosques, and secular humanitarian centers in forty-six places in Belgium.

At the same time, UDEP Liège had brought forward the organization of their February mass demonstration. Aided by the know-how of the militant organization CRER, the networks of coalition organization FAM, and the financial resources of the Walloon socialist labor union (FGTB), UDEP was able to mobilize an estimated fifteen thousand people in a march in support of the sans-papiers in Brussels on February 25, 2006. While the march was a success, the solitary action by UDEP Bruxelles had sown the seeds for future internal conflicts with UDEP Liège. As Tarik explains, they felt as though the struggle to achieve "regularization for all" had been thwarted by the regularization of the occupants of Saint-Boniface Church. This had as an unintended consequence that other undocumented immigrants were strengthened in their belief that the best recipe for success was the formula "occupation + hunger strike = regularization."[14]

The tensions between UDEP Bruxelles and UDEP Liège increased even further in the context of legislative developments. In May 2006, the law of 1980 was being revised in response to the unprecedented wave of mobilization. The Francophone green party Ecolo enlisted UDEP Bruxelles to help them draft a proposal. The proposal foresaw permanent regularization criteria that would regularize the following categories of sans-papiers: refugees who have been waiting for longer than three years for a decision about their status; immigrants who cannot return to their home country because of reasons independent of their will; those who are severely sick or disabled; those who have developed sustainable social ties in the country or have a project for a socio-economic contribution to Belgium. Ecolo accepted the proposal of the "UDEP-bill" in parliament, supported by civil society actors and Belgian celebrities. On May 29, 2006, the spokespeople of UDEP Bruxelles, Valerie and Aqib, were heard in the Belgian Parliament with regards to the revision of the 1980 law. The following is an excerpt from their statement:[15]

> We are thousands of people from around the world, often living in Belgium for several years. We live with you, among you. Nothing separates us except that we are undocumented. We are men, women, and children similar to any other person. Our situation of not having papers is not written on our foreheads. You encounter us every day without knowing it.… The government and parliament thus must choose their values. Either solidarity, humanism, democracy, and justice … or the fear for others, the hypocritical economic exploitation of the sans-papiers, and the fear of confronting the far right and its theses.…

Deservingness deepens the divide

Despite the historical self-representation of the sans-papiers in parliament, no permanent regularization criteria were inscribed in the revised law. Several political parties promised that they would consider this issue, but only after the federal elections of June 2007. This entailed a defeat for UDEP and the entire movement. The February 2006 mass mobilization had put the cause of the sans-papiers in the national spotlight. Well-established CSOs used the created momentum to launch campaigns and share their view about what should be done. This led to tensions with UDEP, who felt that these CSOs were now trying to "recuperate" the movement. Tarik explained how the UDEP leadership interpreted this:[16]

> Many of these associations wanted to profit from this mobilization and this sensibilization by "speaking on behalf of the undocumented." … We felt that the associations wanted to build on our actions so that the problem was mediatized, but with the objective of reserving the reflection part of the problem and attempting to find solutions for them. But from the start, at UDEP, we wanted it to be undocumented immigrants themselves who give their views on solutions.… *But the problem is that they have used actions of UDEP for purposes that were not those of UDEP. We wanted to keep our autonomy and independence, and above all continue to give a voice to all the sans-papiers.*

UDEP felt "used" and silenced by the supporting organizations. Consequently, the 2006–07 period was characterized by a series of solitary initiatives by well-established CSOs that focused on raising awareness. A good illustration is a symbolic action organized by FAM in April 2007. Five undocumented immigrants—one of whom had been recently granted citizenship—were put in a glass house on the centrally located Munt square in Brussels. People could read their background files and then had to decide which one of the five should get citizenship. More than forty-six thousand people voted on the spot or online in this action. Self-organizations simultaneously reached out again to universities, students, artists, and the cultural sector to avoid the problems they had experienced earlier with well-established CSOs.

In June 2007, the winners of the federal elections—the Christian democrats and liberals—vowed to come up with a new asylum and migration policy, including criteria for regularization. However, these promises were thwarted by a governmental crisis, exemplified by the government formation lasting 194 days. Due to the crisis, which was fueled by Flemish parties' demand for more regional autonomy through state reform, an interim government led by Prime Minister Verhofstadt was installed between December 2007 and March 2008. Because of its interim character, this government was unable to deliver the major overhaul of immigration policy that had been promised before. It is in this climate of political inertia that we need to situate the reemergence of undocumented activism in 2008.

In many ways, 2008 was a symbolic moment for the sans-papiers movement. Despite ten years of struggle, there were still no permanent regularization criteria inscribed in the law. Samira Adamu's tragic death had occurred ten years earlier. An ad hoc coalition created a campaign around the symbolic numbers "10-20-60," referring to the anniversary of Adamu's death, the opening of the first secure detention center in Melsbroek, and the Declaration of Human Rights. However, 2008 was also the tenth anniversary of the first occupation of the Beguinage Church. Backed by trade unions, the Collective des Sans-Papiers en Lutte (CSPL) occupied the Beguinage Church, the place where it had all started, once more in March 2008. Compared with ten years earlier, the goal was no longer sensibilization, but collective regularization. Asked why they chose to stage their action in the church, the spokesperson replied: "This is a symbolic place. This is where the struggle began. But this struggle is far from over. There are still many people who long for regularization. That's why we are back here in this church today."[17] Despite the renovation of the church after a major fire, the sanitary and living conditions of the men, women, and children who were participating in the church occupation were precarious. What started out as a fairly small group of fifty occupiers quickly grew to become a group of about 170, representing more than forty nationalities.[18] When six undocumented activists got themselves arrested and imprisoned in April 2008, the church occupiers decided to start a collective hunger strike. While drinking tea and sugar water was still allowed, the hunger strikers stopped eating food altogether. A buddy system was installed to make sure that participants would not cheat.

People were lying on mattresses side by side with posters hanging above their heads saying, "we won't leave here without papers," "until death," and "regularization is the only solution." Other church occupations in the Brussels region quickly followed in Vorst and Elsene. In an interview with a reporter, one of the protesters expressed his feelings as follows: "Europe needs laborers anyway, right? Well then, here we are, we can work. The only thing we ask for is humane conditions to do that." This example demonstrates the self-identification of the occupiers as "workers" in contrast to the occupants of the Saint-Bonifacius Church, who presented themselves as "refugees." Asked about the legitimacy of hunger strikes as a means of political protest, Priest Daniel Alliët answered:[19]

I would prefer to see a resolution without church occupations and hunger strikes as well, but we need to understand where these kinds of actions come from. Hunger strikes emerged in England at the end of the nineteenth century, when women did not get the right to vote. It was a means of the poor, the weapon of the ones without a voice, and it has advanced democracy. A hunger strike is a fight for justice, and nothing else.

In the end, activists put their lives on the line during a hunger strike that lasted fifty-six days. The action did not directly lead to the collective regularization they were demanding. Nevertheless, Minister of Interior Affairs Dewael decided to give the 161 protesters a temporary work permit for nine months. Fabio, one of the undocumented workers involved, reflected on this success as follows:[20]

This is a victory of undocumented workers in peril of their lives and their health. Their solidarity shows that we can win. It is an example for all workers that struggle is bearing fruit. But it is terrible that people have to put their lives on the line in order to get a permit for residence and work, so as to not be exploited.

While the actions in the Beguinage Church were put on hold by the government's concessions, eighty-five protestors in Elsene broke Bobby Sands' hunger strike record in an action that lasted more than seventy days.[21] In total, about nine hundred hunger strikers received their papers. Yet because the results were not in accordance with people's suffering, UDEP Liège interpreted this as a defeat.

Between 2007 and 2009, the sans-papiers movement's internal struggles would reach a high point over the question of the negotiation of regularization criteria. It became increasingly clear that there was a split within the sans-papiers movement between rejected asylum seekers and undocumented workers. More specifically, the latter group, which was in the minority, felt as though the former group was overpowering them. In the summer of 2007, Didier Reynders of the Walloon Liberal Party brought together immigrant rights associations and political parties to write a memorandum to explore solutions for the "migration crisis." The national coordination of UDEP in turn tried to prepare an answer to this memorandum. However, while this was being prepared, the government secretly invited the spokesperson of UDEP Bruxelles, making an offer to give papers to a list of twelve undocumented leaders.[22] Next, the government gave papers to some people on the list, but not to others. When this deal was leaked, intense internal struggles ensued, causing several people, including the UDEP Bruxelles leader, to quit the movement. One year later, UDEP ceased to exist. This example illustrates the efficacy of the government's strategy to "break" the movement by way of selectively making concessions to some sans-papiers. In the vacuum after the collapse of UDEP, seven former UDEP members founded the Organization for the Sans-Papiers (OSP).

In March 2008, a new government was formed, and migration policy became the responsibility of a designated minister of immigration and asylum, the liberal Minister Turtelboom. Plans for a new collective regularization were taken up as part of the government agreement, prompting the sans-papiers once more to be hopeful for change. In May 2008, Turtelboom released a circular explaining the government's plans for a collective regularization that would require applicants to have had legal status before and that privileged work over durable social ties as a criterion for regularization. The proposal was quickly denounced by civil society actors as violating earlier promises that had been made during the negotiations around the government agreement. The plans for regularization were then stalled for months due to the economic crisis and internal government problems.

On January 20, 2009, ten months after the government had announced plans for regularization, yet another group of about 230 undocumented immigrants knocked on Daniel Alliët's door at the Beguinage Church. The same pattern of radicalization of actions that had been observed before unfolded; in April, a collective hunger strike commenced. Alliët was not in favor of the hunger strike this time, but he still supported the sans-papiers:[23]

> I am not in favor of a hunger strike. The people only have things to lose at this point. They dig their own grave, a forgotten grave, because the media attention to the hunger strikes is totally gone.... Due to the results of last year, they still cherish the illusion that they are able to accomplish more in the Beguinage Church than elsewhere. I still support them because I understand their decision for a hunger strike. It is a desperate act and like any desperate act it has its sense.

Thousands of sympathizers demonstrated in the streets of Brussels for the regularization of the sans-papiers in March 2009.[24] The local media reported that on June 5, 2009, almost one thousand people without documents were simultaneously on hunger strike in Brussels.[25]

On June 7, regional and European elections took place, resulting in defeat for the Flemish Liberal Party of Minister Turtelboom. As a direct consequence of the election results, the federal government was restructured, with Turtelboom becoming Minister of Internal Affairs while the Walloon Christian-democrat Wathelet became the new State Secretary of Migration and Asylum Policy. On July 18, 2009, more than a year after Turtelboom's circular had been issued, the Belgian government finally issued new criteria for regularization in Article 9bis of the Alien Law. The criteria included long-duration asylum procedures, families with school-going children, urgent humanitarian reasons, and medical reasons. The negotiated criteria were primarily aimed at providing solace for "deserving" sans-papiers, such as refugees. By contrast, the criterion of sustainable local social ties, which applied to the "undeserving" clandestine undocumented workers, was applied "once only" between September 15 and December 15, 2009.

Conclusion

In this chapter, I have demonstrated how representational gaps emerged between privileged and underprivileged subjects within the Belgian sans-papiers movement. Privileged subjects assumed a leading role in the early stages of the movement. When the "sans-papiers issue" was first put on the political agenda, well-established CSOs found themselves in a position allowing them to act as "representational brokers" for the sans-papiers (Nicholls 2013). The incorporation of the CSOs in civil society and their networks with government actors gave them considerable advantages over the sans-papiers in terms of political know-how and leverage. As privileged subjects, they tended to rely on incremental, "realistic" strategies to determine how to frame issues in such a way that they would resonate with policymakers. When these organizations tried to represent the sans-papiers, it was assumed that they would readily step on board. In practice, however, leadership was taken out of the hands of the sans-papiers by the self-appointed professional spokespeople of the movement. While claiming to represent the cause of the sans-papiers, the leadership of these organizations dictated the agenda, both in terms of policy dialogue and messages. The role of the sans-papiers was effectively reduced to "representing the grassroots." Political representation was done "for" or "in the name of" undocumented immigrants instead of "by" undocumented immigrants.

This chapter has also shown how negotiating terms of inclusion and exclusion during the regularization campaigns legitimized and solidified prevailing understandings of deservingness that underpin a "moral economy of deservingness" (Chauvin and Garcés-Mascareñas 2012). Forced to consider the "political reality" of the day and age, privileged subjects made concessions during negotiations with government representatives. The sans-papiers' stance that legal status should be extended to all undocumented migrants regardless of their background was one of the first things to be thrown overboard. Instead, clear boundaries were drawn by the state and well-established CSOs during the negotiation process, resulting in a highly uneven distribution of political openings for undocumented migrants with different profiles. More specifically, asylum seekers were perceived as "deserving" sans-papiers, whereas "clandestine" workers were increasingly framed as "non-deserving." Even among underprivileged subjects such as the sans-papiers, varying levels of deservingness persisted.

4

Papers for all!

The rise of sans-papiers' activism in Brussels

"Nobody speaks to the sans-papiers, but everyone thinks they are an expert on the sans-papiers." (Abas, SPBelgique member)

On July 19, 2011, SPBelgique members Abas, Anouar, and many others participated in an act of civil disobedience in Brussels. The sans-papiers were "celebrating" the second anniversary of the dossiers they had submitted during the regularization of 2009. For the occasion, they made a cake out of cardboard representing the "chameleonic response" to people's demands for regularization. There was also a letterbox where people symbolically submitted their demands with the heading "work permit B = legal exploitation," referring to the procedure through which regularization could be applied for via a work permit. Most of the protestors were either people who had been waiting for two years to hear back from the administration or who had already received a negative response. The slogan of the action was "we live *here*/we work *here*/we stay *here*/but not without rights." Some 150–200 people participated in the march, which started at Saint-Josse Square, passed by the seat of the CDH, the Walloon Christian-Democratic Party, and on to the cabinet of then current state secretary for asylum and migration, Melchior Wathelet. Banners around people's necks referred to their work situation: "undocumented worker, work injury," "lived here for eight years," "undocumented baker," yet another "construction worker." A handful of protestors had made handcuffs from cardboard and kneeled on the ground.

While they marched through the streets, the group's leaders chanted, and the public responded. One rhythmic chant referred to the ideals driving the protestors: "liberty—*for all*. Equality—*for all*. Fraternity—*for all*. Solidarity—*for all*. Respect—*for all*. Papers—*for all*. For whom?—*for all*." Another chant reflected the climate of despair and frustration that characterized the political moment: "The government—*we've had enough*. Lawyers—*we've had enough*. Meetings—*we've had enough*. It will come tomorrow—*we've had enough*. And then there's nothing—*we've had enough*." No speeches were given. Instead, people chanted, walked, and sat down in front of the CDH office for about half

Citizen X. Thomas Swerts, Oxford University Press. © Thomas Swerts (2026).
DOI: 10.1093/9780197844038.003.0005

an hour. While seated, the crowd tried to make as much noise as possible by whistling and screaming so that those inside would hear them. When we reached State Secretary Wathelet's office, the chants became louder, and people became more and more excited or "fired up." The protestors had to stand on the sidewalk across the busy Rue de la Loi. People started chanting, "Mister Wathelet, come down please!" The undocumented marchers who had "handcuffed" themselves behind their backs lay face down on the street, symbolizing how the lack of response to their demand for regularization had hijacked their lives. When no response came from the cabinet, the protestors suddenly moved to the middle of the street and sat down, chanting loudly "so-so-so/solidarity/with the sans-papiers." The protestors were eventually allowed to speak to a representative of the cabinet after all.

When spokesperson Abas addressed the crowd after the meeting, this is what he had to say: "When we ask a question, it is always the same answer: for the moment there is no government and there is an economic crisis. I said one thing: it is not us who caused this crisis, so why do we have to pay for it? So we have to continue fighting, we can't stop here." The police finally intervened and threatened to arrest people if the demonstration did not stop. Escorted by dozens of police officers, the protestors were forced to leave the perimeter. In an interview a year later, SPBelgique member Faisal told me that this had been one of the actions that were "special" to him:

> We really noticed that everybody was sick of this and *we all made the decision to show that we still exist there.* We stopped the traffic for thirty minutes.... Really, the interventions that were chosen were symbolic.... They were really words that told the truth about the sans-papiers and also about politics.

Symbolic events such as this act of civil disobedience reflect the efforts of the sans-papiers to gain an autonomous voice in the public debate after the regularization of 2009. In analogy with the rise of undocumented youth activism, gaining a voice also required the sans-papiers to create activist infrastructures where they could innovate and experiment with political repertoires. Whereas schools and online fora offered such a space for undocumented youth in Chicago, churches, squats—and to a certain extent community centers—played a similar role for the sans-papiers in Brussels.[1]

Symbolic actions without a government

The regularization of 2009 put an immediate end to the mobilization of the sans-papiers. In my interviews with sans-papiers leaders, they emphasized that the compromise "crushed" the movement. Many sans-papiers filed their case in the three-month window provided by the government. Local integration centers such as Foyer opened their doors to collect applications. Affiliated lawyers were mobilized to give legal assistance to people while applying. It is estimated that this measure led to the regularization of around twenty-three thousand people in 2009 and almost fifteen thousand in 2010. However, as is the case with all one-shot regularizations, some undocumented immigrants either had to wait for years to get an answer or were denied papers. Because of the way the regularization was set up, it was primarily undocumented workers who experienced difficulties regularizing their status. The "B Permit" procedure required applicants to demonstrate a work contract from an employer with a minimum duration of one year to be eligible, and a renewal request had to be filed by the employer two months before the expiration date of the work permit. This system significantly increased the power of employers vis-à-vis undocumented workers. Instead of providing sans-papiers with legal rights and guarantees that could secure their status, the B Permit system in fact led to an increase in precariousness and exploitation.

The first response to this situation was an action by the newly founded Collective of Undocumented Workers in September 2010, which was followed by a demonstration held by OSP. In January 2011, the members of the former collective launched a new initiative, the Collectif Sans-papiers En Attente (Collective of Undocumented Immigrants in Waiting) that would be open to all sans-papiers, regardless of their status. Supported by a local nonprofit organization, Link-Meeting—a local community center cofounded by Priest Daniel Alliët—they created a support group for people applying for regularization. The collective, which would later rename itself SPBelgique, formulated the following global demands (SPBelgique 2012):[2]

- A regularization law based on a just and lasting vision, with clear and permanent criteria.
- The end to precarious regularization as is the case for the "B permit," which we consider as a way to legalize exploitation.
- Considering the waiting period for people whose application is still unanswered, we believe that two years of waiting for a procedure is outrageous.
- We call for decriminalization of undocumented status. Because being illegally present on Belgian territory is an offense punishable by law, undocumented people live in fear of being identified and do not dare to fight for their rights. They are afraid to go out into the street to protest, to complain in case of attack, to go to the hospital in case of injury, to speak openly, to express their point of view, etc. It is unacceptable that this can happen in a democratic country like Belgium.

As these demands show, SPBelgique formulated its demands in a maximalist way. In contrast to UDEP, SPBelgique was more modest in its scope of action and outreach.

In 2011, SPBelgique organized sixteen actions, six of which they self-categorized as "symbolic," six as "mobilization," two as "occupation," and two as "juridical complaint" (SPBelgique 2012). The symbolic actions were primarily experiments in innovation regarding the political repertoire of the sans-papiers in a political climate in which there was little to no interest in responding to their demands. For example, they organized an action theater, where they founded the fictitious recruiting agency "Belgium Global Talent" to address the exploitation of undocumented workers. During the summer months, they organized Popular Assemblies (*Assemblées Populaires*) in the Stalingradlaan in Brussels, a neighborhood with a high concentration of undocumented immigrants. These public assemblies took place around La Pasionaria, a statue shaped like a megaphone that symbolizes immigrant voices. At the same time, SPBelgique tried to spur the "convergence of struggles" by participating in a European march against austerity, a march against global poverty, the "occupy/indignados" movement, and No Border camps.

The response to these actions by government actors was limited to say the least. This in part concerned the deadlock created by yet another government crisis through Flemish parties' demands for more autonomy via state reform after the elections of June 2010 (Laureys 2013, 37). However, this time around, the right-wing Flemish nationalist party (N-VA) and the left-wing Socialist Party (PS) had won the elections in Flanders and Wallonia, respectively, thereby hindering the government formation process. In the end, Belgium would be without a government for eighteen months. An interim government led by Prime Minister Leterme oversaw current affairs, thereby prolonging Wathelet's tenure as the state secretary for asylum and migration, although no significant changes in asylum and immigration policy could be made during this period. However, de facto practices, such as the promotion of "voluntary return" and the intensification of arrests, detentions, and deportations, gained ground. In June 2011, the policies of voluntary return and increased cooperation between local authorities and immigration officials were formalized in a circular issued by Wathelet. After eighteen months of negotiations, a new government agreement was finally reached in December 2011. The Di Rupo government aimed to reform the Belgian migration and asylum policy in accordance with newly issued European directives. The Flemish liberal De Block replaced State Secretary Wathelet, promising to make the asylum procedure shorter and more coherent. In practice, she continued Wathelet's policy of emphasizing voluntary return and deportation while intensifying repressive measures. A new task force, SeFor, was created by the Office of Alien Affairs to better coordinate the joint efforts of local authorities and the police to locate, arrest, and detain undocumented immigrants.

Radicalization and hunger strikes

In this climate of increasing repression, the sans-papiers' actions continued in despair. In January 2012, a group of twenty-five undocumented squatters in Ixelles had been ejected by the police, forcing them to sleep in the open air in Fernand Cocq Square. Students of the Free University of Brussels formed a support group that was able to secure them temporary lodging in a university building. The sans-papiers were allowed to stay there until March, when renovations were scheduled to start. In the middle of the winter, twenty-three sans-papiers, men who originated from Morocco, Algeria, Mauretania, Ivory Coast, and Burkina Faso, autonomously decided to go on hunger strike. With their action, the hunger strikers demanded a one-year residence permit and a work permit. Spokesperson Mohammed explained the action as follows:[3]

> We have tried many things, we have done protests, actions, we have sent letters to the Office of Foreign Affairs, to the minister of Migration, to the Prime Minister, to work, to have papers, to be regularized. So this is our last solution.... We have been here for a long time. We live in this society, we have integrated ourselves, we have appropriated the habits of the Belgians, we have made friends ... we want to work here, we want to help the Belgian economy.

The university tried to convince them to stop the action, to no avail. After six days, five hunger strikers had to be hospitalized because they refused to drink water. Forty-five days later, the hunger strikers still had not received any papers. Moreover, they were on the verge of being ejected from the building. At a press conference, Pastor Daniel Alliët expressed his support: "In order to say in this atmosphere, which is completely unfavorable, 'we are doing it,' then you really have to be desperate. Desperate, we are not leaving, our human dignity demands: stop this semi-slavery, we want to work here in dignity." About one hundred protestors went to the cabinet of State Secretary Maggie De Block with a petition signed by 1,225 people. Hunger strikers Mohammed and Oumar came along to meet a cabinet member. However, she refused to talk to the hunger strikers and threatened to have them thrown out. Furthermore, she urged the student support committee to convince the hunger strikers to stop the action because the government was not planning to make any concessions. At day fifty-five, hunger striker Jamal sewed his lips together. With this act, he protested the fact that they were not being heard, despite putting their lives on the line. He wrote the following open letter:

I'm Jamal, I'm twenty years old, one of the twenty-three hunger strikers. For the moment we are on hunger strike for the fifty-fifth day and there is still no response to our demands. We are twenty-three human beings who suffer and still continue to suffer. I think this is unjust and therefore I decided to sew up my mouth. We demand the right to live in dignity and recognition as a human in a legal situation…. I started this hunger strike because I tried all possible procedures to get papers but they did not work. I cannot live any longer without rights. I want a normal life like everyone else. We do not want to live on the streets without purpose; we are not animals but people…. It is time that we show the authorities that the sans-papiers are supported by a large part of the population and that we are not willing to let them die due to general indifference.

A few days after Jamal's desperate act, Roosemont, director-general of the Foreign Affairs Service, visited the hunger strikers accompanied by two doctors. Protestors were asked to sign a declaration stating that they did not want to receive medical help if they fell into a coma. Afterwards, the doctors officially declared that the hunger strikers were not in danger. After seventy-six days, the hunger strikers' position was becoming extremely precarious. Spokesperson Mohammed justified the continuation of their action as follows:[4]

The hunger strike is our last hope, it is our last struggle. Because we have struggled with actions, protests, assemblies, debates, with blockades, all of this we have already done … we have tried many things before we went on hunger strike. Going on hunger strike is hurting ourselves…. It is not blackmail. We demand our rights … to be able to live in dignity here in Belgium…. Our situation right now is precarious. We only drink tea, coffee, and water with sugar. This is kamikaze. Death can come at any moment because of lack of proteins and vitamins.

Meanwhile, the action continued. Signs above the hunger strikers' mattresses read "Maggie De Block, why don't you feel our suffering?," "I am twenty years old. I am looking for a better future," and "I am sick of living without rights." After ninety days, the public debate started to revolve around the question of whether the police had to shut the action down. Meanwhile, State Secretary De Block took the radical stance of refusing to negotiate with or even speak to the hunger strikers, declaring that the hunger strikers "demand more rights than other people. In a democracy everyone has equal rights. Starting a hunger strike out of nowhere is a means of leverage that we will not give in to."[5] From this point on, the state secretary would systematically denounce any form of protest by sans-papiers alike as "blackmail." The media, prominent intellectuals, and public opinion easily picked up on this framing. Moreover, the hunger strikers were being publicly accused of "cheating" with feeding tubes. After 102 days, the action was stopped without any concrete results.

The European March

Faced with this political deadlock at the national level, SPBelgique tried to switch gears by participating in the European March of the sans-papiers in the summer of 2012. In that year, The French self-organization Comité des Soutiens 75 (CSP75) reached out to SPBelgique and a handful of organizations from across Europe to participate in the *Marche européenne des Sans Papiers et migrants*. For CSP75, marching had been one of the seminal forms of action in their political repertoire:

> Marching is our usual mode of action at the CSP75.... We have been marching for many years like this, collectively, peacefully, tirelessly, deploying our banners, our slogans, our chants, our rhythmic music, our drums, and our demand of regularization for all the sans-papiers. In this way we occupy public space and we draw the attention of people who pass by, thereby forcing reflection. And this is exactly what we will do during the European March, everywhere we will pass.

In order to ensure the transnational character of the march, the organizing committee reached out to collectives all over Europe. Participating actors would form a new transnational coalition organization, the CISPM. The CISPM comprised SPBelgique from Belgium, the International Legal Team from Germany, the Collectif Bleiberecht from Switzerland, and the ad hoc created Coalizione Internazionale dei Sans-Papiers e Migranti in Italy. A division of labor was implemented whereby these collectives would organize the march's passage in each country. In practice, this meant the local organizations had to take care of the logistical and financial practicalities, such as providing a place to sleep for the marchers, providing food, getting authorization from the local police, and so on. After weeks of deliberation, the CISPM came up with a marching schedule that envisaged protests in twenty-one cities in seven countries. In one month, the marchers crossed seven borders, traveled 1,900 kilometers, and staged protests in twenty cities. They marched hundreds of kilometers on foot to reach the European Parliament in Strasbourg.

As described in this book's preface, Fariss, Ilyas, Nassim, and Anouar represented SPBelgique during the march. We had traveled by car from Brussels to Strasbourg to welcome the Belgian marchers at the end of their journey. We were chasing the noise of the marchers' chants through the streets of Strasbourg. When we spotted the marchers, we witnessed an explosion of colors, sounds, dance, movement, and emotions. The marchers were wearing their signature yellow and blue T-shirts with the printed words "*Liberté de circulation et d'installation pour tous*" ("Freedom of mobility and settlement for all"). Ilyas, a member of SPBelgique, was the first person to recognize and embrace us. His face was glowing, and he was chanting, "*Des papiers pour tous!*" He proudly showed us a tank top with the words "*Kein Mensch ist illegal*" from Germany and a flag from an Italian labor union as if they were symbols of victory. "I traveled more than 400 kilometers by foot," he said. "Can you believe that?" He then recounted, "At the border between Switzerland and Italy, we stood face to face with the police, but the police did not intervene while we crossed the border! This was a special moment for us." He said, "It was both symbolical but also very emotional." We ran into SPBelgique members Nassim and Redouan as well. "Isn't it fantastic that the police are making way for us, instead of vice versa?" Redouan joked. Afterward, they claimed that marching had changed their lives for good. As Nassim put it, "We have shown that borders don't exist anymore for us: the sans-papiers."

Without a doubt, crossing borders was one of the most symbolic acts of the march. By crossing seven borders, the marchers wanted to demonstrate the contradiction between "Fortress Europe's" emphasis on external border enforcement and the virtual absence of internal borders in the Schengen area. For many undocumented immigrants, it had seemed impossible to be able to travel from one country to the other without papers, but the experience of the march showed them otherwise. This is well illustrated by the testimony of marcher Paka: "For me, a strong and new sensation of freedom has never left me: I have lived in France for the past twelve years and I have never had the opportunity to leave. The fact of having crossed seven borders has made me feel like a bird freed from its cage" (*La voix des sans-papiers* 2012, 2). The CISPM leadership hailed the successful crossing of these borders as nothing less than a "peaceful revolution." As Annan proclaimed, "even if borders exist, there are no borders anymore; there are only borders for people; for misery, there are no borders; for the crisis, there are no borders; for money, there are no borders." According to the CISPM, they had shown "to all asylum seekers, sans-papiers, and migrants that in Europe, borders only exist on paper."

Beyond the symbolic act of crossing borders, the CISPM was nevertheless still worried about the march's outcome, because "we don't know yet whether we will be heard at the European Parliament." In fact, being heard by the European Parliament had been one of the march's primary goals—the objective was to demand the freedom of circulation and settlement for all, accompanied by a harmonization of the right to regularization for all undocumented immigrants in Europe. As SPBelgique member Faisal explained: "European directives determine national laws, yet we do not know to whom we need to address ourselves, at the national level or at the European level?" By pointing fingers at each other, Europe and its member states made it impossible for undocumented immigrants to voice their concerns. By speaking directly to representatives of the European Parliament, the marchers wanted to hold Europe accountable for this situation. However, they would soon be confronted with the fact that the issue is exacerbated for two reasons: first, the far-reaching sovereignty of the member states in the realm of migration policy and, second, the absence of a state-citizen relationship at the European level. Hence, the marchers' attempt to supersede the nation by addressing the European Parliament would once again result in a referral back to the national level. This is ably illustrated by the following events:

On the first evening after the arrival of the marchers in Strasbourg, the country delegation leaders held a meeting of the CISPM bureau until four in the morning. About twenty people sat around the table, arguing about what they were going to demand in the upcoming meetings. The rest of the 130 marchers were already asleep in the gym hall that the city of Strasbourg had made available. The next morning, I talked to Abas. He said that there had been a lot of arguments between the delegations from the different countries, each stemming from their respective claims and the needs in their countries. "The situation is very different in Belgium than it is in Italy or Germany," he said. Moreover, there was a general sense that the French leaders were trying to control the other delegations. The next day, a group of ten people were getting ready to go to the first meeting with members of the European Council. We walked to the European Council building together. When we arrived at the massive government premises, we were screened by security. Next, they told us we had to wait in the lobby. There was not enough space for people to sit in the lobby, so we had to stand up. Everyone was silent and you could feel the tension in the air. "Smile," Alexander said, "we have reached the end." After a wait that seemed to take ages, the woman at the reception told us we had to go to another building for "safety reasons." On our way there, people were getting a bit worried. On arrival, the security awaited us. "Only three people can be allowed entrance," they said. "This is ridiculous," Abas stated. "We have come all this way marching with people from five different countries, so the least you can do is let five people in." "Impossible," the security replied, and the leaders took a moment to deliberate. They decided that representatives from France, Italy, and Germany would go in, while those from Belgium and Switzerland had to stay outside. Heavily disappointed, the rest of the delegation left while we installed ourselves on the building's steps to wait. Afterward, the others reported back on what happened at the earlier meeting. "The meeting was canceled since people were wearing T-shirts with slogans," they explained. "Since this is not allowed inside European institutions, they offered that we could change our T-shirts for 'neutral' T-shirts from the building's cleaning workers." At that point, the marchers had decided to focus their efforts on the members of parliament instead.

The next day, the big meeting with Euro-deputies from the European Socialist Party and the Green Party was on the agenda. Marchers and supporters had gathered in front of the European Parliament. The marchers assembled a drumming band, and African rhythms were being played. A dance circle was formed, and people were shouting chants like "Solidarity with the sans-papiers," "Yesterday colonized, today regularized," and "Tomorrow, what do we want? Papers! For whom? For all!" Citizen allies and undocumented immigrants, men and women, old and young marchers: everyone joined in. I walked alongside the march's leaders when they approached the European Parliament building. "This is the first time sans-papiers are going to enter the European Parliament," someone whispered. Once inside, the CISPM leaders explained the trajectory of the march and the demands for "freedom of circulation and settlement" they were putting to the European Union. A representative of the European Green Party delegation replied as follows:

> Knocking on the door of the European Parliament is an excellent initiative. This first European March is very pertinent because it permits you to address your demands at those institutions that try to uphold fundamental and non-discriminatory rights.... One cannot deny that we see more progress with regards to so-called security control guidelines to secure the borders of the EU than advances in terms of positive rights recognized at the scale of the whole Union.... The EU is competent to set out global policies, but the member states remain masters of migration on their territory. ("La marche Européenne des sans-papiers transcende les frontières," note viii)

In other words, the European deputies brought the disappointing news that not they but only the member states had the authority to address the marchers' demands. What this outline shows is that there are challenges involved for undocumented immigrants with regard to making claims at the European level. The grounds on which the different delegations formulated their claims were reflective of the politics of deservingness in their respective nation-states. This alludes to the fact that, for undocumented immigrants, engaging in transnational mobilization is not always straightforward. As Abas explained:

> [Participating in the CISPM] is not easy because it is ambitious, even utopic. It makes you dream but there is still reality; the everyday reality of sans-papiers

and the urgency of the situation, of the moment, so in order to say: "Yes, I am going to wage a struggle at the international level," and that at the same time we do not succeed in getting regularization at the national level, leaves you with your thoughts a little bit.

The National Solidarity March

The long-term effects of the march were primarily felt in the much-needed boost it gave to SPBelgique at the national level. However, once again, no direct results were recorded. In the meantime, State Secretary De Block had become one of Flanders's most popular politicians due to her strict, repressive, and nonnegotiable stance on irregular migration. Months of small-scale actions largely went unnoticed until SPBelgique organized a two-week-long march through Belgium in April 2013. The goal of the march was to rebuild a national movement from scratch. As Faisal put it, "For us, the goal is not to march just for the sake of marching. Our goal is rather to show to the sans-papiers that there is still a sans-papiers movement in Belgium—that it has not disappeared, we still have demands and we are still here."

Representational conflicts between privileged and underprivileged subjects nevertheless arose again during the preparation of the march. A small group of people who had actively participated in the European March committed themselves to laying down the preparatory groundwork for the solidarity march. The organizing model of the 2012 European March was used as a framework: partner organizations in each city would provide the logistics and mobilize support. What happened in the first weeks of preparation was that almost no sans-papiers turned up for the meetings. Usually, the meetings comprised about ten to twelve people, of whom only one or two were sans-papiers. Despite efforts to motivate the sans-papiers to be more involved, this situation did not change over time.

When the time came to mobilize the sans-papiers to participate, their lack of involvement in the planning process turned out to be an obstacle. The *soutiens* who presented the "Solidarity March with AND without Papers" to the sans-papiers stressed how the march was conceived as a two-week national consultation, around which the grievances of local organizations in Ghent, Antwerp, Sint-Niklaas, Mechelen, Liège, Brussels, La Louvière, and Leuven would be compiled to then formulate demands to the government. This course of action immediately caused resistance among some of the sans-papiers present. "We need to occupy a church and demand regularization, not talk all day," one of the sans-papiers said. The suggestion straight away led to enthusiasm among some of his peers. However, this line of action was in direct opposition to what the organizers of the march had in mind. The call of the "radicals" was hence silenced. Throughout the march, this remained an issue. Some people felt as though they had been denied the ability to speak for themselves. As a marcher told me, he felt "they were being exploited by the associations who organized the march, because they could not even talk about hunger strikes." While the "moments of exchange" were going on, they secretly made lists of people who would be interested in participating in a direct action after the march.

The organizers of the march faced issues over representation—not only internally, but also externally. The marching committee had sent out a call to well-established CSOs and self-organizations all over Belgium. The response was limited and the organizations that ended up participating were the usual suspects. A couple of weeks before the march, SPBelgique received a call to participate in a meeting organized by Bruxelles-Laïque to "relaunch the sans-papiers movement in Belgium." Once there, well-established CSOs that had played an important role in the movement before—such as CIRÉ, Bruxelles-Laïque, CRER, CRAC-PE, a support group from the ULB, and labor unions—were present. During the meeting, the organizers explained the importance of the current conjuncture because of the increase in repression and the unwillingness of the government to discuss the issue. "We have to create a movement around the sans-papiers," one of the organizers said, "and we are here today to launch it." For SPBelgique, this statement entailed a denial of their efforts over the past year. The meeting organizers then made a case for the formation of a "Front des Migrants" (Migrant Front), a coalition organization that would have as its objective putting the case of the sans-papiers back on the agenda. When SPBelgique's members tried to make the point that this was exactly the goal of the Solidarity March they were organizing, they were not only ignored but silenced. "The organizations present here have years and years of experience working in the field," one of the organizers said. Faisal responded by raising the question: "Do the sans-papiers have a voice in this platform?" He continued by recalling the problems during the negotiation of the 2009 regularization and said that he felt the sans-papiers were not properly represented. Next, sans-papiers who had been mobilized to take part in the initiative were urged to present themselves at the invitation of the meeting organizers. These "representatives" were strategically selected by the organizers to ensure the "participation of the sans-papiers community."

I talked to SPBelgique leaders a couple of weeks later to hear how they had experienced this event. Faisal said that "the sans-papiers movement does not exist in the heads of these associations; they ask: 'where are the sans-papiers?' only to say that, politically speaking, there is no movement so that they can recuperate the movement." In this regard, he expressed an ambivalent attitude toward support organizations in a later interview:

> The associations are two-faced. They can give you what you want but they also have their own, well-determined political agenda, you see, so it is give and take … it is like we have become politicians toward them while we are not politicians, you see?

Hamid told me how he interpreted this turn of events as yet another move from these organizations to exploit the sans-papiers and "speak for them." He had left the last meeting of the Migrant Front angry because he was told to shut up at a certain point, and he did not intend to attend the meetings any longer. What is central to these issues is the fundamentally different types of political understandings that privileged and underprivileged subjects invoke in order to justify strategic choices. As Abas explains:

> The problem here is that we have been confronted with what we call the paternalism or maternalism toward the sans-papiers. There are certain big organizations in Brussels … that always position themselves as the spokespeople for immigrants and asylum seekers, which do good work from time to time, but … we feel like we do not have our place with them; we do not have the same standing and often we are just there to provide *testimonies* while they portray themselves as having all the *knowledge* and *expertise*, and that it is them who know how to solve the situation and for them it is not even necessary that there is a sans-papiers movement because it is them who do the work.… This destroys what we are doing, and that is frustrating. And sometimes we even say that before we go and demonstrate against the government we should go and demonstrate against them.

"Refugees are the sans-papiers of tomorrow."

Merely three months after the Belgian Solidarity March had been brought to a successful conclusion, SPBelgique was overtaken by the actions of yet another group of rejected asylum seekers. Between July 15 and 19, 2013, hundreds of Afghans, including families with children, occupied the Beguinage Church in Brussels once again. The occupation was supported by head priest Daniel Alliët and was intended to protest the deportations of rejected asylum seekers to Afghanistan. Priest Alliët explained why he supported the action as follows: "We are here to say to you: we want to help you to mark the occasion. There is a line that cannot be crossed: one does not send young people, women, children to a country in a state of war."[6] That year, State Secretary De Block had made the return—either voluntary or forced—of rejected asylum seekers a top priority. Afghans, who had benefited from protected status in previous years, were increasingly being denied protection, and forty-six persons were effectively deported in 2013. The protestors' reasoning was that it was inhumane to deport rejected asylum seekers to Afghanistan, since it was a country that was still at war. Afghan activists thereby drew a sharp distinction between "refugees," who were running away from violence, and other sans-papiers, who were portrayed as economic migrants, as the following excerpt from a focus group shows (Willner-Reid 2015, 12):

> Afghanistan is one of the worst countries for war in the whole world now. From other countries they are all coming because of work, but we are not. We are not coming because of food and so on, we are just coming for the security of our lives. This is the big difference between our country and their country, because our country is at war.

During the occupation, a week of reflection took place in which people discussed possible tactics and actions. After several weeks of protest, about two hundred Afghans, including dozens of families with children, then occupied a building in the Rue du Trône in Brussels. A spokesperson for the occupiers, Said, communicated the following about the occupation:[7]

> De Block may well say that they do not deport Afghan children; they do not give them and their parents the right to live here in dignity or work either. Hundreds of Afghan families are forced to survive on the streets in a clandestine way. The services of De Block do nothing to help them. These people want there to be a definitive end to their illegal existence and demand a quick solution.

A nine-year-old Afghan girl spoke to the media about why her family had participated in the action: "We have already been in Belgium for seven years and we can't go back to Afghanistan because we want to stay here and we will also stay here. We don't want to have to go through what our moms and dads went through in Afghanistan; we want to go to school."[8] The occupation of the building in the Rue du Trône was a symbolic way to protest their nonrecognition as refugees in need of help. A banner by one of the occupiers illustrated the main question that was at the center of their struggle, namely: "Who is the real refugee?" The number of occupants quickly grew to more than four hundred people. This group would become better known as the 450 Afghans collective in the months to come. Up to four families were living in each room. The fact that the occupiers chose a building run by Samu Social, a social center that served as a refuge for homeless people during the winter, indicated how they acted "as if" they had been recognized as refugees with the right to shelter and housing. However, the doors were not just open to anyone. Only Afghans were allowed to join the occupation, and proposals to join forces with other migrant collectives were swiftly dismissed.

In order to put pressure on the state secretary, the 450 Afghans collective started to organize weekly protest actions close to the Belgian Parliament, in the Rue de la Loi (Street of the Law). The place where they staged their protests is a busy intersection in Brussels, in the political heart of the city. During one of these protests, I ran into SPBelgique member Mohammed. It had been a while since I had seen him around. A lot of supporters had shown up that day, and I recognized many familiar faces of citizen activists who would also turn up for SPBelgique's demonstrations. The 450 Afghans collective itself claimed to be supported by no fewer than sixty organizations, including trade unions, immigrant rights organizations, student organizations, churches, and trade unions (Willner-Reid 2015, 10). Everywhere I looked, people were sitting down, blocking traffic at the intersection. I asked Mohammed what he made of the scene. "The turnout is great," he said, "but it is not going to change anything for us." By "us," he was referring to the rest of the sans-papiers in Brussels. The framing of the Afghan activists was deliberately intended to distance themselves from other undocumented migrants, for whom the outlook for being regularized was dire to say the least. SPBelgique's ongoing efforts to unite the sans-papiers under one banner were thereby seriously hampered.

On September 25, Afghan protestors were waiting for a meeting with a member of the prime minister's cabinet when the police used force to clear the intersection. While the previous protests had taken place in a nonviolent manner, the police now used tear gas and dogs against the protestors, including families with children. The protestors reported that fifty people had suffered from bites by police dogs. About seventy protestors were arrested and immediately taken to secure detention centers in Bruges, Merksplas, Vottem, and Zaventem instead of the police station. One of the protestors released the following testimony through social media about the violence that had been inflicted on his body by the police:

After the police had arrested us in Rue de la Loi Brussels, they have beaten me a lot in the bus: they have touched my genitals, they have beaten me with a helmet to my head and also kicked my mouth. When we arrived in Merksplas, the police put me in a separate room in the basement where they have beaten me one by one, took off my clothes and asked me to say sorry and beat me.

One day later, on September 26, the police intervened to stop the occupation of the building in the Rue du Trône, which had been ongoing for about twenty days at that time. The owner of the building had requested a court order to initiate the eviction of the occupiers. Refusing to move became a way for the Afghans to demand their right to stay. Over time, those demands became more specific, including a moratorium on deportations to Afghanistan, freedom for all detained Afghans in secure centers in Belgium, a one-year residence permit with permission to work for all Afghans whose asylum was rejected, and a residence permit for five years for Afghans who had been in Belgium for three years or more without papers. Meanwhile, Afghan protestors reoccupied the building in the Rue du Trône twice, despite their eviction. Two highly publicized marches were organized, in December 2013 to Mons and January 2014 to Ghent. After the protesters had been able to meet with the state secretary, most of the Afghans resubmitted their asylum applications and transferred from their occupation to open refugee centers. By the summer of 2014, one year after its initial spark, the Afghan movement had almost completely disappeared from the public eye.

Movement disintegration and collapse

In the same period, SPBelgique was running on its last legs. In view of the attention that was being paid to the "refugee issue," the skepticism that several members had displayed from the very beginning about the European and Solidarity March, and the fatigue that its leaders experienced, the organization's rank and file became harder and harder to mobilize. SPBelgique was still well represented at the occasional protests led by the 450 Afghans collective, but the demands for regularization for all sans-papiers slowly but surely became overshadowed. On top of that, SPBelgique had the rather heavy responsibility of accommodating the CISPM, which was staging a second European March in June 2014, during their passage through Brussels. Given the fragile state of the collective at the time, this turned out to be too much to bear. Five years after its inception, the SPBelgique leadership therefore announced the dismantling of its organization with a press release titled "The struggle will continue":

> Four years ago, four undocumented people decided to relaunch a mobilization of undocumented migrants around the issue of regularization, a process that led to the creation of SPB. Since then, the law has not changed, the borders are still closed and the closed centers still full. But this collective at least had the merit of moving and denouncing at a moment when almost no one dared to reopen this question of regularization. This group also had the merit of finishing with "we are not dangerous, we are in danger" or "give us the papers, we want to

work" and asking the real questions: rights, equality, freedom of movement.... With the little support it received, this collective was able to maintain at least the flame of hope through demonstrations, rallies, popular assemblies, occupations, a march in Belgium and Europe, briefings, debate and movie screenings, collective meals.... It is neither the experience that is lacking nor the will, but it is the division that stifles initiatives.... The struggle existed before this collective, and it will continue exist afterwards ... this collective has only tried to pursue what others have already begun.

And continue the struggle did. As outlined in the Epilogue, the organizing model of SPBelgique provided the later foundations for the "Coordination des Sans-papiers de Belgique" (Coordination). SPBelgique activists continued to play an active role in the movement by founding initiatives such as CollectActif, a community-oriented initiative that expanded the target group beyond the sans-papiers to include refugees and homeless people. Furthermore, former marchers of the European March created the collective "la Voix des Sans-papiers" (the Voice of the Undocumented) in 2014. A decade later, they keep the flame of self-organization alive in Brussels while linking their right to regularization to their local presence via occupations. Thus, as was the case with former IYJL activists, the legacy of SPBelgique continues to have ripple effects on the movement long after the organization was dismantled.

Conclusion

The findings presented in this chapter paint a by now familiar picture. Just like undocumented youth struggled to gain precarious agency in Chicago, the sans-papiers faced a similar uphill battle to do so in Brussels. In response to the representational conflicts described in the chapter, self-organizations emerged that functioned as activist infrastructures where undocumented migrants could experiment with new modes of self-representation. The institutional support provided by churches, universities, community centers, and local neighborhood councils contributed to the emergence of these spaces. While lacking the organizational continuity and material resources of their more established counterparts, self-organizations proved to be highly effective in politicizing undocumented migrants in Brussels. Rather than rationally calculating which political strategies and demands were the most "feasible" or "appropriate," time and time again the sans-papiers rallied around the universalistic demand for "papers for all, without exception." These "unrealistic" and "unproductive" demands clashed more often than not with the views of privileged subjects looking to cut deals around regularization. This should come as no surprise, since these organizations cater to the political representatives' demand to put "emotions aside" to negotiate compromises as "experts." Nevertheless, as shown, putting emotions aside often entails silencing the voice of the sans-papiers altogether.

This chapter has also shown how prevailing understandings of citizenship and deservingness affected the internal dynamics of the sans-papiers movement. Despite efforts to overcome internal differences and unite forces, opportunistic activists proved time and time again how much easier it was to mobilize around particularistic rather than universalistic demands. This observation, taken together with a complete lack of what I call elsewhere "institutional receptivity," helps to explain the volatility and episodes of movement collapse and resurgence that characterize the Belgian sans-papiers movement (Swerts 2021). Moreover, the plentiful examples of failed and successful hunger strikes illustrate a lack of movement coordination and collective memory.

PART II
ACTIVIST TRAJECTORIES

In the second part of this book, I analyze and compare the activist trajectories of undocumented migrants on both sides of the Atlantic. I use the term "activist trajectories" here to designate the individual and collective biographies of undocumented migrants that give insights into the lived experiences, challenges, and key turning points in their activist paths. Compared with the first part of the book, the epistemological vantage point is radically shifted toward the perspective of undocumented activists themselves and the experiential knowledge they draw on to gain precarious agency (see Chapters 3 and 4). The starting point is that undocumented migrants are not born activists, but rather have to become activists. Becoming an undocumented activist involves a deeply personal, highly challenging, and internally conflictual process through which embodied, discursive, and emotional understandings that have been engrained into the minds of undocumented migrants due to the lived experiences of illegality that have to be transformed. This process of transformation is at the same time a profoundly *social* one, since it relies on activist infrastructures such as IYJL and SPBelgique.

Three main arguments are made in the following chapters. First, lived experiences of illegality serve as a crucial experiential basis for future political subjectivation in undocumented migrants' activist trajectories. Despite obvious differences between contexts, populations, and levels of precarity, the life stories of undocumented activists presented in Chapters 5 and 6 display remarkable commonalities as they unfold themselves in the urban context of Chicago and Brussels. These commonalities mainly stem from the detrimental impact that precarious legal status—and the corresponding subjection to illegalizing migration regimes that it implies—has on undocumented youth's and the sans-papiers' lives as unrecognized residents in the city. I distinguish between three fundamental modes whereby undocumented youth and the sans-papiers experience and know precarity at the local level. *Embodied understandings* refer to lived experiences of mobility and immobility developed through migrating to and settling in a city of residence. *Discursive understandings* refer to lived experiences of being "called names" without having the opportunity to "talk back" and being treated as rightless, voiceless subjects in interactions with educators, employers, and bureaucrats. *Emotional understandings* refer to lived experiences of fear, trauma, shame, and anger caused by the subjection to and internalization of state violence, exploitation, and marginalization. While the comparison between the trajectories of undocumented migrants in both cities reveals important contextual differences in terms of the relative intensity of exposure to immobility, stigmatization, and state violence, the analysis highlights how lived experiences of illegality crystallize in similar ways into self-understandings.

Second, I argue that undocumented migrants' potential to become activists who can challenge the status quo is essentially rooted in these lived experiences. Becoming an activist does not require the erasing of an undocumented migrant's previously accumulated embodied, discursive, and emotional understandings. On the contrary, I argue that undocumented activists' precarious agency precisely stems from the strategic performance and public exposure to experiential knowledge steeped in vulnerability. What is therefore required to transform this knowledge into workable *political* understandings that turn bodies, stories, and emotions into activist tools is the presence of "activist infrastructures." The cycle of recruitment, training, and mobilization that undocumented activists go through is propelled forward by the strategic use of embodiment, narrative, and emotions every step of the way. By creatively borrowing existing scripts from the political context in which they were immersed, and by infusing these scripts with their lived experiences, undocumented activists are able to expose the institutional cracks in prevailing understandings of citizenship. Furthermore, self-organizations can function as activist infrastructures that enable undocumented activists to experiment with and enact prefigurative understandings of citizenship rooted in unconditional inclusion and community belonging.

Third, I suggest that the reliance of undocumented activists on scripting and publicly performing their vulnerability as a political strategy also entails potential pitfalls. Put differently, the strength of undocumented activism is simultaneously its weakness. Unsurprisingly, acting out their traumas and inner fears in public, risking arrest and deportation, and literally putting their life on the line can become draining for the activists involved. This is particularly the case given the fact that there are no such things as "quick wins" in irregular migration politics. Moreover, undocumented activists face overt or covert forms of repression from the government. When institutional receptivity is low, undocumented movements also risk being "silenced" or "ignored to death." Furthermore, shifting niche openings that benefit some groups over others can reinforce categorical divisions and cause rifts within movements. The challenge for undocumented activists then becomes how to nurture their precarious agency and keep it safe in the wake of a volatile and hostile political environment.

5
Growing up undocumented
Youth activists' life stories

Little seemed to separate Cynthia from her peers at the illustrious University of Chicago. From our first encounter, Cynthia struck me as someone who blended in perfectly with the witty students that roam the "quads" at the secluded campus in the leafy Hyde Park neighborhood. Guarded by one of the largest private security forces in America, the couple of blocks flanked by Lake Shore Drive to the east and Washington Park to the west are a haven of tranquility in Chicago's South Side. Yet even though Cynthia was studying in one of the best schools nationwide for her field, she never stopped feeling out of place. The relative safety of Hyde Park stood in stark contrast to the gangs she was told to watch out for in Back of the Yards, the working-class neighborhood in the South Side where she spent most of her youth growing up. In her first year, she did not have anyone to talk Spanish to in a dorm filled with predominantly white, middle-class students. Relating to them was difficult because they did not know "where she was coming from." That was because noncitizenship operated as an invisible boundary separating Cynthia from her peers. The stigma of illegality combined with the threat of deportability formed dark clouds above Cynthia's otherwise bright-looking future. Back at her parents' place, Cynthia recalled, "I don't want to say you had an idea of who was undocumented and who wasn't, but it was sort of one of those things." As if the ethnic, cultural, and socioeconomic markers that firmly put her in the category of "minority student" were not enough, her lack of legal status made her feel really isolated. The story of "where she was coming from" was more complicated than a loaded phrase like "from the South Side" could fill in.

Cynthia was born in Mexico City. Her parents were sixteen and eighteen when they got married. Living in a house with her aunt and her grandmother, family members helped to raise her. When her dad realized he could not provide for the three of them in Mexico, he decided to take his chances in the United States. When Cynthia was eighteen months old, her mother joined her father, and she was left behind with her grandmother and aunt. More than a year after she left, her mother returned from the States seven months pregnant to give birth to her second child in Mexico. Cynthia was too young to remember crossing the

Citizen X. Thomas Swerts, Oxford University Press. © Thomas Swerts (2026).
DOI: 10.1093/9780197844038.003.0006

border a few months later. Back in Chicago, the family lived in a cramped two-bedroom apartment with the families of her uncle and her cousin. As soon as they had saved up enough money, they relocated to Back of the Yards, the neighborhood that housed the Union Stock Yards until the demise of the meat-packing industry in the seventies. Throughout elementary school, Cynthia took bilingual classes before transitioning into all English classes. She became a straight A student in high school, and her dad used to say: "You'll end up in Harvard one day and you're gonna make lots of money." Meanwhile, her parents worked full-time jobs to pay the bills for the house they had bought. She was the one responsible for picking up her two younger brothers from school, taking care of the house, cooking, feeding, and baby-sitting them until her parents got back from work.

Cynthia always had an idea she was undocumented, but she did not really understand what it entailed. She recalls overhearing conversations as a child, where her family members used terms like *fronteras* and *nogales*, words meaning that someone was coming or was on their way to Chicago. When her grandparents and her aunt came to the United States, she remembers her dad asking other family members, "Where are they, how did they make it across?" Still, her legal status did not affect her life directly, since a lot of her friends at school were in the same situation. In sixth grade, she was confronted with her legal status for the first time when she had to fill out forms for a summer program. Forced to leave the social security question blank, she ended up lying to her teacher that her mom did not have it. Like so many other undocumented youths, high school proved to be a turning point for Cynthia. Not able to take driver's education, she was regularly confronted with questions like "why aren't you driving?" or "where's your car?" Ashamed for her status, she learned to make up excuses or lie about the reasons why she did not drive. The only friends she could confide in were undocumented themselves. Between them, the running joke was that they would just marry someone to get their status. Afraid that people would change their perception of her if they found out, she painstakingly tried to avoid raising "little red flags" and did not intervene when others made offensive remarks about undocumented immigrants.

When college came around, Cynthia's legal status started to become a major source of emotional stress. Unable to apply for most sources of financial aid, she was accepted to several schools that still required her parents to pay thousands of dollars they could not afford. Her application to the University of Chicago was a last-minute long shot. To her great surprise, the big envelope she received in return contained an acceptance letter with a funding offer. The day she found out the news, her parents took her aside and told her, "We're really proud of you for getting in, but we also want you to understand you may not be eligible to get the money, and if that's the case, then we're really sorry." The combination of her parents' guilt and her own desperation led her to break down behind the wheel at a red traffic light. One phone call later, the administration confirmed she could start the program despite her status. Yet what should have been a joyful experience became an agonizing one when she was confronted with the limitations her status brought with it. Since internships and study abroad programs required background checks, she started tutoring elementary school kids on the side instead. When the tutoring program's policy changed and they also asked for a background check, self-doubt kicked in. "I don't want to be here, I don't belong here, I shouldn't be here, I made a mistake, I'm going to end up failing my classes, I can't concentrate because there's so much going on," were the thoughts that haunted her mind. Disappointed by the barriers she faced, Cynthia slipped into depression. The only friend from high school she shared her struggles with felt worlds away from the life on campus. She became sleep deprived, regularly staying up crying until two in the morning. Feelings of deep frustration, isolation, and powerlessness started to consume her life.

***

If the story were to end here, Cynthia's biography would be a tell-tale example of how illegalizing and criminalizing migration regimes manage to crush undocumented youths' hopes and aspirations. The roadblocks and hurdles that the specific group of 1.5 generation undocumented migrants experience in the United States in their educational and professional careers have been meticulously studied by now (Gonzales 2016)). The emotional toll that living in constant fear of deportation takes on mixed-status families and romantic relationships has likewise been documented (Dreby 2015). The bottom line in existing scholarship on undocumented youth is that lived experiences of illegality add up to reinforce vulnerability, insecurity, and lack of community solidarity (Abrego 2011). Cynthia's story does not undermine that thesis—quite the opposite. However, as we will learn in the following chapters, the analytical apparatus employed to capture the vulnerability that characterize these experiences is ill-equipped to account for precarious agency. While many authors in the field acknowledge the capacity of undocumented youth to mobilize and resist illegalization and criminalization, it is far less clear how this agency is essentially rooted in precarity. However, recent attempts by undocumented scholars to theorize undocumented life by taking lived experiences of illegality as an epistemological starting point give pointers (Abrego and Negrón-Gonzales 2020; Bejarano et al. 2019; Anderson and Solis 2021). Ramirez, for example, highlights the need for undocumented migrants to be in "constant negotiation with their undocumented status and with retaining agency against the current and historical xenophobic political climate that relentlessly tries to strip them away from that possibility" (Ramirez 2020, 155). While they initially maintain agency by *not* disclosing their undocumented status, these suppressed lived experiences become politically potent when "coming out" as undocumented (see Chapter 7).

Adopting the hermeneutical perspective introduced above helps to tease out the intricate connections between lived experiences of illegality and precarious agency. In this chapter and the next I argue that we need to reach a deeper understanding of how undocumented youth come to see, experience, and interpret the world that surrounds them before we can grasp their desire to act for change. In this chapter, I therefore introduce the personal life stories of IYJL activists. These stories not only allow the reader to get an intimate understanding of these youths' trajectories, but also contain lessons on the dialectical relationship between subjection and subjectivation. Encompassing her early childhood until the present, the narrative opening of this chapter provides a detailed account of how the salience and impact of precarious legal status creeps up on undocumented youth's aspirations as they make the transition into adulthood (Gonzales 2016). With every hurdle they face on their life trajectories, they "learn to be illegal," as Gonzales has aptly put it (Gonzales 2011). Going from "being illegal" to "being an activist" can seem to be an insurmountable step. Yet this is precisely what Cynthia managed to do from the moment she stepped forward as an active member at IYJL. In order to appreciate the process of transformation that took place in doing so, I focus on discursive, emotive, and kinesthetic understandings as interrelated and interacting *modes of "being in the world."*

The stories presented in this chapter echo many familiar themes that can be found in the stories of the approximately 1.5 million undocumented youths who have grown up in the United States since childhood. This "new second generation" is highly diverse in origins and socioeconomic backgrounds. Moreover, factors such as race, education, and place of residence further stratify the extent to which undocumented status affects patterns of social (im)mobility (Zhou and Gonzales 2019). While legal status can be regarded as a "master status" that trumps all other forms of achievement and merit, "privilege without papers" is nevertheless unevenly distributed along racial and class lines (Gonzales 2016). Taking into consideration the vast diversity in lived experiences of illegality within the undocumented population in the United States, we should therefore place the life stories of these activists in context. Most of the respondents were female and born in Mexico. This is representative of IYJL's membership. Further, they were between one and ten years old when they migrated to the United States. This corresponds with living undocumented in the United States for a period of between ten and twenty-one years. Despite the hardships they had to go through, IYJL activists were an exceptional group, of which a majority had a college degree.

Embodied lived experiences

Life as an undocumented migrant becomes deeply ingrained in embodied understandings. These understandings are shaped by accumulated lived experiences of mobility and immobility. For citizens equipped with the right travel authorizations or visas, crossing borders means little more than passing border security before checking in for a flight, driving past a checkpoint, or collecting stamps in a passport. Yet for unwanted subjects, such as people who flee from economic deprivation, persecution, or conflict situations, crossing a border often represents an insurmountable obstacle that stands in between their bleak current situation and their dreams of a better life. The mobility of undocumented people, understood as their capacity to move freely through space, is severely limited by the proliferation of borders and bordering practices (De Genova and Peutz 2010). Setting up borders has been shown to be a costly and ineffective way of governing irregular migration flows. Nevertheless, calls for more investments in border patrol officers and physical infrastructure continue to dominate the immigration debate. This can be explained by the symbolic function the border plays as a spectacle rendering the mobility of certain migrant bodies "illegal" (De Genova 2013). Circumventing spatial limitations and restrictions puts the undocumented at risk of being subjected to physical violence, abuse, exploitation, and trauma.[1]

Once across the border, illegalized status also exacerbates the risk of having to live and work in precarious conditions in the city. A study in Chicago confirmed that undocumented youth are more likely to live in neighborhoods that are residentially unstable and exhibit high concentrations of migrants (Lara-Cinisomo et al. 2013). Often forced to move due to the instability of their informal housing situation or the unsteadiness of their parents' jobs, "mobility" can become negatively associated with residential instability and lack of a real "home." While obviously restricted in their mobility to venture out of the country, undocumented youth also experience restricted mobility within city limits. Faced with the tangible threat of apprehension and deportation during traffic controls, a mundane activity like driving around in a "car city" such as Chicago can turn into a potentially hazardous activity. Furthermore, from a young age, undocumented youth learn how to avoid running into the law and concealing their status when questions are asked (Gonzales 2016). In this respect, I argue that lived experiences of mobility and immobility creep into undocumented youth's embodied understandings in ways that can be directly observed by closely examining their stories. First, I focus on how undocumented youth activists in IYJL experienced migrating to the United States with their parents. Next, I outline how their families settled in Chicago and how they experienced growing up in their neighborhood and getting around town.

Crossing the border

The experience of migrating to the United States is without a doubt a life-changing event for undocumented youth. Often leaving at a young age, they are unable to grasp what crossing the border and starting a new life will entail. Furthermore, some youths do not expect to stay in the United States for a long time but end up staying longer than anticipated. The fact that their parents make the decision to move on their behalf can make it harder to accept their everyday reality as undocumented.

The story of Ulises contains several key themes that can also be found in other IYJL members' stories.

> I was born January 11, 1991, in Puebla, Mexico.... I lived there with my two brothers and my mom and dad for probably two years. Up until April of 1993, that's when my dad decided the income he was making from his job was not enough to sustain three little kids.... It just wasn't what my parents expected, and my dad ever since he was a kid dreamed of coming to the US, and we already had family on my mom's side and on my dad's side here in the US. My mom's side goes all the way back to the seventies. Her grandfather already passed away. He used to work at a meat-processing factory in Texas and he was also a bracero....[2] But they ended up moving to Chicago and my grandpa and my grandma from my mom's side, they ended up living in Mexico but they had most of their kids in Chicago into the eighties, up until '93.... So we ended up moving to Chicago with my aunt and my aunt's brother, and my dad was there from April of '93 and he found a job in a bakery and he's a pastry chef so that's what he did. But he wanted us to be there, so he got us tourist visas ... and we flew from Mexico City to Chicago O'Hare.

Several elements of Ulises' story speak of the more general conditions that undocumented youth experience migrating to the United States. The decision to migrate was made by his parents when he was not old enough to understand what was going on. The family history of migration is based on the stories that had been passed down to him by his family members. In terms of the reasons for migrating, finding a job in the United States was the main motivation for his parents. Previous family contacts in the United States are also a recurring feature of many undocumented youths' migration stories. In Ulises' case, Chicago was an obvious destination because of the extensive family presence there. Many people told me how parts of their families had moved to the United States as part of the bracero program, just like Ulises' grandparents. The bracero program was set up between 1947 and 1964 to attract "strong-armed" Mexican day-laborers to work primarily in agriculture (Calavita 1992). While the decision to migrate to the United States is often portrayed as being made by people who do not know what they are getting themselves into, this example shows that many immigrant families have roots in the United States that go back a long time.

The older undocumented youth are when they migrate, the more conscious they are of the embodied experience of migration. Jobito's story is a good illustration of this, as he still remembers how it felt to cross the border with his mother and sister.

I was born in Mexico. I lived there until I was eight and moved to Texas—Dallas—because that's where my father was. He had moved there for us, he had been gone for a couple of years ... and he had saved some money for the family to move.... My mom paid a "coyote," my family sold the house and everything in order to pay this coyote. Me and my little sister crossed the border in a car with some random lady, and then a bunch of kids I didn't know.... I'm pretty light-skinned, I was blond when I was little, so it was easily passable, like I looked American. So they told me if a guy points a gun at you, you have to say, "I'm an American citizen," and it was the first thing I remember how to say. But luckily I never had the gun pointed at me, and my little sister went to sleep, so we just crossed and went to a motel, and the coyote was there and a bunch of other people who crossed the border. And one of the guys was a citizen who was waiting for us, and my mom had to run across the border, across the desert, and she said that both of our male neighbors crossed with her.

The experience of crossing the border with a coyote (a person who is paid to smuggle people) clearly made an impression on the then eight-year-old Jobito. Symbolically, the first words he learned were the ones that would determine the following fifteen years of his life: "I am an American citizen." At such a young age, Jobito learned how to hide his immigration status from officials by "acting normal" and posing as a citizen.

While the stories of Ulises and Jobito pay testament to how they traveled to the United States by car and by plane, others crossed the border on foot. Regular media reports, like the shocking image of the drowned bodies of Oscar Alberto Martinez Ramirez and his two-year-old daughter on the bank of the Rio Grande at the US-Mexico border, serve as a reminder of the potentially fatal risks involved. IYJL member Juana recounted in detail how she and her brother, eleven and three years old, respectively, experienced crossing the desert at night and seeing someone being arrested by the border patrol:[3]

I remember having a mix of emotions while walking through the desert at night. When we ran out of food and water, I was worried about my little brother. He was only three years old. Hungry, thirsty, tired from walking miles and miles on end in the blazing sun. I was scared. He was scared, but I didn't want to show it. I kept telling him that everything would be OK. I remember me begging him to not cry and hold it in; for fear of getting caught. One night, as we came close, we heard people yelling. We saw bright lights and ran as fast as we could to hide. My heart was racing. I jumped over a bush. I scraped my hands and knees. They were bleeding, but I didn't care. I just wanted to be safe. As I hid, I saw a mother being taken away from her little kid by an officer. I remember her screams, her crying out to her son, her holding on to that little boy's hand so tight and her perseverance to stay with him, which only reminded me more of my brother and how I didn't want to lose him.

The lived experience of having to stay silent, run, and hide corresponds to what leading a life in the shadows looks like for deportable migrants (De Genova 2002).

The previous stories reflect the specific context of emigration from Mexico to the United States. Most of the youth of Mexican descent that I interviewed indicated that their families had moved for economic reasons. This stands in contrast to Ara, who was one of the few non-Latinx members of IYJL. Ara came to the United States with her parents at the age of seven because they were forced to leave their country. This would have an impact on Ara's activist trajectory since she became involved in the movement while working around the Palestinian question.

I was born in Kuwait, where they don't have birthright citizenship, which really sucks for me. We weren't expelled, but we were about to be expelled from Kuwait in '90, '91, we left in 1990.... And so the Palestinian leader at the time said, yes, Iraq has the right to go into Kuwait, and in retaliation, Kuwait was like, oh you think they have the right? OK, so kick out all the Palestinians. That makes no sense, but that's unfortunately how politics has worked in the Middle East. So right before we left they actually froze all the bank accounts, and we had to leave. We went to Jordan, we couldn't really make a living, and we came here.

Regardless of the specific migration trajectories that these youths followed, leaving the country where they were born and moving to the United States changed their life forever. By now, they have lived most of their life in a country other than the one they were born in. While some still have recollections of their home country, others do not have any memories of the place where they were born. The experience of having to migrate with their parents is something they all have in common. Hence, these youths' embodied lived experiences of mobility constitute a first shared experiential basis on which they can build a sense of political belonging and community.

Settling in

Borrowing words from former mayor Rahm Emanuel's reply to the Trump administration, "Chicago has been a city of immigrants since it was founded."[4] From the influx of Europeans seeking a better life in the "New World," to the millions of African Americans moving up north during the Great Migration, to the arrival of Mexican workers in the industrial plants, migration has undeniably left a permanent mark on the city. The rich history of migration that shaped Chicago can be sensed palpably in its one hundred neighborhoods, many of which have a distinct culture and "vibe" that can often directly be attributed to the migrant communities that populate them. The number of residents with a Hispanic background in neighborhoods like Pilsen, Back of the Yards, or Little Village ranges from about 60 to 80 percent (US Census 2010). Such immigrant neighborhoods attract substantial populations of undocumented immigrants. A 2014 study commissioned by ICIRR puts Little Village on top, with an estimated population of twenty thousand migrants.[5] Since most of its residents are Latinx, it is easier for undocumented migrants with a similar background to "blend in." Family members who are already living there might be able to help recently arrived families settle in and temporarily put a roof over their head. However, for migrants who have few preexisting networks in their new city of residence, migrant neighborhoods are also a logical first stop in the search for a new home away from home. Besides the obvious advantages such neighborhoods offer in terms of arrival infrastructures, like job opportunities in the informal economy, services in the mother tongue, or even religious offerings, such neighborhoods also offer a place to hide from the authorities (Meeus et al. 2019). The concentration of people with an ethnic background in arrival neighborhoods casts a shadow on undocumented migrants that allows them to remain relatively invisible from the public eye. Since many families in these neighborhoods have a mixed status, its residents are more likely to offer informal support and be relatively understanding of the precarious situation people may be in.

The prevalence of immigration-related themes in undocumented youth's experience growing up becomes palpable through play. Alice Goffman has argued elsewhere that playing games like chase in deprived neighborhoods can be seen as ways of embodied learning (Goffman 2014, 21). Likewise, while undocumented kids do not necessarily "know" what their lack of legal status means, they realize the threat ICE poses. As Tamara recounted, in seventh grade, kids at her school used to scare others who were "fresh off the boat" by pretending that immigration officers were there to arrest them:

> When I was in seventh grade, I specifically remember this one new guy who was obviously coming from a small rural place in Mexico. He barely even knew how to write Spanish, so it was like really difficult for him. And I remember that people in the hallway were making fun of him.... My peers [at school] would yell out "la migra, la migra" or "immigration is coming," so it was like a regular tease, "la migra, la migra, hide, hide!"

Playful jokes aside, this example shows that, as kids, undocumented youth were already instilled with a sense of caution and fear of the authorities. Yaxal, for example, remembers how her parents used to stress that they always had to wear their seatbelts in the car in case they were stopped by the police. The one time her mom did get pulled over by the cops "that was kind of scary because, to us, police officers, you never ever want to talk to them."

Safety concerns were nevertheless not limited to the police. Living in deprived urban neighborhoods also goes hand in hand with a heightened risk of exposure to gang violence and criminal activities. Ilene told me that while she liked growing up in Little Village for the most part, the gang violence was an additional cause of stress:

> I like my neighborhood. I love Little Village. In the summertime it's got lots of vendors, and lots of families come, and they walk and play, lots of little kids everywhere.... The only not so great thing is that the boulevard where I live is kind of a division between rival gangs, and there's a little street over there that you can probably see, it's like a dead end street and sometimes, because they know cars can't move in that direction, there's certain people who will stand out there and kind of antagonize the people on this side, and they might shoot at each other, or around. And because my house is kind of right around that thing, we've had bullets hit the house, and recently one bullet went through the window two houses down ... and one of my friends lives there.

The interviews with other IYJL members confirmed the feeling that they had as kids being simultaneously "at home" and "trapped" in their neighborhood. Since neighbors knew who they were and where they were from, they felt a sense of safety despite their undocumented status. Yet playing outside was often deemed too dangerous for their own good. Raquel, for example, recalls how she was never outside of her house in Little Village as a kid, "so my life in the neighborhood consisted of me waking up, going to school, going home, because of, like, gangs ... my mom never wanted me to be outside." Similarly, Ulises' mother also did not let him go out much in Humboldt Park. As a ten-year-old child, he was given very specific instructions "to stay on that side of the street" and to not go "past any of the corners on that side of the block." For many of these youths, Chicago formed their horizon, since traveling beyond city limits rarely occurred. Cynthia, for example, told me she had never really left Chicago since she was three years old and that she had only traveled out of town for a weekend. Embodied lived experiences of urban immobility are perpetuated throughout their youth and gain especially in importance when they prevent teens from joining the coming of age of peers.

Getting around

When people try to come up with a visual image of downtown Chicago, chances are that they spontaneously picture the elevated "L train" that meanders through the city's central neighborhoods. Despite its aging infrastructure, Chicago has a vast public transport network. Yet the farther you move away from the Central Business District, the more likely it is that you have to rely on a car to get to your destination. Wilson has previously demonstrated that poor neighborhoods in Chicago are spatially and socially isolated from the resources and services that are available in more centrally located middle-class neighborhoods (Wilson 1987). Apart from the increase in urban mobility that traveling by car brings with it, obtaining a driver's license also has a symbolic quality in the US context. Since a driver's permit can be obtained at age sixteen after taking the required lessons, it represents a "rite of passage" indicating the transition into adulthood. The fact that high school students take driver's education classes together turns this into a collective experience emblematizing "coming of age" and the freedom to get around. As Raquel recalled, for example, her status only started affecting her in her junior year of high school, when she knew that she could not sign up for driver's education. "I took the class because it was required for everyone to take the book portion, but when it got to the driving stuff, I couldn't do it," she said. Hence, trying—and failing—to get a driver's license is often a sobering experience for undocumented youth that confronts them with their "illegality" willy-nilly (Gonzales 2011).

Growing up in a mixed-status family, Ulises' parents had driver's licenses, while he and his brothers did not. The limits this posed on his mobility in the city increasingly became a source of frustration for him:

Back in high school, people were like sixteen and they were driving, and I'm eighteen or twenty and ... I can't get a license. I think that's what frustrated me the most in life. Can't move around in the city, like in Chicago you can basically get around ... through public transportation, but ... usually you've got to walk like blocks to get to a bus or train station.... So there's going to come a point, when [it would be useful] to go grocery shopping, to just get around to get to work, you know, in this car country, in this car city.... *You know, there's certain things that you just can't do, which just seem so normal.*

As Ulises' experience exemplifies, not being able to drive serves as a daily reminder for undocumented youth of the privileges they lack. Even when simply going out for a drink with friends, it is often difficult for undocumented youth to let their guard down. Jobito told me he is constantly aware of his surroundings whenever he leaves his house, because "every decision you make is tied to being undocumented," raising questions such as "Should I go this bar? Are they going to check my ID?" Being mobile in the city is not without risks for undocumented migrants. In the opening chapter, we already learned how Reyes faced deportation proceedings after he was arrested for DUI. Several undocumented youths told me that driving without a permit became stressful for them, since they feared what would happen if they accidentally broke the law or had a car break down. Santiago's father taught him how to drive a car with automatic transmission when his family was still living in Miami. When he moved in with his sister in the Chicago suburbs, they told him he could use their car to get around. Half an hour after his sister's boyfriend taught him how to "drive a stick shift," he had to drive a car with manual transmission on Chicago's wintery roads himself:

The first time I drove by myself was after a major snowstorm. And I actually hit black ice.... It became very stressful for me to drive. Because I felt like I had to hide who I was and I had to be very aware of what laws were out there and I couldn't break them.... I was breaking a law driving this car, and it was stressing me out considerably, especially when this car had electrical problems and left me stranded, and I had to call someone to help me out. So it was very, very stressful and I just couldn't stop thinking about how many risks I was taking.

The experiences of urban immobility recounted above constitute embodied ways by which undocumented come to interpret themselves, the urban environment, and their (lack of a) place within it. In the next section, we turn to the question of how undocumented youth experience being discursively labeled and stigmatized as "illegal aliens."

Discursive lived experiences

The "I word" was hardly ever mentioned during interviews. Every time these youth are called "illegals" or "illegal aliens," the line in the sand is redrawn between who is deserving of citizenship and who is not. No matter the efforts of scholars, reporters, or activists to wipe out that line by "reframing" citizenship according to different terms, anti-immigrant discourses seem on the rise (Patler and Gonzales 2015). In June 2019, President Donald Trump announced that ICE would begin the process of "removing the millions of illegal aliens who have illicitly found their way into the United States" and that "they will be removed as fast as they come in."[6] Such quotes recognize the normalization of the familiar trope of the law-breaking, deportable "illegal alien" in political, academic, and media discourses. Like other US residents who follow politics and the media, undocumented youth are aware of the existence of such vitriolic language and the stigma that comes with it (Abrego 2011). In fact, as one of the IYJL organizers told me during an interview, countering such illegalizing discourses is important in view of the detrimental effect it has on their personal life:

> There's been a big issue where reporters ... use the word "illegal." They have the responsibility to use terms that are not criminalizing us, to use terms that are not disrespectful to us, and are not harming us in any other way. And so they might see it as just one little word, and that it might not affect anything, but to someone that's undocumented ... using that word is just pushing us back further and further.

Indeed, the daily confrontation with the "I word" in everyday speech is a slap in the face for undocumented youth who often identify themselves as Chicagoans.

Before undocumented youth can feel personally addressed or hurt by such stigmatizing discourses, they first need to learn how to see themselves as "undocumented." Awareness about one's legal status does not come out of thin air. Lived discursive experiences of illegality comprise overhearing conversations between family members as a kid, being told you cannot go to the college of your choice, or being exploited by your employer at work. Both insiders who are intimately familiar with youths' status and outsiders who need to "check their profile" during bureaucratic proceedings might be the bearers of bad news. Once it sinks into the hearts and minds of undocumented youth, their status can turn into something they want to hide from their peers or feel ashamed about. The interviews indicated that the roadblocks youth encountered in their educational trajectories stood out as pivotal moments that shaped their discursive understandings as "undocumented" residents.

Educational roadblocks

Growing up undocumented does not necessarily mean growing up *knowing* that you are undocumented. Before these experiences, many undocumented youths have a vague sense that there are issues related to their status. The slumbering knowledge that they have about their legal status recurs in many activists' trajectories, as was the case for Raquel. After 9/11 took place, her mother took her aside and warned her to be careful about sharing her status:

> I always knew. I mean, when my mom told me we were going to go to the United States, she didn't tell me how or what, and I think I realized what we were doing when we crossed the border. And the only thing I knew was that we couldn't get the papers, so we're just going to cross the border and see what happens. My understanding was that we were going to go back to Mexico in a year or two. And it wasn't until 9/11 happened, my mom was like really scared, and that's when she started telling me that, like, the more obvious things in terms of, like, not sharing my status with people.

This example shows that it is often hard for undocumented youth to pinpoint an exact moment of awareness concerning their status. Nevertheless, encounters with roadblocks in their educational trajectories tend to speed up their self-recognition as "undocumented" residents. Classmates or teachers may be among the people undocumented youth share their status with. Yet even to their closest friends, it takes courage to "come out" as undocumented. Many undocumented youth learn how to conceal their status or how to carefully circumvent the topic. In my interview with Xenia, she told me she had always "known" at some level that she was undocumented. Knowing she did not have a legal status caused her to adopt a "quiet" and "closed" attitude to avoid questions being asked:

> I guess that as an undocumented [person], at least in my personal experience you learn to … not have conversations that would lead into that. So I think that I was able to not have to confront those conversations until I was in college. And then with really close friends that I did start opening up.… Once I felt comfortable with my understanding of it and then felt comfortable with being able to explain it to someone or defend myself against someone, in case of their reaction.… But thinking [back], to my, like, my childhood and everything, I'm realizing that I tried to be closed, or private in order to protect myself from having those conversations.

As Xenia's story highlights, there is hardly any need to share your status as a kid. High school represented a tipping point in her awareness about her undocumented status (Abrego 2006; Gonzales 2011, 2016; Zhou and Gonzales 2019). In her case, the first bump in the road appeared while her peers in Spanish class were planning a trip to Spain and she realized that she would not be able to join them. It is typically when undocumented youth are confronted with roadblocks such as college applications, financial aid packages that they cannot accept, and school trips out of the country that they start to comprehend what being undocumented really means.

Bureaucratic labeling

Applying for college is a pivotal moment for many youths. Confused about whether they are eligible to apply for college, they turn to school counselors to guide them through the process. While some counselors may have experience dealing with undocumented students, others do not. This leads to frustrating discursive lived experiences for the undocumented students involved. When they are offered financial aid on admission, they learn that they need a social security number (SSN) to be eligible to receive it. Not having an SSN stands as a symbol for the obstacles they face in their everyday life. Filling out applications becomes a traumatic experience when they have to leave the SSN box unchecked. Ulises explained how applying for college and not being able to accept his scholarships was a "tipping point" for him:

> I even applied to DePaul University, you know I got accepted, I got enrolled. And it wasn't until I figured out my parents couldn't take out a private loan, and they wouldn't be able to ... get any type of federal financial assistance that the grant that the university gave me, I wouldn't be able to collect, and so I could still go for this term, but I'm gonna end up owing money to the school, so like, what's the point.... So I ended up dropping out. So there wasn't an "aha" moment, and a light bulb going off, I think that was it. But I think that was like the tipping point for everything that had piled up and I realized like, I'm undocumented.

Since there are no ready-made categories undocumented youth neatly fit into, they are treated "as if" they are international students. This bureaucratic label comes with a price attached. International students are often ineligible to receive available financial aid packages and are usually charged higher tuition fees. Moreover, the label of "international" can feel like yet another unbefitting stamp on undocumented youth's forehead, saying, "you do not belong here." Ara testified how this type of discursive labeling practice added insult to injury:

> When I applied for [a higher education institution], ... I sent an email to the admissions officer and I told her, "we're in the process of fixing my immigration status." I didn't say I was undocumented.... And she was like, "ok, I'll forward your email to the international program director" or whatever. And at that point

> I was like no! I will not be considered an international student!… I grew up here.
> I grew up pledging allegiance to the flag, shouldn't that be enough?

The discrepancy that Ara notes between growing up as a true "American" and being labeled an "international" points to how discursive lived experiences evoke feelings of "being out of place." In the long run, this schizophrenic situation can corrupt the minds of undocumented youth. Just how troubling such feelings can be becomes clear when we zoom into the frenetic state of emotional disarray that characterizes the lived experiences of illegality.

Emotional lived experiences

Undocumented youths' emotional lived experiences resemble a roller coaster that feels as if it is about to derail at any point. As discussed above, undocumented parents often tell their children not to talk about their status openly. The constant threat of being arrested instills a sense of fear in many families, to which undocumented children are especially responsive. The fear of undocumented children can be the fear of being pulled over in the car, of family members getting arrested, or of *la migra* coming knocking on the door. Constantly living in fear places a heavy toll on the mental health of these youth (Gonzales, Suárez-Orozco, and Dedios-Sanguineti 2013). Unable to openly share these experiences with others, they feel ashamed of their status. Shame leads them to feel emotionally isolated and alone with their problems. Emotional isolation can spiral out of control when undocumented youth start to wrestle with serious mental health conditions such as depression or suicidal thoughts. Legal status can also stand in the way of them fulfilling professional or personal aspirations. Blocked pathways cause undocumented youth to accept jobs on the black market that do not correspond with their level of education. Moreover, romantic relationships can become strained when undocumented youth wrestle with the feeling that they are "not good enough for anyone" (Pila 2016). In this section, I single out three distinct emotional lived experiences that are particularly relevant in view of their activist trajectories, namely, fear, anger, and shame, and explain how they tend to exacerbate social and emotional isolation.

Fear

Fear permeates the lives of parents and undocumented children in different ways (Dreby 2015, 22). While moms may fear becoming a single parent if their husband were to be detained and deported by ICE, dads may fear how their absence as a deportee would affect their family's life. For children, the most pronounced fear is being potentially separated from their parents. As Dreby put it, deportability "disrupts their sense of stability" (Dreby 2015, 53). Whether the threat of deportation is immediate or not, real or imagined, or experienced from close by or from a distance matters less than one may think. Evoking the mere possibility of deportation lurking around the corner can be sufficient to instill fear into undocumented communities and turn them into powerless, docile subjects. Without exception, the undocumented youth I got to know talked to me about how fear had impacted their life at some point or another. As we will see in Chapter 5, overcoming fear by becoming "undocumented and unafraid" was a hallmark of their transition into activists. In order to get a sense of where these youth were coming from, it is worthwhile examining Claudia's story in more detail.

Claudia had come to the United States with her family on a tourist visa. Since her grandfather was a green card holder, they figured they would sort out their status once they were there. Claudia's grandfather passed away when she was nine. Immediately afterward, a family dispute erupted between his adopted son and Claudia's mom over the distribution of his estate in the Philippines. Subsequently, the son threatened to call immigration services on them. Unsure whether the threat was real or not, Claudia's family decided to make a run for it. Family members in California offered protection and a place to stay. She distinctly remembers that they were all terrified, "like someone would pick us up and we would get deported right away." They only took a day to pack and they left the blinds down to pretend they weren't there. When her dad ran to the store to get supplies for their journey, Claudia remembers being terrified he would not come back. A couple of days later, she and her family embarked on the long Greyhound bus ride to California. Carrying nothing but small bags with them, the three days in the smelly bus were some of the longest of then ten-year-old Claudia's life. They had not told anyone where they were going, because they did not want to run the risk that the information could get into the wrong hands. Once they arrived, Claudia hid in a tiny apartment for a month and a half along with her mom, dad, sisters, grandma, and great aunt. When her family calmed down and investigated the possibility of them getting deported, they finally decided that it had been an empty threat after all. Back in Chicago, they tried to pick up their lives again where they left off. Yet, as Claudia recalls, "from that point on my parents drilled it into my head, never to tell anyone about our status."

Anger

Not being able to talk about one's status is one thing. Being confronted with the privileges that peers with legal status can enjoy is something different. Since undocumented and documented youth play side by side on the same soccer teams, attend the same schools, and go to the same churches, the social distance between them seems negligible. However, it is precisely because the things these youths want to achieve and the activities they would like to take part in seem so nearby yet remain decidedly out of reach that they can become a real cause of anger and frustration. These feelings can result in youths blaming their parents for the decisions they made to migrate to the United States when the youths were too young to have any say in the matter. In addition, they can lead to youths envying and distancing themselves from peers and seeking the support and comfort of others who are in a similarly precarious situation.

Ilene's emotional lived experience is worth highlighting in this respect, since it corresponds with that of other youths I interviewed. Ilene and her sister Tamara came to the United States when they were seven and ten years old, respectively. Whereas Tamara experienced migrating as an exciting adventure, Ilene did not want to leave their life in Mexico behind. Since Tamara was older at the time, she felt as though she was part of the decision-making process. By contrast, Ilene had the feeling that she had no choice but to go. The feeling of being too young to have had a say in this decision made it difficult for her to feel at home in Chicago:

> I had two birthday parties for my seven years: one in Mexico and one here [Chicago]. The one here was not very fun. My dad bought me a cake and it had a little Cinderella figure on it and I didn't like Cinderella. It was awkward. And then I was here and it wasn't very fun. I didn't really want to come here; I explicitly said this to my parents. And I felt like they didn't listen to me, and I didn't like that.... And so, I tried to get us to move back to Mexico for a really long time. Like, I just pointed out things that were going wrong in general, and I would blame it on the US. So I did that for like thirteen years and I didn't feel like I really belonged anywhere.

The feeling of not belonging anywhere kept on haunting Ilene while she transitioned into adulthood. In college, she increasingly felt trapped while seeing how her peers were able to get on with their lives. As she recalls, "I started feeling really angry at some of my friends, not for being citizens, but for not taking [full] advantage of their citizenship." Since Ilene dreamt of the ability to travel freely, she resented friends with passports who did not feel the need to explore the world themselves. Ilene's story thus illustrates the feelings of anger, frustration, and, ultimately, powerlessness that many undocumented youth experience.

Shame

The frustration and constant fear that keeps undocumented youth always virtually "on edge" can be an isolating experience that instills feelings of shame and self-doubt. Tamara, for example, remembers being worried what her peers would think of her if they were to find out about her status:

> I remember being like, I don't know if ashamed is the right word … but just worrying about people finding out.… Because it may create bad reactions, bad feelings, or whatever. Like I remember not knowing … how my friends were gonna react.… Because I remember feeling very vulnerable, like I really wasn't that connected to a lot of my friends when I was in high school.

Tamara's example hints at how isolating growing up in shame can be for undocumented youth. The "tipping point" in awareness about youths' undocumented status sometimes triggers a change in behavior, where previously sociable youths aim to protect themselves by purposefully isolating themselves socially. This was the case for Damian, who felt isolated for the first time in his young adult life when he transitioned from fourth to fifth grade.

> It felt very isolating. I felt like my social life changed dramatically.… I used to be the person that would probably be considered the class clown by fourth grade, and by fifth grade I was just by myself, and I felt like nobody noticed that because like, again, I got into "gifted," and so most of my friends were left behind and I got into a different set of classes. So it felt very isolating. All of a sudden I was in this situation and I knew I couldn't tell anybody.

It is a significant step to go from feeling isolated to slipping into depression. Yet several IYJL experienced depressive episodes in their life (see Chapter 7).

Conclusion

In this chapter, I adopted a hermeneutic lens to see what the world looks and feels like from the vantage point of undocumented youth who spent most of their lives growing up in Chicago. Embodiment, discourses, and emotions were identified as three interrelated modes of "knowing" the world that structure these youths' lived experiences of illegality.

Firstly, embodied lived experiences capture the spatial (im)mobility and physical techniques that go hand in hand with becoming an undocumented resident.

In this regard, we saw how the experience of crossing the border and moving to their new "home away from home" in Chicago came to make them associate mobility with risk and danger. Once settled in, undocumented youths learn how to watch out for police and avoid getting into trouble. Despite the residential instability that many mixed-status families face due to their precarious housing situation, youths feel trapped in their neighborhood. Crime and gang violence motivate parents to keep their kids off the streets. Once they grow older, moving through urban space becomes increasingly cumbersome, as driving without a license entails the risk of arrest, and going out with friends without an ID might end up in them getting refused at the door (or worse).

Second, discursive lived experiences of illegality refer to the subjective experience of being labeled and categorized by bureaucrats, teachers, employers, academics, journalists, and politicians. Being named an "illegal alien" or "international student" is a humiliating and denigrating experience for youths who often feel more American or Chicagoan than anything else. The nine digits of the SSN that signify who is deserving and non-deserving of financial aid come to be associated with blocked educational and employment opportunities. While undocumented youth might oppose illegalizing discourses, they often refrain from engaging openly in discussions, because it could expose their status. Many youths therefore end up internalizing undocumented stigma and doubting their personal worth.

Third, lived experiences of illegality cause undocumented youth to become trapped in murky emotional waters. Deportability instills a sense of permanent fear and insecurity into undocumented youth's minds. The fear that sharing their status with the wrong person or committing a minor offense in public might result in deportation causes many youths to become secluded. Having to say "no" time and time again or being confronted up close with citizenship privilege provides a fertile ground for the development of feelings of anger and frustration. Anger can be directed toward unknowing friends, teachers, and counselors, but also toward the parents who got them into this position in the first place. Shame about one's status further leads to self-doubt and encourages social and emotional isolation. When fear, anger, and shame become internalized, it can subsequently result in serious mental health issues (see Chapter 7).

6

Becoming undocumented

Sans-papiers activists' life stories

Compared with the other patrons at the community center, the Anchor, Mehdi stood out in several ways besides his above-average height. Sharply dressed, adorned with a gold necklace, and frequently sporting sunglasses, everything about him seemed to breathe success. Confident whenever he spoke and punctual for meetings, there was an aura of professionalism and accomplishment that surrounded Mehdi wherever he went. "For the first meeting of SPBelgique, I came dressed in a suit," he recalled laughingly. "People figured I was a lawyer or something," he said, thereby distancing himself from the often lackluster, worn appearance of his peers. Medhi basked in stories of the cybercafé he had opened back in Morocco or the bikes he owned in his hometown. He boasted that he had degrees as a mechanic, hairdresser, and informatics engineer. Despite appearances to the contrary, he had more in common with the mixed crowd of sans-papiers, homeless people, recovering drug addicts, and urban poor who frequented the Anchor than he made out.

On a regular weekday, Mehdi had to get up at four in the morning to go to work. His workplace was in a village across the Walloon border about thirty kilometers from Brussels' city center. He had to take a metro, a train, and two buses to reach his job. His employers at the only Asian restaurant in town tended to leave everything from the previous day's shift untouched for him to sort out, and as soon as he got in, he had to start cleaning the floor, tidying the kitchen, and doing the dishes. "There is so much work to do that I cannot even take a break to eat my sandwich, you know, you eat while you continue working," he told me. At the end of the day, he was paid about thirty-eight euros in cash. Minus the transportation cost, rent, clothing, and the little money he was able to send back to his family, he had to make do with a meager budget of 100–150 euros per month. Despite the low wage and the hard work, Medhi considered himself one of the lucky ones. His job situation had been stable for the previous three years, which was more than could be said of most of his fellow undocumented friends.

Migrating to Belgium had been a lifelong dream for Medhi. When he was little, his Belgian cousins would spend their summer holidays in his hometown in Morocco. The stories they would tell about life in Europe piqued his curiosity. On top of that, Mehdi had been dating a Belgian girl online for the past

Citizen X. Thomas Swerts, Oxford University Press. © Thomas Swerts (2026).
DOI: 10.1093/9780197844038.003.0007

few years. She was of Moroccan descent and lived in the Brussels municipality of Schaarbeek. "If you want to marry me, you have to come over here," she had told him, thereby putting his commitment to the test. Determined to visit his "future fiancée," he decided to leave Morocco. He tried to obtain a visa for Belgium twice, but his application was turned down both times. He was subsequently able to secure a work contract and applied for a visa for Spain. Again, his application was denied. At this point, the only remaining option was to cross the Mediterranean. Although the distance between Morocco and Spain is merely 8.9 miles along the Strait of Gibraltar, standing on one or the other side of the border means a world of difference for young men like Mehdi. Yet the Mediterranean is also a treacherous border that has claimed the lives of more than thirty-two thousand people since 2014.[1] Hence, it should come as no surprise that Mehdi found the journey to Europe to be "really, really hard."

His first attempt was a traumatic experience. Through word of mouth, he had secured a place on a Zodiac, a small inflatable boat. The owner of the boat was a friend of a family member. One night, around one in the morning, the smuggler woke Mehdi up, saying, "We are leaving now, take your things." Unprepared, Mehdi was only able to grab the essentials. Not far from the sea, the smuggler inflated the boat. Mehdi started to get anxious when he saw the thirty-seven people and gasoline containers that all had to fit into the seven-meter-long boat. At that moment, he was crying because he realized what he was leaving behind, but also what he was risking. When the boat took off, "the sea was crazy, we could not even see anything," he recounted. As soon as they left, people started jumping out because they knew that there was not enough space for everyone. Mehdi was able to hold on to his seat by climbing on top of a gasoline container. By then, it was about three in the morning. When they noticed the coast guard from a distance, people started shouting "police, police," and they made a half-turn with the boat. People jumped from the boat in the dark, leaving their money and belongings behind. Mehdi followed suit and saw how others ran toward a little forest. "I started running, I fell down, I could not breathe, it was really hard." When the coast guard fired warning shots in the air, they abandoned everything.

After a second attempt by boat also failed, Mehdi left for Tangiers with a friend of his to try a different approach. In Tangiers, they were introduced to a smuggler who promised he could take them to Europe in his truck for a fee of 7,500 euros. The smuggler showed Mehdi around the harbor where the truck was parked, told him how he could sneak past customs and how he should hide underneath the truck. The next day, police stopped Mehdi and his friend at the harbor and told them to get lost. A few days later, Mehdi succeeded in walking past customs by pretending to be talking on his phone. When he finally reached the truck, he was "afraid, but it was a mix of emotions." Once he was in position, he called his friend, who told him he had to get out immediately since the truck would not be boarding the ship after all. As Mehdi was completely covered in grease, harbor security approached him and asked if he was a mechanic. "No, I wanted to take my chances," he replied, "like everyone else." When security threatened to hand him over to the police, he bribed them into releasing him with the money he had left.

Eventually, the fourth time was the lucky charm for Mehdi. Equipped with a fake Moroccan passport, he came into contact with another smuggler, who for a fee of 8,500 euros, promised to take him to Castellón de la Plana in Spain, where Mehdi's relatives lived. When the smuggler and his girlfriend picked Mehdi up in their Ford Focus, they reassured his parents, "Your son will reach Spain, no problem." The smuggler told Mehdi that he had "a contact" within customs, and indeed, when the customs officer approached, he did not even check Mehdi. After customs searched the car, Mehdi had to hide in the trunk until the car embarked on the boat and it was safe to get out. He was then sent to a rented cabin and stayed there until they arrived in Almeria. Then, he had to hide again in the back of the car covered by a blanket. Mehdi remembers the fear he felt when he heard the officer demand the smugglers' passports in Spanish. When the smuggler yelled "Go!" this was his cue to get up from his hiding place and pretend he had been there all along. The moment he set foot in Almeria, Mehdi experienced a joy that he "cannot even begin to explain, even if I wanted to."

Getting from Spain to Belgium was easy compared with the nightmare of crossing the Mediterranean. Mehdi spent the last three hundred euros he owned to pay for the gas and supplies necessary for a relative to drive him up north. The Schengen area ensured that they did not come across border security during their 1,300-mile journey. However, the sense of freedom and mobility Mehdi had experienced earlier quickly faded in Brussels. The romantic relationship that worked well online did not survive offline. Mehdi was initially allowed to stay in his uncle's house, but as time went on, he was forced to work out a different arrangement. With the salary he made working at the Asian restaurant, he had few options available in terms of finding a decent place to live. He teamed up with other sans-papiers to live together in Vorst, before moving to Molenbeek in the Etangs Noirs and Beekkant neighborhoods. Possibly the quintessential "arrival neighborhood" in Belgium, Molenbeek is characterized by large volumes of in-migration and out-migration, as well as a historically dilapidated housing stock (Van Hamme et al. 2016). Everyday life in Molenbeek was tough to bear for Mehdi and his roommates. The computer he had bought with his savings was stolen after a break-in. To make matters worse, their neighbor, who knew they were sans-papiers, regularly called them names and threatened to call the police on them. When he struck Mehdi's friend in the face after an argument, they were afraid to report it because of the risk of deportation involved. In the end, Mehdi took his chances and moved out. Meanwhile, fixing his immigration status became a distant dream.

***

Mehdi's story is a good example of the lived experiences of many sans-papiers who dwell in the streets of Brussels. His biography resonates with the stories of North African migrants who crossed the Mediterranean hoping to find a life of prosperity, happiness, and job security in Europe. As empirical research on the lives of undocumented migrants in Europe has demonstrated, experiences generally fail to live up to expectations (Bloch and McKay 2017). Being confronted with the reality of deportability, criminalization, bureaucratic intimidation, exploitation, and everyday precarity can lead undocumented migrants to accept "living on the margins." The stories of SPBelgique activists confirm that migrating to Europe via irregular means, having to deal with state bureaucracies, finding stable housing, working "black-market jobs," and maintaining social and romantic relationships leave a permanent mark on their understandings. Nevertheless, while these themes might sound familiar to migration scholars' ears, their endings do not.

This is because we know for a fact that these are not just any undocumented migrants' stories, but *activists'* stories. Just as Cynthia's story did not end where we left it in the previous chapter, Mehdi's story does not end here either. Indeed, Mehdi would grow to be a familiar face within SPBelgique, as someone who loyally took part in strategic meetings and proved himself to be a militant during protests. However, the problem with existing scholarship is that it renders undocumented activism theoretically impossible. This concerns the fact that the conclusion about the outcome—namely, debilitating subjection—is already written into the frames of analysis. Several studies acknowledge the creativity and resourcefulness with which undocumented migrants are able to strategically navigate constricted labor and housing markets (Burgers 1998; Burgers and Engbersen 1999; Engbersen et al. 2006). Yet the bottom line in the bulk of scholarship is that their prospects for social mobility remain low, no matter what. Bloch and McKay blame this on the "resource-poor networks" that undocumented migrants are forced to rely on, trapping "individuals into lives of poverty, precarity, and marginality from which relatively few ever escape" (Bloch and McKay 2017, 190). The impossibility to break free from the vicious circle of marginalization is further guaranteed by a theory of—somewhat unreflexive—internalization. In this respect, it is argued that the subjection that undocumented migrants fall prey to encourages them to lay low, hide, and survive in the shadows (Gonzales and Chavez 2012). The internalization of undocumented migrants' underprivileged position in society and their relative social isolation from mainstream society are thereby designated as the twin culprits that account for the reproduction of their precarious status.

In this chapter, it is argued once again that a hermeneutical perspective is better suited to understand the complexity of precarious agency at the micro level. Compared with the stories of IYJL activists, those of SPBelgique activists demonstrate that what it means to be undocumented is "situational" (Khosravi 2010). Most of the respondents were Moroccans, in line with SPBelgique's membership. Because of their shared nationality, most of them applied for regularization through a work permit. The asylum seekers I interviewed came from Bangladesh, Nepal, Guinea, and Senegal, and most were in their thirties. During my fieldwork, I only encountered three female SPBelgique members. The time that people had resided in Belgium without papers varied between six months and eleven years. Compared with relatively privileged IYJL members, the sans-papiers had less access to cultural, economic, and social resources and were more likely to be directly exposed to state violence. Nevertheless, their stories mirror those of IYJL activists in more ways than one. In what follows, I zoom in on the lived experiences of illegality that the sans-papiers encountered on their life paths before they ventured into politics.

Embodied lived experiences

In order to capture embodied lived experiences of illegality, I focus once more on the discrepancy between migrant mobility and urban immobility. Compared with the undocumented youth introduced in the previous chapter, the sans-papiers typically made their own decision to migrate as adults. Migrating necessarily involves physically moving from one place to another, and depending on how undocumented immigrants get to Belgium, this process can be more or less challenging. On one end of the spectrum, undocumented immigrants get a tourist or student visa, book a flight to Europe, and overstay their visa. On the other end, immigrants negotiate a price with human traffickers and risk their life attempting to cross the border. For some immigrants, Brussels is the first destination they set foot in after leaving their home country. For others, it is the end destination after extensive periods of travel. Each of these trajectories can lead to undocumented status, but they involve more-precarious or less-precarious embodied trajectories.

Motives for migrating diverge, depending on migrants' country of origin and personal situation. While immigrants who leave their country for economic reasons are considered to be "unwanted" by the Belgian state, those who can invoke persecution, war, or medical reasons are granted the benefit of the doubt. Yet if their application is denied, they are mercilessly thrown back onto the streets.

I contend that such forms of bureaucratic categorization create social inequalities and injustices between immigrants with different backgrounds. Hence, I will only evoke these labels between parentheses below to highlight how lived experiences of illegality of those who are labeled as "economic migrants" and "refugees" initially diverge and later converge in Brussels. The mobility migrants experienced coming to Europe stands in stark contrast to the immobility they face in the city. Once undocumented, settling in Brussels tends to occur in arrival neighborhoods (Meeus et al. 2019). Undocumented migrants who have family connections often rely on these for aid before venturing off (Bloch and McKay 2017). Many sans-papiers in Brussels therefore flirt with homelessness,[2] others search for alternative housing solutions by squatting in abandoned buildings.

Crossing the border

Crossing the border without state authorization is done by Moroccan migrants who are categorized as "economic migrants" as well as by Central African, Middle Eastern, and Asian migrants who are categorized as "refugees," albeit for different reasons. Obtaining a tourist or student visa may be impossible for people migrating from Morocco due to administrative or budgetary restrictions. Applying for a tourist visa, for example, requires having a job and sufficient financial means to finance the journey. For those who do not possess such means, crossing the border in an irregular way becomes the only option. In this case, people often make use of human traffickers to reach European shores. For example, Ilyas told me how he had paid a human trafficker eleven thousand euro to get across the border from Morocco to Italy. The boat that took them there was too small, and there were about 350 people on board. The police picked them up as soon as they arrived in the harbor of Lampedusa. They were taken to a detention center where they were given food and clothes, and they were allowed to walk away whenever they felt like it.

As Mehdi's story already illustrated, immigrants sometimes have to make several attempts before they make it to Belgium. For example, Jalil made three attempts before he was able to reach Belgium from Morocco. The first time, he was arrested and imprisoned in Greece for six months. The second time, he reached Switzerland, but he was arrested and had to stay in a secure detention center for three months before he was deported back to Morocco. The third time, he managed to get to Belgium through human traffickers who hid him in a truck. These stories demonstrate the risks that economic migrants are willing to take to leave their country. Compared with people who overstay their visa, the journey to Europe leaves a deeper impression on their embodied understandings.

The hardships that traveling without papers in Europe entails became clear to me when I heard Omar's story. Omar traveled through Turkey, Greece, Macedonia, Serbia, Romania, Hungary, Austria, Germany, Italy, Switzerland, the Netherlands, and France before finally settling in Belgium. During his journey, he was arrested, detained, and physically abused. Initially, he had planned to obtain a visa in Istanbul. When this was turned down and he was refused access to Greece, he was approached by someone who said he knew how to cross the border:

We left during the night, we enter a forest and then he shows me a lamp far away, about forty kilometers further and he says, "Do you see that lamp over there?" I say yes and he tells me, "You go straight and after the lamp you are going to come across rails, you follow them to the left and when you continue you are in Greece." I say, "Ok, no problem." So I start walking, because it is a forest and it is night and I don't know. I walk slowly, slowly and then I hear trucks behind me that honk. I look and I see that it is a brigade of officers from the border control. So I start running and running and at a certain point I see a lot of dense trees and I go inside and they pass by and they don't see me. I continue walking, and I bump into people that I don't know. I ask, "What are you doing here?" "We are leaving for Greece." "It would be nice if I could go along with you, that way it is less risky."

After successfully crossing the Greek border, Omar traveled through Albania, Macedonia, and Serbia for several months. From Belgrade, he traveled north to Kikinda and reached Hungary, where he was arrested and "beaten numerous times. They made my life harder." Despite this mistreatment, he succeeded in traveling to Germany. When police arrested him while staying with friends in Munich, he applied for asylum and received a temporary residence permit. He overstayed his visa until he continued his journey via the Netherlands to Belgium. Unsure where to go next, he stayed in Brussels because it "reminded him of Morocco."

For people who may be in danger because of their political, religious, or sexual preferences or have escaped from war-torn regions, irregular entry is usually not a matter of choice. Akash's story is a good illustration of the challenges that Asian migrants face coming to Belgium. In Bangladesh, Akash had campaigned for a local politician in the Bangladesh Nationalist Party. After graduation, he had started a computer repair shop. A local politician later asked him again to be a campaign manager; they lost the elections. Next, members of the victorious Awami League started to extort him. He received death threats, his shop was smashed up, and one of his employees was beaten. When he filed a complaint, the police protected the newly elected politician. He was captured by the

Rapid Action Battalion and tortured for a week. When he was released from the hospital, he borrowed money from family members and planned his escape to Europe:

> I left my locality to ... Chittagong in October 2009. I was hidden there in my friend's house. There is a big cargo ship, because this is a port city.... I first came to Italy by cargo ship, hiding in the ship.... I was hiding with four other guys in a room beside the kitchen for almost one month. They gave me food and everything, but I could not come outside until they told me it was ok. I paid them five thousand euros. An uncle of mine helped me because he had connections with a human trafficker. So after thirty-five days I arrived in Italy. I was there for one night. After Italy I came to Belgium in a truck in two days during the night.

Not all trajectories of migrants who are later categorized as "refugees" bring them straight to Belgium. Sumon, for example, had been on the run since 1999. He first moved from Bangladesh to Amritsar, India. Then he moved to Pakistan. From there, he left for Afghanistan, and he was in Iraq during the war. He managed to move to Turkey and settled in Greece, where he stayed for eleven years. He lived in different cities in Greece, depending on where he could find work as a cook. At first, he could make up to 1,800 euros per month, then his wage diminished to 1,200 euros, and finally to 800 due to the economic crisis. He could no longer make a living and left for Belgium in 2012 to apply for asylum. One year later, his application was rejected, and he became a sans-papiers.

Respondents who had overstayed tourist visas were generally regarded as "economic migrants" in search of a better future. The interviews with SPBelgique members indicated that the decision to migrate seemed to be based more on perceived economic opportunities than on firsthand or secondhand knowledge about these opportunities. In this respect, the myth of Europe as the "land of milk and honey" and the "mother of democracy" speaks to immigrants' imagination. Frustrated in achieving their professional or other aspirations in their home country, they project their hopes for a better future in Europe. Faisal's story reflects these dynamics at play:

> In Morocco, I had a job. I worked in the chemical industry as a security agent in a big firm that does export.... I had my [legal] status, I had a perspective, I had everything so to speak. So ... in the first month of my employment there was a strike, so the labor union was protesting with regard to laws concerning the increase of wages in the chemical industry ... and I was there.... I had to take a test for internal evaluation purposes, and I scored four out of twenty on it because I was a striker. So, in the next couple of years this remained a

problem and I made my calculation considering that I wanted to get married and have kids and so on.... At that moment I got a tourist visa, so I entered in a clandestine way. When you want change, you make decisions and who knows how it is going to turn out.

Faisal gave up a steady job to come to Europe. From the outset, he planned to overstay his tourist visa. Belgium was an obvious choice since his brother, sister, and mother had already become Belgian citizens.

It is often only when undocumented migrants' experiences do not live up to their expectations that they realize what life without papers means. For example, Zouheir came to Belgium from Morocco when he was nineteen years old. Asked how he got here, he reflected on the disparity between his aspirations and the shock of becoming a sans-papiers:

I wanted to come here, in order to realize my dream in Europe. Have a residence permit, have a job like everyone else, work. All the dreams that I had in my head; I have not been able to realize [them], I have not found them. I discovered a different world here; it was not like I had in mind.... I came here on a tourist visa. When I arrived here for the first time, it was new for me. I had to discover the country, the people, everything.... A sans-papiers does not have rights, he has nothing.... We can do nothing. We came here to work, to help our parents. But we have found nothing. We found neither help nor anything else.

Overstaying a student visa is another common trajectory for Moroccan migrants to become sans-papiers. During the interviews it became clear that these immigrants did not necessarily plan to settle permanently in Europe. Instead, respondents became undocumented because they were misinformed or because they experienced problems with their education.

Settling in

Regardless of how or why immigrants become undocumented, everyday life in Brussels is tough. Because undocumented immigrants are not allowed to legally rent, their housing situation is precarious.[3] During the first months of settlement, the presence of support networks of friends and family is of crucial importance to avoid living on the streets. Faisal, for example, was able to stay with his unmarried brother for a while before he found a place of his own. While he appreciated the gesture, he soon came to realize that he would no longer have the same privileges he had grown accustomed to as a Moroccan citizen:

I arrived right here on the Rue Stalingrad. My sister, my brother, and my mother were there. They are Belgians. It is normal that when I arrived here, I did not come empty-handed, … but still, for food and lodging I relied on my brother back then because he was single so we lived together.… I knew that I was a sans-papiers the first month that I was here.… I was used to having my money and my credit card in my pocket, traveling, eating, and so on and now it was a strict minimum.… That touches your dignity; I wanted to be independent.

Finding stable housing is a constant struggle for undocumented immigrants in Brussels (Kagné 2000, 8; Adam et al. 2002, 116–19). Many respondents indicated that they had moved numerous times from neighborhood to neighborhood during their residence in the city. This can be part of the sans-papiers' strategy to avoid encountering domiciliary police controls (Adam et al. 2002, 105). Abas, for example, lived in seven different places in a six-year period, leading him to state that "it is not easy to have this kind of bond with your neighborhood." Since paying rent requires an income, renting housing is dependent on steady employment. Employed undocumented migrants are thus able to afford better housing than the unemployed. Most times, middlemen who have a legal status and often share the same nationality rent a place and then sublet it to several sans-papiers who rent it together. For example, Mehdi told me he lived with two brothers in a house in Jette. The brothers were domiciled and paid the total rent of 650 euros per month for the two-bedroom apartment. He then had to pay 180 euros to the brothers for his room, which he shared with one of them. Nevertheless, renting a place does not guarantee good accommodation. For example, although Mohammed rented a room in an apartment, he still had to share it with four other men. He barely had any belongings, and he slept on a mattress on the floor.

Squatting is a popular alternative. Several SPBelgique activists, including Akash, Mohammed, Jalil, Ilyas, and Mustapha, lived in squats. The housing conditions in these squats tended to be precarious. Jalil told me he and his housemates had been doing construction work for months to make their squat "livable." They managed to get running water and electricity, but there was still no heat when the winter kicked in. Others reported that their squats lacked such basic facilities altogether. For example, Mohammed told me how his room was in the basement of a house, without windows. Perhaps an even bigger challenge than upgrading the physical infrastructure of these squats, however, is keeping the peace among housemates. Amine, for example, left his squat "because people were using drugs and my belongings had been stolen." Eviction represents another tangible threat to housing stability. For example, the police evicted Ilyas and his housemates from their squat in the middle of the winter. When this happens, sans-papiers sometimes become homeless as well. In view of the unstable income of many sans-papiers, lack of funds represents a second avenue into homelessness. For example, when Anouar could no longer afford his place, he was forced to stay in a homeless shelter. "I have been staying in this social center for fifteen days now; it is terrible," he complained to me. "I am stuck with ten others in a room, and you have to be in by nine PM." These insecure, unsafe, and unhealthy housing conditions contribute to the general precarity of the sans-papiers' everyday life in Brussels.

Getting around

The constant threat of being arrested also looms around every corner for the sans-papiers. The fear of being deported is valid. Almost all the respondents told me stories of friends or family who had been deported. Unlike in the United States, the police can stop anyone on the street to check their ID. This means that even an ordinary walk to the grocery store can result in arrest and deportation. For example, during an interview, Faisal told me that he had received a phone call the previous evening saying that a mutual friend had been arrested near her house in Anderlecht. The day of the interview, she had already been transferred to Zaventem to be deported. "Deportations affect everyone," he exclaimed, stressing that the threat is omnipresent in Brussels. Moving through urban space therefore becomes a challenge. The sans-papiers are always aware of their surroundings.

Being undocumented in Brussels alters how people behave, how they physically move through space, and how they see themselves. Being subjected to episodes of state violence, where the threat of deportation becomes partially realized, strengthens these embodied understandings. On an everyday basis, many sans-papiers experience the threat of deportation when they have to get around. Taking public transport is particularly tricky, as the police and metro security officers organize checks from time to time (Adam et al. 2002, 94). As Mehdi put it: "I never had any problems with that because I respect the rules, [but] if you get caught by those who control the trains or the police, you are in big trouble." Most sans-papiers try to avoid taking the subway for this reason. However, this is hard when they have to get to work. For example, Brahim told me he had already been stopped for ticket control in the subway four times while going to work. All of these times he had a valid transport ticket, yet one time, the police asked for his ID and took him to the station. Once there, they told him that they had no time to deal with him. "Besides," they said, "the secure detention center is full." "It was a close one," he smiled when telling this story. Others made sure to always keep a stack of metro tickets at hand to show that they pay for their tickets.

Episodes of state violence toward undocumented immigrants also occur on a larger scale. On a late afternoon in the summer of 2012, for example, the police raided Moroccan cafés in the Rue Stalingrad in Brussels. Close to the South Station, Rue Stalingrad is well known as a place in Brussels where sans-papiers gather. The wide street has many cafés that have become informal gathering places for the sans-papiers. That day, the police orchestrated a raid on the neighborhood. The official reason was that local merchants had complained about the presence of people selling bootleg DVDs and CDs on the street. The police responded by blocking the street exits with dozens of police cars. Undercover agents, the riot police force, and agents of the Zuidwijk neighborhood joined in with the effort. They blocked the exits, searched people, and asked for their IDs. Next, they arrested everyone present—150 people in total. The majority of those arrested were of foreign descent. Buses had been prepared to transport the arrestees to the military barracks in Etterbeek, which functioned as a makeshift prison. Those who were able to present a valid ID were released the same night. Others were detained for twenty-four hours before they were allowed to leave. Ten people received orders to leave the country, six were sent directly to a secure detention center. SPBelgique member Redouan was at the nearby mosque that day. He showed us pictures he had taken on his cell phone of people handcuffed with their face on the ground surrounded by police dogs. When he understood what was going on, he fled the scene through the mosque's exit on the other end of the street. These types of police actions serve to keep the fear alive within undocumented communities.

Discursive lived experiences

When immigrants become sans-papiers, the world they used to know ceases to exist and they are confronted with their underprivileged position in Belgian society. As an SPBelgique member expressed in a blog post, the sans-papiers "*lives in a world parallel to others.*" His new world is nothing like the image that he had one day, long before his departure. And few are those who know him and recognize him." In the "parallel world" that immigrants enter once they become undocumented, the reasons for departure and the specific migration trajectory are used to discursively categorize and sort "wanted" from "unwanted" populations. Undocumented immigrants encounter different challenges trying to regularize their status and get by, depending on whether they are categorized as "economic migrants" or "refugees." For those who overstay their visa, their legal status can change to "undocumented" in a matter of months. For asylum seekers, it can take years before they receive a negative response in Belgium. Only asylum seekers get temporary access to work, healthcare, and housing for the duration of their application. "Economic migrants" are considered non-deserving by the state and are therefore forced to rely on work in the informal sector or family and friends to survive.

Legal status: Interactions with the administration

For those who are considered to be "economic migrants," the only legal options to regularize their status are family reunification—either through family ties with Belgian citizens or marriage or cohabitation with a Belgian citizen (art. 10)—and medical regularization (art. 9ter). Family reunification is strictly monitored by the state. Medical regularization requires the applicant to be receiving treatment that is not available in their country of origin. Besides these criteria, the regularization in 2009 briefly opened a window for regularization through a work permit B. Most of the Moroccan sans-papiers that I got to know through SPBelgique had tried this. A handful of respondents reported that they "bought" a work contract from employers for amounts ranging from 1,500 euros to 5,000 euros, but having a contract proved to be insufficient to secure regularization. Moreover, the waiting time to hear back from authorities was so long that some employers did not follow through with their earlier commitments. Since a permit B is tied to a work contract and needs to be renewed every year, this only represented a temporary solution at best. Zouheir explains how this failed to work out for him:

> In September 2009 they opened the regularization. But despite all this, I have not obtained anything in terms of papers, although I deposited my files.... I received a letter from the municipality saying that I had to bring four pictures and my passport. When I read that, I was very happy because I thought that they were going to give me a residence permit.... When I gave them the letter, they told me that my dossier was negative.... The reason was that I was missing four months because I entered Belgium at the end of 2007 and they demanded March 2007. So that's why they refused. I was very mad because I lost three years of my life.... Moreover, I had purchased a work contract for 2,000 euros from an employer in the construction business.

Other sans-papiers saw their applications rejected because the documents they had submitted to prove their length of residence in Belgium were deemed invalid or because there were problems with their work contract. These shared experiences led undocumented workers to found SPBelgique (see Chapter 4).

Abas's story exemplifies the insecurity and instability undocumented migrants typically experience in interaction with state bureaucracies. After he had traveled to France on a student visa and successfully completed university, he moved to Belgium to pursue an additional master's degree. Yet he no longer had a student visa. So he applied for regularization in Belgium instead, not realizing that this entailed more than a simple administrative procedure to adjust his status. While waiting for an answer, he was gradually forced to accept jobs on the "black market" to finance his studies:

> I tried to arrange everything [papers] and afterwards this was blocked, but it is always ongoing, you know, *that is the worst about this situation, that it is always in procedure and that you have to wait.*... Little by little, the procedure takes up a long time without response.... I started to work in the cleaning sector and the conditions were miserable and I was only working with undocumented immigrants, ... but I did not really have a choice because I had to find a new place to live, because the person who was giving me a place to stay wanted to help out his family and it was only a small apartment.... I was even able to pass my exams in January, ... but in the second part of the year I started to neglect my studies because this job is not adapted to my situation, not well-paid, and *having to wait for my papers became a problem.*

Migrants who are considered "refugees" can make use of state services, including shelter and education, as long as they are "in procedure." The administration ranks refugees according to their country of origin on a priority list. Thus, applications from some refugees are given "priority status" because of the situation in their home country. A series of procedures designed to determine whether an asylum seeker is telling the "truth" are set in place. First, asylum seekers need to have an intake conversation, where they tell their story in their native language. An interpreter then communicates the story to the government official. Next, refugees have to "prove" that they are personally in danger. "Sufficient proof" needs to be given by the asylum seeker that they are no longer able to stay in their country of origin. After the intake conversation, it can be months or even years before they hear back from the administration. During this waiting period, it is virtually impossible for asylum seekers to get information about the status of their application. Once the administration reaches its conclusion, they receive a notification by mail. There is no possibility to appeal the decision, although asylum seekers can reapply.

I talked to several sans-papiers whose applications for asylum had been rejected. For example, Sumon received a negative answer a year after he applied. During the waiting period, he stayed in a refugee center and was taking Dutch language classes. As soon as he was informed about the negative decision, he was evicted from his room and had to survive on the street. In addition, he was kicked out of his Dutch language class. Another example is Rashid, who fled from Afghanistan to Pakistan with his brother and father to escape the Taliban. When his father passed away, human traffickers brought him and his brother to Belgium. They both enrolled in high school and submitted a request for asylum. After four years of waiting, they received a negative response. Their mother had been arrested and deported in the meantime. In my interview with Akash, he gave a detailed account of how he experienced applying for asylum:

> I did not have any relatives or family in Belgium, so they sent me to a refugee center in Anneessens in Brussels. I was there for almost two years from 2009 to 2011 until I got my first negative answer.... It was really tough for me, because now I realize that I am becoming illegal. What should I do, where should I go?... So when I talked to my lawyer he was telling me I did not provide enough proof... that's why they gave me the negative. Then she told me, "can you bring more documents, then you can get asylum." ... So I re-applied and gave them new elements, new proof.... But a couple of months ago I also got my second negative. They said that they were fake documents that I submitted. So now, I am illegal.

In contrast to those who are considered "economic migrants," the housing and education services that those who are considered "refugees" rely on for the duration of their asylum application give them a sense of entitlement. When this access is taken away after a negative answer, the mental shock of becoming undocumented is all the more significant.

Professional roadblocks

Undocumented workers are typically employed in sectors such as construction, cleaning, the restaurant business, and open-air markets (Kagné 2000, 9; Adam et al. 2002, 132–38). Finding a job is not easy for sans-papiers in Brussels. Networks of friends and family are a starting point when trying to find work (Adam et al. 2002, 130). Community meeting places, such as cafés frequented by people with a precarious legal status, also operate as informal work agencies. Certain public spaces, such as the neighborhood around the open refugee center Petit Chateau, are well-known "pick-up" places for day jobs. At any point in the day, you can spot groups of men with backpacks hanging around on the Boulevard de Dixmude and the Boulevard d'Yser, waiting to be picked up by vans for a day's worth of work. One day, I started talking to an African man who introduced himself as "John." John told me he was "a musician" and that he had arrived in Brussels four months earlier. When I asked him what he thought of the music scene, he evaded my question. Suspecting that his legal status could be precarious, I told him about my research. I asked him whether he had been staying in the neighborhood. Confirming that my hunch was correct, he replied that he did not have papers and had been sleeping in the Brussels North station at first and in the park nearby afterward. "It is really hard sleeping outside in the open," he said, "it caused me to start drinking to forget my troubles." "Now things are better," he continued, "since I am staying in a squat." As the squat was not in the neighborhood, I asked why he was there that day. "I was recruiting fellow Nigerians for a job tomorrow," he replied. "I have an employer who trusts me to only recruit hard workers." When I asked him what his aspirations were, he said "to get a fixed job on the black market and find a girl to marry."

Many SPBelgique members engaged in day labor like John did. Mohammed, who I got to know well during the Solidarity March, explained to me how he had to operate big cranes at his job on a daily basis. He had not been given any proper training to handle these machines, nor did his employer take any of the required security measures. A few years after SPBelgique's demise, I recognized Mohammed's face on the news. A scandal had erupted around the prestigious renovation of the Arts-Loi metro station. At the inauguration of the renewed station, the politicians who commissioned the works were posing for the gathered press in front of pictures of the renovation site's workers. The pictures had been put up to honor the men who had been involved in the hazardous business of drilling and expanding the tunnel. Mohammed was featured prominently in one of them. Ironically, word had gotten out that a subcontractor had hired undocumented workers to do the dirty work. Officially, Mohammed and his colleagues had been hired as cleaners. They were "always called on for work that the regularized workers did not want to do," like demolition work, stripping out, and digging the tunnel. "We did it because we do not have a choice," Mohammed declared in a public testimony.

Undocumented day laborers have little possibility to protect their rights as workers. Hence, their employers often exploit them (Bloch and McKay 2017). Working conditions tend to be worse for these types of jobs than for regular employment. For example, when I spoke to Abdul after months of absence from SPBelgique, he told me he was in a "bad place" with his current employers. He had been living-in with his employers in a Flemish town about thirty kilometers from Brussels. They owned a bar and he was allowed to live upstairs in the building. Since he could not afford to pay rent, he agreed to clean up the bar each day after closing time. However, the employers gradually started to give him more and more tasks, while they kept on postponing paying his wages. Abdul told me he felt "trapped" in his situation, but he did not have the mental energy to look for a different solution. Problems with getting paid are not unique to Abdul's story. SPBelgique member Zouheir also frequently ran into issues with malicious employers:

> As soon as people find out that you are a sans-papiers, they pressure you. They give you a lot of work, they pay you less, sometimes they scream at you and so

on.... Sometimes I worked at a bakery in Ossegem [Brussels]. He did not want to pay me. He told me, "take bread with you or a pie, I don't have money for the moment." The police came and everything, they told me that I should not go to this guy again because they knew him. I told him, "pay me, I don't have money to pay my rent," and he refused.... When the police came they told me, "You do not have the right to work because you are a sans-papiers, go back to your country."

Zouheir's experience shows how little undocumented workers can protect themselves from exploitation. Even with the help of an association specializing in undocumented workers' rights, his wages could not be recovered.

Others, like Omar, tried to avoid having to deal with employers as much as possible by becoming handymen or the like. Although Omar could not complain about his workload, people consistently pay him less than usual because they know he is a sans-papiers:

In terms of work, I do cleaning, mechanics, plumbing, TV repairs, computers, installing safety cameras, installing automatic curtains, other things, moving, emptying houses, all the jobs really that present themselves.... There are a lot of contacts, people I know and there are even people that I don't know personally who were given my number and who call me and then I go and work for them.... I present myself the way I am, as an SP [sans-papiers].... When people know you are an SP, they pay you less.

Karim complained about the vulnerable position he was in toward his boss as well as due to his permit B status. Since his boss could always use his B permit as leverage, complaining about his job situation was out of the question:

Working with a B permit at an employer is not self-evident ... they take advantage of the situation you are in.... They either pay you badly, or the boss does not pay you at all, no holidays.... If you do something your boss does not like, or you get annoyed, they immediately say: sorry, I am going to take back your B permit. Then, you are obliged to listen, like a slave. So then, you feel like you always have to do what the boss asks you to do.

Emotional lived experiences

The emotional lived experiences of the sans-papiers are in many ways similar to those of undocumented youth. Fear, anger, and isolation manifest as dominant emotions that capture their affective state of being. Lacking safe spaces like schools, and forced to take jobs on the black market, the sans-papiers are even more exposed to the risk of deportation. This exposure instills feelings of fear and insecurity into their minds. When they are repeatedly confronted with the inability to fix their immigration status, this can turn into a major source of anger and frustration.

Romantic relationships are tainted by the veil of "fake marriage." From the most intimate emotional decisions, such as who to commit to romantically, to the ability to work, live, and reside in the place that they call "home," noncitizenship thus casts a dark shadow on the personal lives of the sans-papiers (Sigona 2012). I encountered these emotions on countless occasions during my fieldwork at SPBelgique. Katia, one of the social workers at the Anchor, confirmed that many SPBelgique members struggled with their mental health. However, "these guys will not talk very easily about their psychological problems," she told me. Hence, I had to get to investigate the emotional lived experiences of the sans-papiers indirectly, through observation of interactions and situations.

Fear

Sans-papiers typically experience fear to varying degrees in their life before they migrate to Europe. Migrants who had fled violence or persecution back home were already intimately aware of what it feels like to live in constant fear. Other migrants who left their old life in relative comfort behind could encounter fear for the first time during their journey to Europe. Regardless of their previous mobility trajectories, the emotional lived experience of fear transforms when they become sans-papiers. While the source and immediacy of direct threat changes, living in the shadows in Brussels still involves tangible risks and threats to their presence. Mohammed expressed the sans-papiers' state of affective precarity as follows during an interview:

> Living without papers means that you do not have the right to a lot of things. You do not have the right to move. Even on a psychological level, ... many people live under great stress, they live in fear of getting arrested, ... and even on the level of mobility, of personal liberty this weighs on them.

Getting people to testify openly about such experiences was hard. However, Mohammed shared a story about Youssef, one of his friends who became mentally ill because of the legal limbo he was in. Having lived and worked in Belgium for six years, Youssef applied for a B permit with a contract provided to him by his employer. When he received a temporary work permit, he told his family that everything would be sorted out soon. A few months later, he received the news that his application had been refused. He gradually lost faith in himself, became deeply frustrated, and blamed his situation on Belgian society.

In order to illustrate how being subjected to the threat of deportation affects sans-papiers' emotional understandings, it is worthwhile to zoom in on a particular episode that Abas shared with me. Abas wanted to visit one of his friends in Paris. Without realizing that he was not allowed to travel without papers, he booked himself a ticket on a Eurolines bus. At the border, police officers stopped the bus and asked for everybody's ID. When he could not present a valid ID, they took him from the bus and transported him to a secure detention center twenty kilometers away. Once there, they brought him before a judge. He was facing deportation to Morocco. He then explained that his procedure for regularization in Belgium was still ongoing. After they heard him in court, the judge decided that he could not give sufficient guarantees that he was not going to stay in France "illegally." He was taken back to the detention center to await a further hearing. In the meantime, social workers tried to convince him to return to Morocco and offered him medication to calm down. When he faced the judge the second time, he said that he had a friend in Lille who could guarantee that he would not stay in France without papers. The judge replied that he would be released on the condition that his Moroccan passport would be declared invalid. On his release, he had to check in at a French police station each day for ten consecutive days to show that he was not going to flee. After he had done this, police officers drove him to the border between France and Belgium. They uncuffed him and asked him whether he had enough money to take the train to Brussels. When he replied yes, he was free to go. In the interview, Abas recounted:

> *It is at that moment that I realized that I was a sans-papiers*, the fear that you have of getting deported, the fear of secure detention centers, for me, for example, … every time that I come across a police officer on the street I am afraid, it is really something that stays in your head. All of this due to a status that changed from one day to the other. Everything collapsed, even my relationship with others because I started to isolate myself; I did not want people to ask questions.

The experience of being arrested and physically held captive in the detention center instilled fear in Abas's mind, leading him to retreat into the shadows.

Shame

Regardless of their migration trajectories, migrants risk becoming isolated when they become undocumented. Rejected asylum seekers who put their hope in the Belgian state, find themselves "ejected" from institutional support structures once their application is denied. As long as they are still waiting for a decision, they can feed off the positive stories of others who are in the same situation, to nurture their own hopes. However, when the negative decision reaches them, it often shatters their dreams and triggers shame about their status. Akash explained how devastating it had been on an emotional level to have his application turned down. It caused him to lose all hope and sink into a deep depression:

> It is really tough to describe my situation. It is really horrible, it is really pathetic, it is really frustrating, it is really devastating.... I am really a little bit shy and afraid as well to speak about my status to others because ... I am feeling bad inside.... This is not my life, this is not my future. *I was mentally depressed, I was stressed.... I was really scared and I became so tired. Not physically tired, but mentally tired. Because, the last couple of years, oh my God, I did not face so much trouble in my entire life. It was really catastrophic and devastating. My life, my dreams have been torn apart.*

Akash indicated how he did not want to share his status with others too much because of shame and the emotional stress that it causes him.

Many SPBelgique members were also hesitant to talk about their emotional lived experiences because of shame. Several respondents indicated that their families back home, who often contributed to financing the expensive journey to Europe, were not entirely aware of their undocumented status and expected something in return (Bloch and McKay 2017). Recalling Mehdi's story at the beginning of this chapter, he still sent remittances to his family despite the precarious work circumstances he was in. "Getting real" with family members would force them to admit that they had failed to realize their aspirations (Van Meeteren et al. 2009). In Tarik's personal memories, he explained how expectations from people back home can weigh heavily on undocumented migrants who "fail to succeed":

> The worst that can happen to a sans-papiers is having to return to one's country after spending years in Europe empty-handed, without money, without plans, without papers. He finds himself confronted with the unspoken accusation by his entourage. He is often accused of having wasted time, money, of not having been able to build a future for himself, of having wasted his life. This pressure can become a very heavy mental toll to bear.

Besides family relations, romantic relationships also fall prey to the uncertainty that comes with being a sans-papiers. Marriage seemingly offers an easy way out of the personal deadlock that many sans-papiers are in. Mehdi, who was introduced in the beginning of this chapter, had planned to get his papers through marriage from the outset. After his "online" girlfriend dumped him, he eagerly tried to find a new partner. In total, he had been—unsuccessfully—engaged to five girls. The sixth proved to be "the real deal." He and his fiancée passed the bureaucratic tests designed to detect fake marriages at the local municipality where she was registered. Mehdi eventually got married, received his papers, and now lives with his wife and two kids in a small town. Likewise, at least four former SPBelgique activists were eventually regularized after years of living in Belgium undocumented, through either marriage or cohabitation. This illustrates the stakes that are at play regarding romantic relationships between undocumented and documented persons.

Undocumented status can cause havoc among married couples too. Anouar's emotional lived experience was telling in this regard. Back in Morocco, he had passed higher education, and he was active in civil society as a human rights organizer. In this capacity, he organized protests against the Moroccan king. Afraid of possible repercussions, he left the country with his wife and seven-year-old kid. He overstayed his visa when he joined his family in Brussels and three years passed, during which he failed to regularize his status. Meanwhile, his second child was born in Belgium. Family reunification represented a logical solution, were it not that he would have to return to Morocco for five years before being eligible. Slowly but surely, the stress around his legal status started to affect his marriage and led to a painful divorce. Anouar was kicked out of the house and had to fend for himself. While this worked out quite well in the beginning, things spiraled out of control afterward. Depressed and frustrated about the hopelessness of his situation, he lost the urge to work. Unemployed, he could no longer afford to pay his rent. Unable to cope with these changes in his personal life, he resorted to alcohol. From that moment onward, I caught him drinking half liter cans of beer before noon on more than one occasion. Over the course of my fieldwork, I witnessed his transformation from a neatly dressed, distinguished, reliable man into the unshaven, depressed, and bitter shadow of his previous self that he had become.

Anger

Deep-seated anger and frustration were omnipresent during my fieldwork at SPBelgique. Since many SPBelgique members were unemployed for long stretches, their everyday life lacked structure and purpose. This added up to all-consuming frustration that terrorized the mental state of many sans-papiers. Zouheir described feeling empty and numb through the utter hopelessness and desperation of his situation. Asked to describe a typical day, he responded as follows:

> My typical day passes in emptiness. I wake up in the morning, I dress myself, I go out. *I just go out to forget about my situation.* Doing a little tour of the city center and afterwards I come back home. Life for a sans-papiers here in Belgium is really hard, he does not have the right to work, he has nothing. He has nothing in terms of rights.

Zouheir's description of a typical day points out how time ticks away slowly in sans-papiers' lives (Willen 2007). Blocked in the ability to realize their dreams, the aspirations they once had are indefinitely suspended in favor of mere survival. The following deeply personal testimony of a SPBelgique member reflects how sans-papiers are mentally affected by having to "live life in pause mode":

> My world has never been so sad and gloomy as that day, the day I neared the end, the day of the beginning. At that moment, I asked myself: What attaches me so much to this life? Is this faith? Is it the fear of hurting others? To live at all costs, wanting to survive. Is it the instinct of life, or the survival instinct? A life in pause mode, an awakening without awakening, an endless drift, brief, obscure ideas, that I do not dare to develop.... Doubt flies, panic dominates, and my life oscillates again and again. I dreamed of a simple world, of a just world. But today, my only dream is freedom. *My life no longer resembles anything: the days follow up on one another, the days are similar and the same nightmare always comes back: that of the return without an appointment, that of the end before the end. An endless cycle, a fatigue that accumulates, a perception of reality altered by suffering and a dream that lasts only the time of a sleep: this is my life.*

Conclusion

This chapter has investigated how lived experiences of illegality shape the understandings of SPBelgique activists at the micro level. While the pathways of those who are categorized as "economic migrants" and "refugees" initially diverge, they converge when rejected asylum seekers become undocumented. Although the sans-papiers' state of "being in the world" is essentially situated, scrutinizing embodied, discursive, and emotional understandings proved to be useful entry points to explore this state of being.

First, migrant mobility and urban immobility affect how the sans-papiers understand their society of residence and their place within it. Depending on the motives and available means for moving to Europe, the migration experience involves varying levels of risk and trauma. Moroccan migrants were often able to avoid having to cross dangerous borders like the Mediterranean by overstaying visas. Others, who either lacked such means or were fleeing persecution or war back home, were forced to migrate to Europe irregularly. Their "irregular" bodies were often subjected to violence by border police during the journey. These hardships would prove to be a taster of the obstacles they would face trying to settle in and get around in Brussels. Lacking the right to rent, the search for housing is accompanied by threats of eviction and precarious living circumstances. Targeted raids in popular immigrant neighborhoods and arrests on public transport ensure that the sans-papiers have to remain vigilant at all times.

Second, I singled out interactions with state bureaucracies and employers as seminal discursive lived experiences of illegality in which migrants are confronted with the reality of their precarious legal status. Interactions with state institutions force migrants to produce proof of their deservingness that fit ready-made bureaucratic categories. What followed for many SPBelgique members I interviewed was an agonizing series of suspended hopes, a life "in pause mode," and the subsequent rejection of their application. Migrants lose state protection with the stroke of a pen when they discursively transform from "asylum seekers" to "illegal aliens." Migrants who applied for regularization through work struggled to "prove" their worthiness by supplying work contracts that were often obtained through bribing malicious employers. Having to wait years to hear back about the decision, they found themselves in a vulnerable position toward their employers. The experience of being exploited by employers confronts migrant workers with the underprivileged position that an "S-P" holds in the urban informal economy.

Third, precarious legal status causes high levels of emotional stress, insecurity, and fear of deportation for undocumented immigrant communities in Brussels. Lived experiences of being arrested and detained help to keep this fear alive. Hesitance to talk openly about their status seems more prevalent among SPBelgique activists than among IYJL activists. Often lacking family connections in their city of residence, many sans-papiers tend to keep to themselves. For those who are in touch with relatives, either in Brussels or back home, shame prevents them from discussing the problems they face. Social isolation therefore represents a tangible threat to the mental stability of sans-papiers. Feelings of anger and frustration tend to accumulate under these precarious conditions. Such feelings often negatively affect the personal and even intimate relationships sans-papiers have with housemates, friends, and partners.

***

The previous two chapters have shown how embodied, discursive, and emotional lived experiences shape the process through which both youth activists and sans-papiers activists learn what it means to be undocumented. We have also seen how undocumented migrants' confrontations with prevailing understandings of citizenship vary in intensity according to the local context in which they are embedded. Such prevailing understandings range from nationally defined citizenship requirements and deportation policies, to locally enforced practices of inclusion and exclusion from educational, welfare, and work institutions. The hermeneutic perspective that was adopted shows that gaining awareness of their precarious legal status requires migrants to internalize and position themselves vis-à-vis these prevailing understandings. It is precisely because subjects actively participate—in hermeneutical terms—in this positioning that the possibility of political subjectivation becomes plausible. Yet for political subjectivation to occur, it is necessary to explore the collective synergies that emerge when undocumented migrants share and act out lived experiences of illegality in concert. This is what I will turn to next.

7

I define myself!

Making activists at the Immigrant Youth Justice League

From a young age, Claudia learned to hide her legal status at all costs. Although she confided her status to her high school counselor, there was no reason to do so when she started going to college at UIC.[1] The first couple of years, Claudia was solely focused on her studies and unaware of the struggle around the DREAM Act. When the limitations that she was bound to face on the job market started sinking in, Claudia experienced an existential crisis. No longer motivated to go to school, she took the first semester off and reconnected with Andre, an old friend of hers who also happened to be undocumented. Earlier that year, Andre had been one of the many Chicagoans that ICIRR had mobilized to step on a bus and attend the March for America in Washington, DC. On March 22, 2010, tens of thousands of immigrant activists and their allies had gathered on the National Mall to rally for comprehensive immigration reform and a path to legal citizenship for undocumented migrants. Inspired by the youth he met at the event, Andre persuaded Claudia to join him for a rally around the DREAM Act. Together with two others, Claudia and Andre embarked on the seven-hundred-mile drive from Chicago to DC in the summer of 2010. In hindsight, Claudia described the many hours they spent together as "cathartic." Being able to talk openly about her personal struggles without fear or shame with peers who had gone through similar experiences was an eye-opener for her. At the scene of the rally in DC, Claudia was overwhelmed by the sensory overload of the protest spectacle. That day, twenty-one undocumented youth, including ten IYJL members, were involved in sit-ins at the offices of several senators, urging them to push for the DREAM Act. Claudia remembers being amazed by the fact that so many people were wearing "undocumented, unafraid" T-shirts. Her first response to the civil disobedience action was that they were "nuts" and that she would never even consider doing such a thing. However, witnessing the sit-in and the rally and shouting "undocumented, unafraid" together with her friends made her feel "part of something" for the very first time in her young adult life. Back in Chicago, she decided she would go to an IYJL meeting to see what it was all about. Claudia did not immediately feel at home there. Due to her Asian American background, she felt isolated among the majority of IYJL members who had a Latinx background. Although IYJL activists usually

Citizen X. Thomas Swerts, Oxford University Press. © Thomas Swerts (2026).
DOI: 10.1093/9780197844038.003.0008

started the meeting by sharing their status and the issues they were struggling with, Claudia did not speak out right away. It was only in the company of a close friend that she brought with her to a smaller planning meeting for a rally that Claudia finally decided to "come out" to the other two IYJL members who were present. When she said it, they were surprised because Claudia had been attending meetings for three months by this point. Since she never openly talked about her status, they had assumed she was an ally. But they bonded over the experience, exchanged numbers, and offered her further emotional support. Claudia increasingly started to share her status at meetings and found that the more she said it, the more welcome she started to feel. Gradually, Claudia thus became *recruited* as a potential IYJL member.

A turning point in Claudia's activist trajectory presented itself in December 2010, when a fellow undocumented activist lost the battle against depression. IYJL decided to respond by creating a forum called "Dreams Deferred, Life Denied," where people could share their own issues publicly during a "Die-In" at Federal Plaza in downtown Chicago. Dressed in blue graduation gowns, Claudia, Cynthia, and Reyna testified about their personal struggles while others lay down on the ground in solidarity pretending to be dead. Pictures of the undocumented activists who had lost the fight against the mental demons that haunted their minds were hanging on a fence behind the speakers. As an ally, I had been responsible for securing stage props in the form of old books that I had obtained for free at a university library giveaway. As always, Noah, a more tech-savvy ally, was responsible for amplifying and filming the speeches. It was here that Claudia shared her status for the first time in public:

> Here I am, my name is Claudia and I was born in the Philippines…. Since I was five years old, I was told to never tell anyone about my family's dark secret, *to never tell anyone what I am.* In high school I was one of a handful of Asians in a school dominated by affluent white students, *not only that, I was also undocumented, out of status, without papers….* In my junior year, when all my peers were beginning the college application process, I hit a wall. I broke down to my counselors and told them my situation, because I was desperate and scared I wouldn't be able to go to college…. With the help of those same counselors, they helped me get to UIC, where I pursued my passion in English and art education. For three years, I withstood straining obstacles, I commuted over two hours every day to and from school because my family could not afford campus housing on top of paying full tuition, I barely had any friends at school because I lived so far away…. And earlier this year, I fully realized I would not be able to reach the requirements necessary to earn a teaching degree. I grew extremely tired of busting my ass in school and feeling so guilty wasting my parents' hard-earned money if I could not even make anything of myself in the

long run. I suffered a major depressive episode, coupled with crippling anxiety, and I was hospitalized twice. I stopped going to school and felt helpless, afraid, and ashamed. I felt worthless. *Not until I discovered the IYJL, and joined the movement, was I able to openly discuss my experiences and struggles. I met courageous students who channeled their frustrations into fighting for the rights of undocumented youth like myself. I have only recently mustered up the strength to come out of the shadows and speak out. All of the suffering made me stronger. I no longer look over my shoulder to see if anyone is listening when I say: "I am undocumented."*

While watching her speech, I witnessed how her voice trembled with emotion and she had to stop several times to catch a breath of air. Claudia looks back at this event as an emotional moment. Progressively, she started to consider "coming out" as a way for her to connect to people. Claudia's participation in the die-in served as a stepping stone for an even more public and high-profile event: the Coming Out of the Shadows Rally. As an accepted IYJL ally,[2] I was able to witness the backstage process in which Claudia was trained as a speaker. I initially participated in making banners for the rally with other IYJL members upstairs, while speakers were getting trained downstairs. When I entered the training room, people were practicing their speeches. They spoke loudly with powerful voices, and people had tears in their eyes. Claudia got interrupted during her speech by one of the organizers. "Less acting," she was told. "OK, you felt frustrated, but why?" A few moments later, Claudia came into the room upstairs and sat down crying, and Ilene talked to her. "It is just so difficult to have to tell my story over and over again," she said. Ilene comforted her and reassured her that coming out would be a great experience. At this point, Claudia had proved her potential to represent IYJL publicly while she was being *trained* to become an activist.

Claudia's mobilization as an activist occurred during the first coming-out rally that I witnessed on March 10, 2011. The eight undocumented youths who would be "coming out of the shadows" on Dailey Plaza in downtown Chicago were prepared one last time. A local theater group had agreed to lend their stage for the occasion. As an ally, I had been asked to wear a yellow safety vest, stand in front of the stage, and act as a liaison with the police if necessary. A crowd of youth, parents, allies, activists, scholars, journalists, and sympathizers greeted the eight speakers as they lined up on stage. When Claudia's turn came, she shared her childhood memories and reflected on the strength that activism has given her to continue pursuing her personal dreams and aspirations:

I grew up feeling less than others, but my undocumented status only pushed me to work ten times harder to prove that I matter and deserve the life my parents sacrificed to give me. I did and continue to do what I think is right to make my parents proud and to persevere through all the obstacles in my education. And thus far, I have no regrets. But that's not to say I fully accept my situation. No, I still cry. I still cry for the dreams suspended in limbo as I reach with all my might yet remain constrained and stuck in place.... To all the dreamers out there in my community, to all the young people hiding out in your bedrooms wishing with all your heart that something would change, that this country would finally recognize you as an American and allow you a chance at a real future, *all I can say is you can't wish for change, nor can you go at it by yourself. The time is now to emerge from the shadows because you are not alone. Come out of the shadows and take action. Be honest with yourself and those around you. Reclaim your identity and accept yourself, regardless of discrimination and hate. Look at yourself in the mirror, in the eyes, and say, I am undocumented, but I am not ashamed. My name is Claudia. I am undocumented. I am unafraid. And I am unapologetic.*

The speech that Claudia delivered was simultaneously a deeply personal account of the hurdles she had faced due to her legal status and a perfect reflection of the intense training sessions she had undergone to craft a compelling story for mobilization purposes. By physically getting on stage that day and performing her rehearsed life story in front of an audience of supporters and allies, she turned into an IYJL activist. Compared with the previous die-in, Claudia delivered a much more composed performance. By evoking the emotional transformation she underwent, from feeling afraid, ashamed, and less than others to feeling proud, honest, and hopeful as an activist, she struck a nerve among the spectators. A mere four months later, Claudia stepped up once again by blocking traffic and getting arrested during an act of civil disobedience against Secure Communities. By putting her body on the line, she instantly became known as one of the "Chicago Six." The Chicago Six would go on to represent themselves in court to challenge the charges of "reckless conduct" and blocking traffic filed against them by the state and the city. IYJL justified the action in a blog post by stating that "telling stories and coming out was just not enough.... For these undocumented organizers, once again, the issue is both personal and political."[3] Talking to a reporter during one of the trial dates, Claudia corroborated this reasoning by noting that her "activism is important," because "without it, I'd be living in fear of being deported." Now, she continued, "I no longer see myself as 'illegal,' I now see myself as 'undocumented.' And after overcoming fear and stigma, that feeling is truly liberating." Claudia had thereby completed her transformation from an isolated student who suffered from anxiety and depression into a full-blown activist.

***

Claudia's transformation into an undocumented activist shows the power of self-organizations like IYJL to function as *activist infrastructures*, understood as relatively autonomous and protected spaces where members of illegalized communities are recruited, trained, and mobilized as activists and gain precarious agency in the process. In contrast to the instrumental and rather calculated ways wherein undocumented youth were initially incorporated by established organizations into the movement, self-organizations created a milieu of self-determination and self-representation based on community experiences. Scholars have used terms like "free spaces," "prefigurative spaces," or—closer to the terms used by undocumented activists themselves—"safe spaces" to designate the importance of "small-scale settings within a community or movement that are removed from the direct control of dominant groups, are voluntarily participated in, and generate the cultural challenge that precedes or accompanies political mobilization" (Polletta 1999, 1). Autonomous, relatively protected spaces where activists can strengthen the bonds between them, explore their identity, and think about ways to challenge the status quo via their activism are far from unique to the immigrant rights movement. In fact, previous scholarship has demonstrated how the civil rights movement, gay rights movement, feminist movement, disability movement, and squatters' movement have all relied in one way or another on such spaces to prepare disruptive acts of activism and turn potential members into activists (The Roestone Collective 2014). This is especially the case for movements that aim to disrupt the status quo, because they require "environments where uncertain activists can forge the relational and emotional bonds needed for high risk and disruptive actions" (Nicholls 2021).

Undocumented activism represents a clear example of what McAdam has called "high-risk activism" (McAdam 1986). McAdam rightly observed that movement participants tend to initially be engaged in low-risk activism, only to be gradually "pulled" into high-risk activism by the deepening of their ideological commitment to the movement and the development of strong ties with fellow activists. Previous lived experiences of vulnerability, however, do not feature prominently in McAdam's recruitment model. In fact, he emphasized that "the absence of personal constraints that may increase the costs and risks of movement participation" increases the "biographical availability" of potential high-risk activists (McAdam 1986, 70). As Claudia's story and those of IYJL activists illustrate, their biographies would seem to make them *unavailable* for a career as an activist. Yet Claudia put her life as she knew it—including the many family and personal connections, the city she grew up in, and the investments she made in her education—on the line when she came out in public and got arrested. Indeed, all migrants with a precarious legal status who participate in mobilizations where their status is disclosed run the risk of arrest, detention, and deportation. What is missing, then, is a framework that can help us understand how self-organizations enable undocumented migrants to be precarious and agentic at the same time.

Turning vulnerability into strength is one of the main goals of self-organizations such as IYJL. The "making" of undocumented activists typically involves three stages: *recruitment, training, and mobilization.* Recruitment and training tend to occur "backstage" in self-organizations (Goffman 1959). The hesitance undocumented youth feel to openly talk about their status means they first need to be assured that participation is safe. "Safe spaces" like IYJL therefore presumes relational work that ensures a certain level of comfort, seclusion, and invisibility for potential members (The Roestone Collective 2014, 1347). Once undocumented youth are recruited as potential members of the organization, and by extension, the activist community, they need to "prove their worth" in practice. This involves attending weekly meetings, performing organizational rituals, and eventually representing the organization in interactions with outsiders. Membership thus represents less the status of organizational affiliation than a moral qualification that is collectively bestowed on undocumented youth by their peers meaning they are "fit for duty." Training then comprises moments when organizational leaders transfer activist know-how and firsthand knowledge to potential activists and "test" whether an individual's understandings are in line with the organizational understandings. *Mobilization* tends to take place "frontstage" in self-organizations (The Roestone Collective 2014, 1347). Movement members are then given the opportunity to "perform" their precarity in front of others and regain their agency in doing so. For this to work, self-organizations need to be sufficiently visible, stable, and recognizable to allow other civic actors to respond. Maintaining a careful balance between visibility and invisibility therefore constitutes an integral part of the process through which activist infrastructures produce undocumented activists (Swerts 2017).

The common denominator in each of the three stages of subjectivation outlined above becomes visible when applying the political hermeneutic framework introduced in the first chapter. In this and the next chapter, I will argue that the making of undocumented activists depends on the politicization of three of the few resources that are readily and intimately available to them, namely, their *stories, bodies, and emotions.* First, discourse analysists and scholars who have advocated the need for a "cultural turn" in social movement studies have argued that sharing stories can play a pivotal role in recruiting new members, building a sense of community, mobilizing support for social movements, and gaining a voice in the public debate (Polletta 2006). Second, cultural sociologists and feminist scholars who have criticized "mainstream" social sciences for rendering bodies invisible have argued that a marginalized position in society can become "inscribed" into the body, with bodies also operating as potential "sites of opposition" (Pitts 1998; Bourdieu 1998; Butler 1990; Wacquant 2004). Third, symbolic interactionists and social movement scholars who have rejected rationalism as a catchall explanation for various types of social action have emphasized that emotions are socially constructed in meaningful interactions with others, and can be used for socialization purposes and to motivate people to actively engage in and support collective action (Jasper 1997; Gould 2009).

While the argument can persuasively be made that stories, bodies, and emotions hold sway over movement dynamics in varying contexts, this is particularly the case for undocumented movements (Nicholls 2013; Swerts 2015; Escudero 2021; Abrams 2022). Every undocumented immigrant who is potentially interested in becoming a movement member arrives at their first meeting or rally armed with their own discursive, embodied, and emotional understandings (see Chapters 5 and 6). Their stories, bodies, and emotions contain the seeds for undocumented migrants to explore what they have in common with others in a similar predicament and what sets them apart from others. By physically gathering in meeting rooms and other "safe spaces" at regular intervals and sharing their emotional state of mind without having to fear possible repercussions, they develop a sense of community and belonging. The emotional energies that performing community rituals and sharing stories release can subsequently be molded into tools for mobilization through training and disciplining. The malleability and theatricality of stories, bodies, and emotions furthermore allow undocumented migrants to experience agency in taking control of their own lives and in publicly performing their innermost struggles, needs, and desires to outsiders. Hence, this research confirms the argument made in recent undocumented scholarship that undocumented youth "are transformed through the process of becoming activists" in "the spaces created through their political and community engagement" (Garcia Cruz 2020, 121).

In the remainder of this chapter, I will show how precarious agency is produced at the intraorganizational meso level by putting discursive, embodied, and emotional understandings to work to recruit, train, and mobilize undocumented youth activists for movement purposes.

***

Recruitment

In order to recruit potential movement members, activists need to create a "safe space" that allows undocumented youth to physically gather, meet, and exchange lived experiences of illegality. As shown in Chapter 5, "simple" things like walking around the neighborhood or taking public transport can become tricky for the undocumented. Schools and universities are among the only places where the stress of having to constantly look over their shoulder is relatively absent for undocumented youths. Long before activists campaigned to pressure schools and universities into becoming "sanctuary campuses," the legal protection offered by the *Plyler v. Doe* case had already turned school buildings and university campuses into spaces of sanctuary for undocumented youth. This offered a supportive environment for the creation of self-organizations such as IYJL. The following interview excerpt shows how Cynthia interpreted the role schools played:

> Schools have always been a sanctuary for students, regardless of immigration status. Like for me, personally, I always regarded school as a way to get away from, for example, the risk of facing deportation or talking about the issues that we face, so we always saw school as a way to not live in fear.... *So I think the role of schools is, like, not only a way for us to educate and empower ourselves but also a way to feel that we are in a position where we are safe to get organized.*

I previously introduced the story of Reyes. Tracing the origins of IYJL as an organization leads to the informal meetings that took place within the protective walls of schools between undocumented youths who felt emotionally connected to his case. Tamara was one of the people who made other undocumented youths aware of Reyes's story through her job at a local radio station. When Reyes showed up wearing an ankle bracelet to a meeting in February 2009, she decided to try to help him as much as she could. It was around December, when all of his legal options were running out, that activism became the last resort. At that point Tamara realized that it was not only a person's life they were fighting for but also a friend's life. This insight made her quit her job, and she opted to focus on being an activist instead. Here is how she recalls the first conversations about founding IYJL:

> IYJL was an idea that came about in conversations with Reyes, Marcinda, and Manuel, and we were sitting in a room saying we need to have an immigrant youth organization of some kind, because around his campaign, for example, none of the organizations were youth. Like, none of them were reflective of *what we thought, of what we felt, of who we were, and so there needed to be a space.*

It is important to note here that there was a need at the time to "create a space" that was reflective of undocumented youths' lived experiences and understandings, since the people who worked at the support associations around Reyes's campaign were often older professionals. What started as a campaign to safeguard one person from being deported quickly became a safe space where undocumented youth could get together, share their feelings, and organize politically.

Inspired by Harvey Milk and the gay rights movement's "coming out" strategy, IYJL organized their first "Shout It Out" event in December 2009. The idea behind the Shout It Out events was that they would offer a place where undocumented youth could share their stories in a protective environment. Reflecting on these first experiences, Ilene explained why hearing the stories of others immediately "sold" the movement to her:

> The other groups that I'd been in, we never talked about being undocumented.... When we were in IYJL, all sitting around that table and talking about our statuses and our stories, I was like, I've finally found a group where people know what frustrations I'm going through and can actually identify with them. And I don't have to explain what it feels like because they know. And they know how frustrating it is, and some of them have already dealt with it and can actually help, and some of them are just starting to go through it and so *I think that when we met at the space and were able to come across some stories, that was beautiful and probably the best feeling I've ever had. And I fell in love with IYJL, and I think I fell in love with every single person in IYJL.*

Community rules about confidentiality are typically negotiated at the start of Shout It Outs, and attendees subsequently go around the circle sharing their life stories with each other. During the first Shout It Out that I attended, Claudia welcomed us. "First of all," she said, "we should all know that this is a safe space for people to come out and feel supported." Hence, everyone was told to respect the community agreements. "What is most important," she said, "is the guideline that says what is said here stays here; what is learned here leaves here." Raquel started by telling her story to the group. While she was talking, it was quiet in the circle. At a certain point, she started crying. People passed around a box of tissues. Ulises shared how he had been lying in bed worrying all night about his legal status and the problems this was causing at school. Next up were some people who were coming out for the very first time. Miguel was a math student. He shared his experiences of crossing the border and growing up undocumented. He was part of a mixed-status family, which meant that his younger siblings were American citizens. He became very emotional while he was talking and started to cry. The other youths who shared their stories that day cried as well. When I interviewed Ulises afterward, he talked about the emotional bond that Shout It Out events create:

> When you listen to others' stories, you feel a certain level of connection ... it's enlightening, and sometimes even emotional, but in a good way.... *I can talk to them and share my story and connect with them at an emotional level and they might be able to understand me, understand what I am going through.*

When Ulises that day shared his worries related to his educational future, I noticed that this indeed changed my sense of personal connection with him (see Swerts 2015, 2018).[4] Whereas I had talked to him previously before or after meetings, hearing his personal story allowed me to get a better sense of what he had to go through emotionally on a daily basis. Seeing Raquel, another IYJL member who I had come to know as a confident youth leader, break down and cry in front of me moved me to the point that tears came to my eyes as well. When it was my turn to speak, I felt nervous because I thought I had nothing to offer. "But you migrated to the US too, right?" someone suggested, leading me to recount my experiences moving from Belgium and getting settled in Chicago. Through these exchanges, I was confronted with my own positionality (see Appendix). Yet I could not help but feel that what I was able to share as an "ally" with legal status was somehow not enough.

For many of the undocumented youth I met during my research, the Shout It Outs represented the first time they had disclosed to others the experiences related to their status. Hence, Shout It Outs are highly transformative events for undocumented youth that represent a first step in the transformation of their discursive, embodied, and emotional understandings into *political* understandings. In doing so, they break the circle of social isolation that governed their lives before and look for acceptance and recognition from a community of peers. Jobito recalls how he first experienced hearing other people's stories:

> The first time I heard other people talk about being undocumented ... I just cried for that whole day, I think most of us did. It was just a big group of us who sat around the table and talked about being undocumented.... I think we cried because ... *it was just so raw, the emotion, and good to be able to say it out loud, and have the group. Like, more than just one person, more than just you, knows how it feels to say you're undocumented.*

A good example of how coming out to peers can lead to recruitment was Carl. I had briefly talked to Carl at an IYJL Open Meeting before. After the meeting, we bonded over the fact that we were both musicians. He shared with me that he played in a death metal band, which was his favorite pastime. However, he could not invest as much time as he would have liked, because he was undocumented, and he had an outstanding student debt of twenty thousand dollars hovering over his head. He therefore had to combine two jobs where he made a meager nine dollars an hour to pay off his debt. He expressed how frustrated he felt seeing all his friends being able to attend college without having to worry about finances. The next time I saw Carl was at a "mental health workshop" organized by IYJL. Here, Carl told his story again to the assembled group of IYJL members and allies, albeit in slightly more detail. "I have only told this story to two people before," he said, before being comforted and supported by those present. Next, the attendees had to perform a "trust exercise" that consisted of making eye contact with your neighbor for a whole minute. By creating an environment in which undocumented youth get the feeling of being listened to and being recognized for who they are, they gradually become recruited by the organization.

Recruitment crystallizes into proto-membership through repeated presence. Physical presence and emotional availability are minimal requirements that need to be met by any aspiring IYJL member. This is reflected by Ulises, who explained what it means to be an IYJL member as follows:

> When there's, like, an event, try to the best of your ability to go or try to help in some way or spread the word. Just being there for them [IYJL], emotionally and not only physically in terms of, like, organizing. So that's what I think it means to be a member. *To be a member ... you have to be present.* Even if it's not all the time, and even if it's one week, you have to be present.

The more that undocumented youth attend meetings and rallies, the stronger their connection to the broader activist community becomes. For Jorge, for example, becoming an IYJL member also opened up an entire world that was "out there" but previously unavailable. He expressed that he was "definitely proud to be a member of IYJL" and that becoming an IYJL member also makes you a member of a nationwide community of undocumented youth. Since he came out publicly, people have approached him through social media, and his social networks have dramatically expanded. For undocumented youth, becoming a member of self-organizations such as IYJL therefore offers a ready-made identity; a "label" that gives purpose, instills pride, and evokes esteem in interactions with peers.

Training

Once constituted, activist infrastructures can start to serve as the "backstage" that can be used for political training, innovation, and experimentation. During the training phase, the discursive, embodied, and emotional understandings that start to take shape in the recruitment phase are corroborated, adjusted, and aligned with organizational understandings. Because self-organizations like IYJL consist of small, relatively exclusive groups of undocumented activists who try to remain autonomous from the sphere of influence of well-established CSOs and engage in high-risk activism, getting members in line and reflecting on political tactics together are of crucial importance. Their autonomous character, therefore, in part depends on the strength of the organizational rules and rituals put in place, with an eye to regulating membership and training potential activists.

From the very beginning, the "points of unity" make it clear that undocumented youth take the lead in the organization: "We believe in the right of those most affected to lead our own movements for liberation, and thus believe in an organization where undocumented youth are at the leadership, working with the support of allies." In this sense, it is certainly no coincidence that "immigrant youth" cast themselves as the superheroes who spearhead their own version of the well-known Justice League formation of the DC Comics Universe. Instead of Superman, Batman, The Flash, or Wonder Woman, it is undocumented youth who don their capes, join forces, and take up the fight against the oppressive and unjust immigration system. "Undocumented, Unafraid" T-shirts sporting the IYJL logo quickly became the alternative protective armor that IYJL members— including allies like me—would wear at rallies and other public events. In a reversal of roles, citizens are assigned a supportive role as "allies," while the "most affected" are regarded as the only legitimate movement leaders (Swerts 2018). From the perspective of IYJL, defining and upholding this clear-cut distinction between undocumented youth and allies was imperative to preventively demine potential conflicts over representation (see Chapters 3 and 4).

All potential movement members had to agree and comply with the formal IYJL norms, which were adopted consensually by existing members (see BOX 7.1 below). These norms were usually written on the blackboard as a visual reminder of the rules of the game for newcomers and regular attendees at the start of every meeting:

Box 7.1 IYJL Norms

What is said here, stays here, what is learned here leaves here
  No one knows everything, together we know a lot
  Leave space for humor and play
  One Diva, One Mic
  Keep it simple
  Here comes first
  "Yes, and…"
  "I" statements: Recognize we speak from our own experiences
  Don't speak for others
  Be aware of time and be on time
  Be curious
  Express discomfort
  Boundaries: Everything is an invitation; draw your own boundaries and
    respect those of others
  Take Risks: Green, Yellow, Red
  Attack/tackle the issue not the person
  Assume best intentions
  Check your privilege

Decision-making at IYJL was usually carried out through a simple majority vote. However, on several occasions there had been discussions that got out of hand or people had left the room yelling. In order to defuse heated discussions, norms like "agree to disagree," "don't speak for others," and "'I' statements" had been put in place. It is important to note here that the last norm, "check your privilege," mainly applied to citizen allies. Since more and more would-be allies presented themselves at IYJL over time, an "ally sheet" was drafted, urging allies to familiarize themselves with policies, laws, and other practices that affect undocumented immigrants; use their privileges to mobilize support; and learn to let undocumented people take the lead.

Membership was also built by undocumented activists through organizational rituals. A key one that I encountered week-in week-out during my fieldwork was the coming out as undocumented (or ally) ritual that typically took place at the start of every IYJL meeting. My first encounter with this ritual was at a meeting in August 2010. At the time, the DREAM Act debate was still ongoing, and there was a general sense of urgency in the air. The meeting was called, "Why we can't wait." IYJL members went around the circle introducing themselves to newcomers by saying, "My name is … and I'm undocumented." The organizational ritual of disclosing one's legal status was also an invitation for others to do the same, as a display of personal strength. During the weekly meetings I attended in the two years after this initiation, I experienced how this organizational ritual facilitated the transformation of recruits into movement members. Cynthia, whose story was introduced in Chapter 5, was one of the people who had just joined the movement when I started my research at IYJL. When I asked her how she became a member, she reflected on how this organizational ritual had affected her:

I remember going to my first meeting…. They said introductions, and they all said their names, and they said, "I'm undocumented," and I was like, "Why are they doing this?" … And I remember there was a minibreak in between a meeting, and someone came up to me and they were like, "Where are you from and why are you here?" and I'm like, "Oh, you know, this is where I'm from, and I'm undocumented," and so I was like … "Why did I just say that?" … And they were really open about their status, and that's what I think attracted me most about the group, cause, I've never … been around people who were so open about something that you're not supposed to talk about…. *So I've been with IYJL for a little over a year now … and at the beginning it might have been about you because you found someone you could talk to, you found a group of friends you were comfortable with, because you found people who are active. And eventually it becomes not so much about you, and you realize this is about everyone else.*

While Cynthia came across as shy and insecure when I first met her, I witnessed how she transformed into a confident leader over time. In the beginning, she barely participated in the meetings, but when she slowly started to share her story with other members of the organization, her engagement in the movement solidified.

Being an IYJL member meant different things depending on one's citizenship status. I quickly became aware of these differences when I was first involved in the coming out ritual. Whereas founding members would introduce themselves, saying, "Hi, my name is X and I am undocumented," citizens would in turn use the expression "Hi, my name is X and I am an ally." Even when everybody in the room knew each other, IYJL members swore by this formula as if it were an initiation rite that had to be completed before anything could take place. It did not take me long to embrace the ally label, as it offered me a ready-made identity within the movement. The "asks" they made of me ranged from driving people around to using resources on campus, being part of the security team during rallies, or building the stage for coming out rallies. Yet since I was involved with IYJL as a researcher first and foremost, I questioned whether my use of the label was justified. A session I attended with other citizen members helped to reassure me about my ally status. While undocumented youths gathered in the room next door, our task was to think about some questions: Why did you join? Why did you stay? What is your role? What can we do better? Noah expressed the view that allies should have "no asks," "check their privilege," and be self-reflexive. Scott admitted that people asked him, "Who are you?" when he joined and that having to disclose his intentions had been intimidating. Several allies highlighted that it was at times unclear for them how they could "step up." To my surprise, Emily then said that the way I had volunteered to preside over a session on college applications for undocumented youth had inspired her to take more initiative herself. In this way, she commended how I had shared my know-how of the educational field as an ally. Through trial and error, I survived what Emily called the "informal interviewing process" at IYJL:

> There's an informal interview process. So I think, like, the norms of IYJL that are written on the board aren't necessarily the real norms of IYJL. You can't be with IYJL and not be immensely angry about the way the system is structured.... There's a humility that you have to have because otherwise you won't stick in the group because you have to accept that sense of humility to fit in. And I think that's why a lot of the allies come and go, they're not used to that. *You have to have your own pain I think, your own personal pain. You can't come from a position of a lawyer, like, you can't come there to watch or experience in full, like, you have to be there to work and do stuff.*

At regular intervals, organizational "retreats" were organized to reflect on political strategy, come up with new ideas, and transfer firsthand knowledge about high-risk activism from more seasoned activists to recruits. In November 2011, I participated in a retreat that took place at a farmhouse in the neighboring state of Michigan. I volunteered to drive a couple of IYJL members over there in a rented car. The farmhouse had been temporarily made available by an allied community organization. In the first "workshop," Raquel and Ilene talked about the importance of building trust and getting to know people as the basis on which "safe spaces" could be built. "Through stories," Raquel continued, "we can pose a problem and make an ask of the audience." Ilene added that coming out also allows them to communicate "that we made the choice to not only be angry but to act." IYJL members then shared how they had been able to persuade people to act by establishing an emotional connection with them. Moreover, they stressed the need for activists to move beyond "self-help" toward "soul-searching." As an exercise, the workshop participants were asked to share their life story, which had to include a "climax" and a clearly formulated "ask" toward the end. Like the other attendees, I thus had to revisit the story I had told earlier about my "personal connection" to the issue, with the additional instruction that it had to demonstrate "a progression in awareness, biographical details that allow for emotional identification, and steps to take action." All of this needed to be accomplished in thirty seconds, because that is the amount of time that mainstream media typically award to stories. Compared with the previous version of my story, I added that becoming an ally at IYJL had "confronted me with my own privilege as an international student with a temporary immigration status," which led me to "openly support the movement and convince others to do the same," ending with the ask "to other citizens to check their privilege and become an ally." While I never had to share this story in public, the other participants and I nevertheless learned what it would take to "come out" and "step up" as an IYJL member in public.

In another workshop, people gathered for training in civil disobedience. Tamara, who had participated in several acts of civil disobedience across the country by this point, walked the participants through all the necessary steps, from planning the action to talking to the press afterward. In terms of the target of a civil disobedience, "be realistic about your target; stop all deportations is most likely not going to happen." Besides deciding on an overall messaging strategy, "visuals are really important too," she explained. "You have to think how you want them to interpret the event." Hence, the clothes activists wear, like the graduation gowns or "Undocumented, Unafraid" T-shirts, have to be carefully chosen in function of the message they want to convey. Next, Tamara explained that there is a lot of "backstage action" involved, with different roles for different people: a legal team needs to be on standby in case of arrests, "safety marshals" need to secure the site of the civil disobedience and negotiate with police, media need to be contacted and a press release needs to be written in advance, people in charge of logistics need to locate the site and figure out how to get there, a fundraising campaign needs to secure the bail needed to get out of jail, and last but not least, "caretakers" need to be appointed who can call people's family and provide emotional support. As an experienced activist, Tamara furthermore stressed that when talking to participants who are new to acts of civil disobedience, "you have to ask each person individually why they are participating, because you want people who are risking something to feel that you are taking care of them and that it is OK if they were to still change their mind." As the date of the actual act of civil disobedience approaches, she continued, "build a trust team," where you "start with storytelling and trusting each other" and you also "practice walking together as if you are already there." Lastly, Tamara trained the participants how to act and behave during the act of civil disobedience itself:

> You have to give them your name and birthday, but only give them the address of your lawyer.... Write down the phone numbers of your lawyer and the legal hotline with permanent markers on your bodies and on the side of your shoe and try to memorize these as well.... Take enough clothes because it gets really cold in jail, and take off any piercings beforehand. Tell them if you have a medical condition. Depending on where you are arrested, expect to be cuffed around the hands or legs.[5]

Both examples pay tribute to how undocumented youth used IYJL as an activist infrastructure to reflect on tactics and mold potential activists' political understandings.

The more likely it was for members to potentially be engaged in a specific political action in the name of IYJL, the more intense the training became. In 2012, I investigated how Xenia and Yolanda, two undocumented sisters who had been recently recruited by IYJL, experienced the training process for the coming-out rally on March 10. They paired with Raquel and Jobito, who had spoken in previous years, to prepare their speeches. Tamara helped in the training too, saying, "With them [Raquel and Jobito], you should expect to share your story, cry, connect emotionally, and practice your speech." Weeks after her coming out, Yolanda told me that she had gone through several stages before she was able to deliver her speech in the right way. First, she shared the unscripted version of her story, as she would tell it to a friend, in pairs. When she then had to share her story during a Shout It Out, she physically choked. Writing it down made her more comfortable the second time. By the last training session, she felt ready to speak at the large rally. Xenia told me that she immediately knew she would want to be one of the speakers for the rally. However, at the beginning, she did not fully understand what speaking at the March 10 event really meant or who the audience was supposed to be:

> At the meetings, we were discussing what the target was. Then I started learning that the target was undocumented [persons]. I thought that our personal stories were meant to be heard and that the target was going to be everybody ... but then they said that it was the undocumented ... so I had to think about how I would talk to another undocumented [person] in a way that, in my mind, I would have to convince them to get involved and active. *So I think I went through a whole process of understanding ... what it meant to speak on March 10th ..... That day we had a final training and ... that's when they were pushing me to be more expressive, more descriptive. I think that was the hardest part of the process, to be more open than I was expecting.*

During the training, Xenia learned that undocumented youth were the target audience. She also learned that her speech had to be an emotional and expressive story to have the mobilizing effect the organizers had in mind.

Mobilization

Activist infrastructures like IYJL recruit potential movement members and train aspiring activists in the backstage of "safe spaces." It is there that they learn what it takes to become accepted as members of the activist community. It is also where they are confronted with the fact that their discursive, embodied, and emotional lived experiences of illegality are not necessarily signs of vulnerability but potential signs of strength for those aspiring to become full-blown activists. The transformation from a "regular" movement member into a participant in a coming out of the shadows rally or a civil disobedience event is a rare, yet life-changing experience that only happens to a selected few. More-experienced leaders were usually in charge of scouting potential candidates for high-risk actions at IYJL. Given the struggles over representation discussed in Chapter 4, IYJL was particularly wary of only lending its stage to activists who complied with the "perfect, deserving DREAMer" profile. Regardless of their biographical profile, however, they had to demonstrate a willingness to "perform" and "act out" carefully crafted organizational scripts and messages through performative stagings in public space. These performances required IYJL activists to show themselves, share their stories, and convey their emotions in such a way as to maximize impact and resonance with the movement's allies, the public, politicians, and the media.

The die-in I mentioned at the beginning of this chapter is a good example of a low-key event that helped to test the potential of newcomers like Claudia and Cynthia to become activists. Staged in downtown Chicago in front of a small crowd of movement members and allies, the event primarily served to make the issue of "mental health" struggles among the undocumented activist community relatable and discussable. Cynthia's story was introduced previously in Chapter 5. By the time Cynthia took the mic to give her testimony, I had come to know her well. Being aware of her background and the obstacles she had faced, I was still shocked to hear her express her most intimate emotional struggles in public as follows:

> If you look at my arms, you'll see faint scars, they've been there for years. Some from eighth grade, high school, even last month. They're scars of frustration, of anger, of disappointment. I'm tired of having to live this way every single day.... I am tired of having to see my parents worry about what's going to happen to them and what's going to happen to me.... *Why can't I decide my life? I lost control, and that's why I resort to that, when I feel like I have nothing, no choice, no voice.* And it's gotten to the point where, what if it goes a little deeper? Maybe that's better. Maybe that's the way to go.... I am just tired to listen to people say that I am not good enough, that I don't deserve to be here; it is getting to the point where they are telling me that I do not deserve to be alive, and that's not fair.

In response to the stigmatization that undocumented youth like Cynthia undergo, some turn toward inflicting harm on their own bodies. Whereas Cynthia flirted with the idea of committing suicide, Raquel was still recovering from a suicide attempt she made a day after her high school graduation a year earlier. Worries about financing school, the pointlessness of her education, and having to pass on opportunities served as constant reminders of her limitations. "That's when a funeral started to look less expensive than four years of education at the school of my choice," she said in a trembling, but loud voice. In dramatic fashion, IYJL members dressed in graduation gowns laid down pretending to be dead on the ground to demand attention for the issue of mental health.

In 2012, I witnessed my second coming-out rally. As I outlined in the previous section, sisters Xenia and Yolanda had both been trained to give a speech. Xenia spoke first that day. When Yolanda was up next, she gave the following speech:

> Hi, my name is Yolanda. When I was four, I immigrated to the US along with my sister and my mom, not really knowing why we were leaving our home in Mexico. I just knew that I was probably going to be reunited with my dad. At that moment, all I wanted to do was remember the way he looked, I wanted him to carry me in his arms and, most importantly, I desperately wanted my

family to be back together again. It did not take me long to consider Chicago as my new home. But as I got older, I began to realize that I was nine digits away from even beginning to consider a piece of the American Dream. The worst reminder came the night my dad called to tell me that my mom had been pulled over. Knowing that she did not have a driver's license, I tried to prepare myself mentally for how our lives would change.... I felt helpless while I waited at the steps of my school. I couldn't even reach out to my teacher who was standing a few feet from me, because he had no idea that I was undocumented. Every minute that went by, I felt myself becoming paralyzed with hopelessness.... I would leave the home I have grown to love if my mom was forced to leave it. I should not have had to decide between my mom and my home. In fact, no child should have to decide between their parent and their home, yet thousands of kids have to feel the pain every single day because of racist, abusive, and dehumanizing laws. So I stand here today because I don't want anyone to feel like they don't have a voice. I know what that feels like. I will not let my struggles, my dreams, and my existence be pushed aside or used in the name of politics. My life is not a political token. As a human being I have a right to be happy, we all do. I invite you to stand up and fight with me for the justice we deserve. The government can attempt to take away our rights, but it cannot take away our will to fight. I am not backing down. I define myself. My name is Yolanda, I'm undocumented, unafraid, and unapologetic.

The remarkable commonalities between Claudia's speech a year earlier and Yolanda's speech are immediately noticeable. These commonalities illustrate the institutionalized norms that "model stories" need to comply with for mobilization purposes. In a way similar to Claudia's speech, Yolanda started off by recounting the story of how she had migrated to the United States as a child. The narrative then went on by invoking emotions of fear and helplessness concerning the threat of deportation and the consequences of her legal status, as in Claudia's case. Her speech ended with a call to the audience to "stand up and fight."

Undocumented youth activists have also used their bodies strategically in situations where publicly resisting in silence conveys a stronger message than raised voices. As I explained in Chapter 2, civil disobedience tactics that have been used here are sit-ins in politicians' offices, sit-downs aimed at blocking the street, and forming human chains. Civil disobedience as a tactic probably involves the most risks for undocumented youth activists. However, it is precisely the embodied and emotional experience of putting their life on the line that makes it a seminal turning point for undocumented youth who transition from regular members into full-blown activists. IYJL member Raquel, for example, explained how she emotionally and physically dealt with being arrested during the senate sit-ins (see Chapter 2):

> I think what the sit-ins did was put the spotlight on something that we had been asking for a really long time.… I think it was really smart the way that it was like putting a shame, it was kind of a challenge, not only to the system, but also to specific politicians. And it felt good to do. *I was scared, but I think that one of the things that we remember, that I remember a lot, is when we get arrested we always walk with our head up.*

Besides the action being an effective way to "shame" politicians into action, it also affected Raquel on a personal level. The collective experience of "walking with their head up" during arrest can be interpreted as a sign of strength and pride. Ilene recalled a similar experience of embodied resistance during arrests at acts of civil disobedience in Georgia and Arizona. When she looked at the pictures of herself getting put into a van afterward, she noticed that she and the others were smiling. In Arizona, they were also holding up their heads intentionally because they had seen how undocumented immigrants had been walking with their heads down during Operation Streamline.[6] She recalled:

> It was really just empowering to take that back and be like I am making my own choice today, about what's gonna happen to my life. And I'm taking the risk, but I know that I'm taking it and I have support behind me, so I'm not scared to do it.… I think that that has been one of the most powerful things that has happened. *Civil disobediences are powerful in general, but I think when you're undocumented, and you have that possibility, I think it's even more powerful.*

In April 2011, IYJL member Santiago was one of seven undocumented youths who got arrested during an act of civil disobedience in Atlanta to protest a new law forbidding undocumented students from enrolling in five state universities. When I talked to Santiago about his arrest in Georgia, he said he had experienced it as a liberating and life-changing event:

> I feel like Atlanta gave birth to me in a lot of ways. Like I needed that physical acknowledgement of a reality that I've dealt with metaphysically. I'm thinking that I've been incarcerated this entire time, like the way that I thought was incarcerated. Someone putting me in handcuffs and putting me in jail was very liberating for me. It was an acknowledgment of something real in my life. It just made it real. *It just gave birth to me.… That was the first thing that I did in my life.*

Reflecting on the experience, Santiago clearly explained how the embodied experience of being arrested and incarcerated caused a change in his awareness about his own vulnerability as an undocumented person and the agency that he was able to regain by becoming an activist.

The legal aftermath of the walk-out and sit-down of the Chicago Six Claudia participated in represents the risky character of carrying out civil disobedience. Faced with criticism from more well-established CSOs that the timing was not right, IYJL member Araa defended their collective decision as follows:

> Every time we make our status public, and risk arrest, we are also risking deportation.... For this, we have been called "reckless" and "irresponsible." I completely reject the argument that what we do is reckless. An organizing team ... meticulously, carefully, and strategically planned the walk-out and sit-down with a greater goal in focus, and an entire community standing by in support. We talked about the risks, the legal consequences, our rights in detention, our choices, our fears.... *We cannot bear to live in humiliation another day,* and we won't wait for the media to tell our stories for us.

Sometime after they had all been arrested, the Chicago Six were interviewed by a local radio station about the experience. Ilene's detailed account of how she personally experienced the action shows what it feels like to be arrested:

> I got dropped off and, like, I was seeing how it was actually going to happen. Mario was mentioning a lot of the plans, so it was all, like, not sketchy, but, like, really up for anything because we really didn't know what would happen, because this was our first time in an open public hearing about Secure Communities in the area.... *And I was very angry, and very much needed to get out that anger and that message in a way that would help other people understand what was going on and talk about what was going on....* When I was actually in jail, it actually hit me we are doing this, and this is happening.... I was there in jail, in this little cell, very cold, you know, thinking about my family and it suddenly hit me.... How did those other people who are prosecuted under Secure Communities feel when they are in jail as well, you know, knowing that they didn't do anything criminal but that they can be deported any time? *So, I think that's one of those things you don't really feel until you are in jail.*

The case of the Chicago Six was neither the first nor the last time that IYJL members resorted to mobilizing their bodies in their struggle for justice. At the occasion of Obama's presence in Chicago for a fundraiser, IYJL staged an act of civil disobedience to demand that the DACA program be extended to undocumented migrants, regardless of age. When I arrived at the scene of the protest, I bumped into other IYJL members. While I had not been part of the planning of the action, I was immediately enlisted to hold a big banner saying, "Tell ICE: Don't deport Lourdes Moreno Carrero," showing a picture of Lourdes and her family, the number people could call, and a sample script for potential callers to follow. At the Hilton hotel where Obama was scheduled to speak, activists unfolded a banner stating, "Deporter in Chief." Next, twelve activists, including IYJL member Ilene, formed a human chain and sat on Michigan Avenue circling a banner with the inscription "400,000, Not 1 More Deportation." As one of the participants, Ilene was quoted as saying to the press that: "It doesn't make sense to keep deporting people that could qualify for immigration reform. We want our families to still be here when a path to citizenship opens. We're calling on the President to give our parents and everyone in our community the same relief he gave us." Even during a highly risky and nerve-racking action, Ilene was thus able to spread a composed message about why IYJL as an organization was doing this again.

Despite IYJL's unrelenting actions, constantly having to publicly share your story or risk arrest also entails a real danger of triggering activist fatigue. During my fieldwork, I noticed how certain IYJL activists who had been very active as public speakers in the beginning, started to turn down speaking engagements and become frustrated during meetings. Raquel provided some insight into how activist fatigue can creep up on IYJL activists:

> A lot of the things we do in IYJL, we get caught up in this way of telling our story. I think it has a lot to do with the kind of storytelling we've been doing for over a year now, *so it kind of becomes like automatic. At the same time, I feel like every time we tell our story or I go to speak at an event or something, it's emotionally draining.*

Similarly, certain IYJL members expressed reservations about the ability of the organization to sustain acts of civil disobedience in the long run. Together with six other undocumented activists, IYJL member Xenia participated in an act of civil disobedience in 2013, when they formed a human chain by linking their arms with locks and blocked the Broadview Detention Center Road. Despite this experience, she raised questions about the movement's capacities to sustain this much longer:

> I think we're still a very small movement, and there's a very small number in the organization. So risking the people, we only have a few opportunities to do civil disobedience before we really affect the chances of changing our status.... It's not a very resourceful or easy choice.... *So I think we have to be creative and think about ways that will not jeopardize individuals in their personal lives.*

Recurring discussions on mental health, "post-action stress," and the intensity of "unhealthy" ways of communicating in the organization also indicate how precarious agency can start to crumble when you need to resort to personal vulnerability time and time again.

Conclusion

In this chapter, I have demonstrated how self-organizations like IYJL function as activist infrastructures in which undocumented youths become activists. I have identified three distinct stages that these youths go through to become politically active: recruitment, training, and mobilization. In each of these stages, discursive, embodied, and emotional lived experiences of illegality serve as the "raw material" that is cultivated and transformed into political tools. Experiences of vulnerability are acknowledged as "real" and "important" in the context of self-organizations. For undocumented youths, the politicization of their personal stories, bodies, and emotions then depends on their ability to take control over their own narrative, decide when and where to be physically present, and turn their fears and frustrations into feelings of pride and empowerment. Below, I outline once more how political hermeneutics serve as the underlying mechanism that enables undocumented youth to gain precarious agency at the intra-organizational level.

First, telling stories, being physically near one another, and experiencing emotions together in the relative protection of "safe spaces" like IYJL enable undocumented youths to become recruited as potential movement members. Through the act of coming out as undocumented and listening to and sharing each other's stories, new members can identify with the undocumented community. Being able to look around a room and realize that all the faces you see sitting around you are the faces of people who know what you are going through, visually reveals the idea of a community of peers to participants. The emotional transaction that takes place during "backstage" gatherings in safe spaces fosters shared feelings of grief, frustration, compassion, hope, and solidarity.

Second, the stories, emotions, and bodies of movement members undergo significant transformations as they become socialized into the movement culture, are exposed to organizational norms and rituals, and are trained to be ready for political action. IYJL membership does not equal a "status" that anyone has or does not have, but rather a critical and emotionally engaged attitude that needs to be continuously proven in practice and validated by peers. While undocumented members are expected to share their stories and speak up, citizen allies are expected to step back and support the organization from a distance by leveraging their privileged networks and access to resources. Physically "being there" during meetings and rallies serves to prove personal commitment, while training is used at times to prepare aspiring activists emotionally and physically for what is to come.

Third, recruited movement members become full-blown activists when they step out into the limelight, presenting their stories and emotions and putting their bodies on the line in public spaces. Well-rehearsed life stories are performed to evoke sympathy and understanding from outsiders for undocumented youths' experiences of fear, frustration, and pain. At the same time, they serve to demonstrate how undocumented youths have been able to regain control over their life and—to use the language of the coming-out rallies—"define themselves." Bodies become organizing tools when they reveal themselves to be undocumented, deportable bodies. By risking arrest and getting arrested, activists experience their deportability firsthand and physically come to grips with the precarity of their illegalized status.

8

So-so-so! Solidarité!

Making activists at the Collectif Sans-papiers Belgique

Zouheir grew up in a small village on the outskirts of Rabat. He left his family and friends behind at the age of nineteen in search of a better life in Europe. Back in Morocco, he had not managed to get his high school diploma because he failed in his final year. Since he knew how hard it would be to get a job without a diploma, he figured he might have a better shot at success crossing the Mediterranean. He first traveled to France on a tourist visa, packing little more than his passport and some personal belongings. When he arrived as a young adult in Paris, he had a hard time getting to know the city and figuring out how things worked. Weeks went by, and after several months, Zouheir's tourist visa had expired and he did not a have a job. He got in touch with an aunt who lived in Belgium, who convinced him to come to Brussels in the hope that he would be able to find steady employment and settle down. When he arrived in Brussels, he tried to enroll himself in baking school and Dutch language classes. However, he quickly learned that he had to have a valid ID card to be eligible for enrollment. This was the first wake-up call for Zouheir that made him realize the dreams he had of coming to Europe would be harder to achieve than he had initially thought. When his money dried up, he started looking for odd jobs to get by. The merchants at the big open-air market at the Anderlecht abattoir proved to be a fairly reliable source of day labor. His job consisted of offloading and loading crates of goods, setting up the merchants' tents, and sometimes selling textiles and socks. This work turned out to be tougher than expected. Employers demanded that he work hard for a meager salary, lowered his wage without warning, and scolded and yelled at him on the job. Scrambling to make a living, Zouheir had to be content with sharing a room in a dilapidated apartment in a working-class neighborhood in Schaarbeek. Days slipped by in emptiness, and weeks became months. Before he knew it, two years had passed. While he kept in touch with his family the first few months, this became less as time went on. Zouheir, now twenty-one years old, began to suffer from social isolation and the exploitation that he had to undergo on a recurring basis. Feelings of frustration, anxiety, and depression started to consume him. He noticed that he could often not muster up the energy to even leave the apartment or look for a job.

Citizen X. Thomas Swerts, Oxford University Press. © Thomas Swerts (2026).
DOI: 10.1093/9780197844038.003.0009

By then, Zouheir knew all too well that obtaining legal status would be the only way to get his life sorted. However, he was confronted by a lack of legal avenues to pursue. Marrying someone or looking for legal cohabitation started to look like an attractive strategy. Before it even came to this, another strategy presented itself in the form of the sans-papiers movement. Having arrived at a turning point in his life, the wave of occupations that swept Brussels in the lead-up to the 2009 regularization campaign appeared to be an opportunity for Zouheir. About six hundred sans-papiers from thirteen nationalities had been occupying an empty office building of the Fortis Bank on the Saint-Lazare square in Sint-Joost-ten-Node since mid-May. The goal of the occupation was to put pressure on the political parties and well-established CSOs that were simultaneously negotiating the criteria for the regularization campaign. Friends who were also undocumented informed Zouheir about the ongoing occupation. He took his backpack and a blanket and decided to join them to see what it was all about. In the end, he only stayed for twenty days because the living conditions at the occupation were simply too much for him to bear. At the time, he had just been involved in a minor accident and still had a plaster cast on his foot. There was no heating or running water in the building, and the rooms were cold, empty, and dirty. The occupiers had to go to the snack bar across the street to use the restroom and clean themselves up. The mayor had been alerted to the situation by residents who complained about fights breaking out and other nuisances. Although the mayor publicly refused to order the police to intervene, Zouheir realized that the situation was untenable. His premonitions came true when a spectacular police intervention involving a helicopter landing on the roof of the building was staged "to clean them up." Zouheir distinctly remembers being affected by the way the police physically treated and verbally abused occupants during the eviction. Nothing was gained as a direct result of the occupation, and activists felt let down. Despite the negative outcome, Zouheir considered this to be a positive experience for him on a personal level. Participating in the occupation made him realize that there were more undocumented people like him who were willing to get out there and take risks to claim their rights.

When the regularization campaign in 2009 finally kicked off, Zouheir had high hopes. The window to apply for regularization at his municipality on the basis of his "sustainable ties" to the country was three months. In order to be eligible for a one-year residence permit, he had to prove that he had continuously resided in Belgium for two and a half years and present an employment contract for at least one year. Assembling proof of residence was difficult since he did not legally rent his apartment. Getting the employment contract was equally troublesome, given the type of day labor he was engaged in. He therefore used all his hard-earned savings to purchase an employment contract from a malicious employer in the construction business. Zouheir thought that it was just a matter of sorting things out administratively at this point and expected to receive his residence permit quickly. However, a year passed without receiving any word from the administration. Many other sans-papiers who had applied for regularization via a work permit were in a similar situation. They got together and formed the "Collectif Sans-papiers en attente," literally meaning the collective for undocumented people who are waiting. It was again through a friend that Zouheir was made aware of the collective's existence. Tired of sitting around waiting, he started to attend the weekly Thursday meetings of the newly formed collective. By the time I got to know Zouheir, he had already received word that his application for regularization had been turned down by the government. He struck me as a friendly, yet shy young guy who felt uncomfortable speaking up during SPBelgique's meetings. Yet, as he told me later, he felt that attending these meetings gave him energy and perspective, because "they give us plans for how we have to do things in order to have rights." Rather than taking a leadership role, Zouheir excelled in offering logistical support for the collective's activities. He was a regular member of the cooking team whenever SPBelgique organized dinners. He also volunteered as a cook at the Anchor, the local community center where the collective's weekly meetings were being held. Besides this, Zouheir was committed to the ongoing effort to recruit fellow sans-papiers to join the movement. He would reach out to potential movement members in occupations, put up posters for rallies around town, and distribute flyers at Moroccan tea houses and night shops in the Stalingrad neighborhood. When talking to potential movement members, he always stressed that participating at SPBelgique would offer them a perspective to change their situation. He often encountered people who were willing to participate in principle but who were too afraid to be arrested during events. When he did manage to convince fellow sans-papiers to attend rallies or meetings, they tended to become rather quickly discouraged by the lack of immediate results. "But you should not be afraid," he told me, "we always have to be courageous and we have to be patient." Regardless of the difficulties he faced recruiting members, he was still convinced that organizing marches and protests was the only way forward to gain victory.

When the time came for SPBelgique to prepare a delegation to attend the European march in Strasbourg, Zouheir was one of the first to put his name on the list. The week before, he had told me that he had lost his job. The march offered a reason to put his time to good use for the collective. Zouheir got in the van with me, Abas, and three citizen allies. During the long drive there, he kept relatively quiet while I noticed he listened closely to Abas sharing his personal story. In Strasbourg itself, he attended meetings and slept next to me on the cold floor in the gym hall where the marchers were allowed to stay by the municipality. He did not speak up during meetings but seemed to absorb everything that was going on. He also joined in when the marchers staged a "circle of silence" in the city center of Strasbourg, thereby temporarily preventing casual passersby from crossing the square. This symbolic action aimed to draw attention to the many migrant lives that had been lost as they desperately tried to reach Europe. Nevertheless, Zouheir's silent presence extended beyond his participation in the circle of silence. That is because "being there" exemplified how he gave meaning to SPBelgique membership. Like so many other SPBelgique members, Zouheir felt uncomfortable and insecure when it came to speaking up in public. He generally waited for the spokespeople of the collective to lay out their vision and only joined in when they started talking about the practical organization of actions. After the European march, Zouheir visibly felt more comfortable taking the lead in organizing events. He set up a fundraising "solidarity" event for SPBelgique during Ramadan, where a documentary was screened, followed by a meal. He led the debate after the documentary and welcomed guests who arrived for the *Iftar*. Zouheir, who had developed a close friendship with Fariss during the European march, was also continuously in touch with Fariss while he was being held in the detention center before his deportation. "Being there" thus extended beyond being physically present at events, to being there emotionally for fellow members during hard times. However, after his friend got deported, I noticed that Zouheir appeared less in the picture than before. His spirits were low, as he seemed to have lost hope of a positive outcome. When I asked him about it, he said: "The future for the sans-papiers in Belgium is dark. There is nothing in the future." Not long after that, SPBelgique ceased to exist and Zouheir retreated into the shadows.

***

The transformation of Zouheir into an undocumented activist contains lessons about the functioning of SPBelgique as an activist infrastructure in Brussels. Despite the obvious differences in contextual and biographical factors outlined in the previous chapters, SPBelgique as a self-organization fulfilled a strikingly similar role to IYJL, as a space in which sans-papiers were recruited, trained, and mobilized. Discursive, embodied, and emotional understandings again played a crucial role in the process through which the sans-papiers gained precarious agency. However, the functioning of SPBelgique as an activist infrastructure also differs from IYJL in several important ways.

For the sans-papiers at SPBelgique, the principle of "autogestion" was guiding from the start. With roots that can be traced back to the tradition of factory occupations within the European labour movement, the term autogestion originally gained traction to indicate the self-management of the means of production by workers (Purcell 2013, 147). However, sociologists like Henri Lefebvre later broadened the concept by contending that "each time a social group ... refuses to accept passively its conditions of existence, of life, or of survival, each time such a group forces itself not only to understand but to master its own conditions of existence, autogestion is occurring" (Lefebvre 2009, 135). Refusing to accept conditions of everyday survival and mastering their own condition of existence indeed motivated the collective attempts at self-management by the sans-papiers. The extreme precarity that characterized their lived experiences of illegality in Brussels (see Chapter 6) created a real and pressing need for an organizational space that could autonomously support undocumented immigrant communities in their everyday struggles to get by. Many sans-papiers in need were partially dependent upon the support and limited access to resources provided by what Felder et al. (2023) have called the "assistance circuit" for sans-papiers in the city. However crucial this support might be, accessing it is rarely unconditional, and having to do so can reinforce feelings of dependency, entrapment, and alienation (Felder et al. 2023). For the sans-papiers, autogestion thus revolved around the capacity to reduce and minimize dependency on the assistance circuit all together by relying on what Abrams identifies as "self-produced, community-based resources" (Abrams 2022, 26). Examples of such resources include collective housing via squatting and occupations, collective meals via food waste recuperation and collective knowledge sharing about regularization and employment strategies. While autogestion might seem to veer close to well-rehearsed concepts like emancipation or empowerment, a crucial difference pertains to its inherent abolitionist critique of the state. Self-management of community resources is presented as a radically alternative way of organizing society that directly challenges and attempts to undermine state power, as dominant institutions "begin to make less and less sense" (Purcell 2013, 148).

The self-management of community resources relied on establishing and maintaining solidarity relations within SPBelgique. Historically speaking, solidarity served as the main rallying cry for the European labour movement that called upon all workers to unite themselves "in a joint struggle around common interests against a shared enemy" (Oosterlynck et al. 2016, 768). As I will demonstrate below, struggle served as an important "source" of solidarity within SPBelgique, where institutions like the Belgian state and "Fortress Europe" were designated as "shared enemies" of the sans-papiers. This represented an attempt to channel the deep-seated emotions of anger and frustration that had accumulated among SPBelgique members whose lives were suspended when they applied for regularization (see Chapter 6). Compared to IYJL, where the legacy of the gay and civil rights movements served as clear sources for inspiration, the labour and squatters' movements fulfilled a similar role for the sans-papiers. This was not only a matter of mutual symbolic attraction, as several SPBelgique members simultaneously participated as undocumented workers in labour union organizing or lived in communal squats. The meaning of "true" solidarity was constantly reinterpreted and redefined in struggle by the SPBelgique leadership. Due to previous negative experiences of being overpowered by established organizations and "soutiens" (see Chapter 4), social workers, professionals, and politicians were often accused of having a hidden agenda to exploit the sans-papiers. Being united across differences was therefore seen as the pinnacle of solidarity at SPBelgique, thereby leaving less room for individual stories and experiences to be expressed. In contrast to the centrality of safe spaces for IYJL, SPBelgique rather revolved around creating a "solidarity space" where the sans-papiers could experience being part of a common struggle and sharing a similar faith. Turning recruits into movement members at SPBelgique therefore did not necessarily require them to "speak up" but to demonstrate their commitment to the cause by "being present" at weekly meetings and "voting with their feet" during marches and demonstrations.

For solidarity between movement members to occur, SPBelgique's organizational practices revolved around what Darling has called a "politics of presence" (Darling 2017). In a context wherein the sans-papiers' mobility is restricted and criminalized, asserting and visualizing physical presence can be seen as a rejection of illegalizing migration policies and an expression of the right to stay (Darling 2017, 190). The physicality of presence was expressed in different embodied practices at IYJL. As will be demonstrated below, such embodied acts ranged from "self-management" practices like volunteering and cooking (see above) to political practices like sit-ins, marching, and border crossings. SPBelgique's reliance on embodied practices has broader significance since it challenges sociological theories that traditionally saw the body as "trapped" in a web of power relations. For Foucault, for example, "disciplined" bodies are institutionally produced through techniques and technologies of surveillance, as the body is the locus where power relations take their grip (Foucault 1977). In a similar way, Bourdieu's theory of the habitus conceives of "mirroring bodies" as bodily practices that reproduce class relations through cultural expression, consumption, and taste (Bourdieu 1998). Theories of the disciplined and mirroring body leave little room for the undocumented to take control over their own bodies. Butler's theory of gender performativity offers a potential way out, as it stresses how gendered and embodied subjectivities are constituted in ongoing and repetitive acts of signification and resignification (Butler 1990). For this reason, bodily agency is to be located "within the possibility of a variation on that repetition" (Butler 1990, 185). Feminist scholarship thus leads the way in demonstrating how a hermeneutic perspective on the body can reveal its potential as a "site of opposition" (Pitts 1998). Translated to the world of the undocumented, precarious agency can be stimulated by resisting the forced immobility and violence that is imposed upon their bodies by the state. However, embodied forms of precarious agency come in different shapes and forms. In Chapter 3, I outlined how the sans-papiers movement initially relied on the use of hunger strikes and bodily mutilation as embodied ways to claim to "the right to be there" (Siméant 1998, 287). Siméant has previously argued that hunger strikes by the sans-papiers are a theatrical "mise en scène" of the domination of the state that shows how much they have suffered and continue to suffer (Siméant 1998, 315–16). Furthermore, Fassin argues that evoking the "suffering body" works because it resonates with state criteria for regularization based on health and illness (Fassin 2001). Yet, as I explained in Chapter 4, there was a clear sense among the SPBelgique leadership that hunger strikes put the sans-papiers in a vulnerable position and came with a toll that is too heavy to bear for the movement. Instead, SPBelgique activists started to experiment with bodily tactics that aim to publicly display their capacity to be self-sufficient (autogestion), present (sit-ins and occupations), and mobile (marches and border crossings).

In the remainder of this chapter, I will outline how SPBelgique recruited, trained, and mobilized the sans-papiers for political purposes and how discursive, embodied, and emotional lived experiences of illegality were transformed in the process.

Recruitment

The roots of SPBelgique as an initiative can be traced back to informal meetings in a café in the Stalingrad neighborhood of Brussels. These cafés functioned as places where sans-papiers could get information about odd jobs, housing, and other everyday needs. Hence, they represented a place of encounter for sans-papiers to casually meet others in a similar position to them (Wilson 2017). Over the course of these encounters, a small group of men found out that they had something more in common than their origins from the Moroccan city of Ouijda. They had all applied for regularization based on the permit B regularization procedure but still had not received a response. By sharing their stories in mutual confidence, they communicated their frustrations and fears with one another about being "in limbo." Hearing each other's stories resonated so much with them that they came to the agreement something had to be done about it. Faisal reflected on how it all started:

> So we were at the café over there [he pointed out the window], and we were from the same city, Oujda, in Morocco.... It was really more like a discussion in the café back then. So we tried to create the movement on the spot.... *Our group had been waiting for a year to hear back, so it was really a group of desperate people.*

As Abas explained, the collective mainly focused on finding a solution for the immediate problem of those who had filed their request for regularization. Political demands about regularization for all were not yet prominently on the table, but only emerged later:

One day in a café we said, "Why don't we do a protest?" We are going to celebrate the anniversary of the regularization. It was like that. The guys said, "Sure, it is not complicated, we make flyers, we ask for authorization." We were still an independent group back then, only made up of sans-papiers.... *Immediately, I felt like this was all I had been waiting for. Before, I heard people talk about the movement and I even visited an occupation, but it was as if I was not ready yet. And above all, it felt like it was not my struggle....* But the regularization of 2009 showed me that it serves nothing to hope and to wait.

By being together in the café to share their stories and experiences, these sans-papiers discovered the need to form a more permanent group, namely, "Collectif en attente Permis B," where problems and possible strategies could be explored.

This initiative saw the light of day at a moment when the sans-papiers movement was virtually nonexistent. As SPB leader Abas explained, "Those who led the movement in 2009 were regularized and the reality is that, once regularized, the sans-papiers quit the movement and picked up their daily lives." Strict regularization criteria and the administration's lack of capacity to process the applications left many applicants in limbo for years. Confronted with similar stories, associations like Link Meeting and Pigment, which were affiliated with the Beguinage church's head priest, had created a parallel group for undocumented workers named "Collectif travailleurs sans-papiers." As Faisal explained, they felt as though the associations were not representing their experiences well, since they were created on the impetus of social workers and "very much framed in terms of which demands could be made etcetera, *so you could not make the demands you want there.*" Nevertheless, Link Meeting and Pigment offered the logistical and practical assistance necessary to consolidate the collective. After a while, both collectives merged their efforts while trying to safeguard their autonomy.

The categories that the Belgian state created to sort and rank migrant populations initially created internal divisions within their rank and file, as Abas contended:

> Little by little, we realized that ... if we really want to speak for the sans-papiers, we had to involve undocumented migrants who are in all sorts of different procedures. This was a problem we faced in the beginning, namely, that ... *the division between asylum seekers, clandestines, or families created a division within the movement.* In order to really be a collective force, we need to gather our strengths. But assembling everyone is not something that is easily done.

The realization that not all sans-papiers had filed for regularization pushed SPBelgique to expand its scope to include all sans-papiers and demand regularization for all regardless of status. Setting up a "solidarity space" that would enable them to overcome categorical divisions and provide more sta-bility than the relatively unstable and ad hoc groups that had dominated the movement in recent years thus became a top priority.

When the "regulars" who attended the Anchor left and the sans-papiers were handed the keys by the social workers, the tired-looking community center vir-tually transformed into a vibrant solidarity space where information about the political situation, survival strategies, material goods, and services were provided by and for the undocumented community. Abas explained the vision behind this as follows:

> The goal of SPBelgique is to make it a collective, a space for assembling, of encounter, of solidarity, and collective and individual initiative.... It is *a space to live in general, it is a way of living,* not in the sense that we live in the same house, but that it is a space of gathering, where people can form themselves, can inform themselves, all of that. Solidarity is very important, we are all in a precarious position, some more than others, so we have to show solidarity.

The use of the term "solidarity," a concept historically associated with the labor movement, is no coincidence here. SPBelgique collaborated closely with labor unions from the beginning and mimicked their organizing model in various ways. Not surprisingly, the first time I encountered SPBelgique members was during a May 1 rally in the Stalingrad neighborhood. When I hopped off the tram and exited the Brussels South station, I was overwhelmed by the sensory overload of the spectacle on the streets. Like every year, labor union members had mobilized in great numbers to celebrate Labor Day. The city was buzzing with excitement. People were chanting and there was a festive atmosphere with marching bands playing, people drinking beer, and unionists having a laugh. Wading through the crowd, I was looking for signs of SPBelgique's presence. After a while, a performance by a handful of people with a migrant background struck my eye. The performers were standing there in silence with handcuffs on and messages attached to their chest saying, "I work 7 days a week," and "Modern slavery for a Permit B." Meanwhile, I noticed how a man at the scene was actively approaching spectators and providing context to people who seemed interested. Close to the spectacle, Mohammed was selling tea to the spectators from a little stand. I walked up to the stand and asked if I could buy a cup of tea. "Of course, you can. All proceedings go to the sans-papiers, you know, their cause is really important," he replied, handing over the cup. I continued by telling him that I was interested to learn more since I intended to study the movement in Brussels. "You should come to the general meeting of the collective in the Anchor then; we meet there on Thursdays," he replied. He subsequently referred me to Maud, a social worker who filled me in on the details and told me where the meeting would take place.

When I arrived at the Anchor the next week at five p.m., I was greeted by Killian, a social worker. I witnessed how movement members were painting big banners for their next march stating, "3 years of waiting in a democracy (?)." I approached Mehmed and explained the purpose of my visit. He immediately offered me a cup of coffee. "Do I have to pay somewhere?" "No," he laughed "it is free, but you can leave a voluntary contribution there if you like," pointing out a jar with coins on the table. I asked him what they were trying to achieve with the collective. "You see that word, *democracy*," he asked, pointing to the banner. "What does that even stand for when people are being treated as animals, as slaves," he continued. "With the collective, we are trying to show that this is not about 'politics' but about real people." At the start of the meeting, he introduced me and my research as something that could benefit the organization. Immediately afterward, people started questioning me. "What will be the aims of your research?" several people asked me, referring to the demands that I would support. I tried to explain that the goal of my study was to better understand the dynamics of the Belgian sans-papiers movement. "But would you support the regularization of the undocumented?" someone rebutted. I replied that personally, I would support this. This visibly led to relief among the attendees. My "disclosure" of solidarity with the cause was a first and necessary step toward gaining access to and the trust of SPBelgique members.

Abas's statement above that SPBelgique was a "space to live" can be taken quite literally. For example, preparing and sharing food was an important way for SPBelgique to put solidarity into practice and recruit new movement members. Over the course of my fieldwork, I would often hear people share stories of poverty, distress, and extreme precarity. In between meetings, the smokers would stand outside on the sidewalk chatting. Although I did not smoke, I learned to join them because members were more inclined to share their frustrations and despair here. During these smoking sessions, I heard how devastating it was for people to frequently lose their job, not get paid by their employers, get robbed of their belongings, get evicted from the shelters and squats they were staying in, and barely be able to survive without cash. As Mohammed explained, such precarity and lacking everyday needs often stood in the way of effective mobilization:

> Sometimes there are a lot of people who arrive, but this depends on the everyday; *each time we have little problems, but this is caused by having to cope with everyday life for the sans-papiers. He tries to look for food, he needs a place to stay.* Consequently, the majority of the sans-papiers do not have enough time to participate in, for example, a march.

The community meals that were regularly organized by SPBelgique catered to the basic need to feed sans-papiers who were struggling to get by.

The organization of solidarity meals also offered ways for newcomers to integrate themselves into the collective and show their worth. A couple of people would typically oversee the *récup*: the practice of going to local shops and market dealers to request leftover food that could no longer be sold the next day. Others would oversee the cooking. Since I considered this to be a good way to make myself useful to the organization, I volunteered to help in the kitchen. This also offered a good opportunity to get to know new movement members like Omar a bit better. I had first encountered Omar during an SPBelgique protest a couple of weeks earlier. "This is my first protest," he confided to me. "I have only attended a couple of general meetings so far." Since both of us were new to this, he stuck around, eventually grabbing my shoulder and leaning on me while we walked through the city center and loudly chanted slogans like "So-so-so! Solidarité. Avec les Sans-papiers" with the rest of the crowd. I was interested to see what joining the cooking team meant in terms of finding one's place within the organization. That Saturday, I managed to be an hour late when I took a wrong train. "There you finally are," Omar joked on my arrival. "We already thought you were going to bail out on us," Fariss said with a smile. In the kitchen, eight people were working hard to prepare the food. There was a clear hierarchy, with Mohammed being the "chef" and people like me and Fatima put in charge of chopping vegetables. When we had a break, I picked up a guitar and Omar joined in with a *qraqeb*.[1] I also talked with Fatima, who was a new face to me. "I have only started to come to the collective recently," she said. "A friend of mine told me I should come. I can't come to the regular meetings because I work late evenings on most days. But there are many ways to contribute to the movement," she laughed while we made our way back to the kitchen. After a long meeting about organizing a march, everybody was hungry, and the meal was finally ready. I was genuinely surprised by the delicious traditional Moroccan dish that Mohammed had prepared with what seemed at first sight like food waste. During the meal, I recognized many familiar faces from the meetings I had previously attended. However, this time around, the atmosphere was less "tense" than usual, and people seemed more relaxed and outgoing while enjoying the conviviality of the moment (Nowicka and Vertovec 2014). I realized that collective meals like this represented a rare opportunity for these sans-papiers to forget their daily struggle for survival and experience a sense of togetherness. Anouar highlighted how he felt that cooking and distributing food was a highly effective way to generate solidarity for the cause:

> When the sans-papiers prepare food for others, irrespective of their situation, documented or undocumented, Belgians or people from a different origin, this surprises people.... *It is symbolic and it provides much visibility to the movement.* If we do not achieve our big goals, there are always smaller things that can be done on the side that can provide an impetus for creativity.

Sometimes the cooking team would use produce from Humana Terre, a community gardening project that three SPBelgique members had initiated on the side at a site of the Free University of Brussels in May 2012. The goal of the project was to investigate alternative ways to "live properly and in dignity" without papers, through gardening. The sans-papiers were given permission by the university to take care of an old, neglected orchard. A small group of sans-papiers started working there every week and planted tomatoes, kale, red peppers, and pumpkins. A greenhouse was built, and weeds were removed. No pesticides were used; everything was produced organically. On July 15, 2012, two months after the project started, the garden was opened to the public and people could visit for a drink and a tour of the garden. In the months after that, the sans-papiers took initiatives including building a traditional Moroccan bread oven made from stone and clay. They also participated in activities such as a festival around the right to food, and they organized "dialogue picnics," where they discussed experiences about living together in Brussels. Children from the school across the street were regularly invited to visit the garden and to learn about gardening, as well as the situation of the sans-papiers. Activities like this could also lead to recruitment, because they demonstrated the power of "horizontal solidarity" (Swerts and Oosterlynck 2020). As Abas explained, "It is not like we are distributing flyers on the street, and we are going to talk about raising awareness concerning the cause of the sans-papiers." Instead, working in the collective garden allowed the sans-papiers to experience feelings of agency and self-determination. Mohammed corroborated this sentiment:

> Motivated, the sans-papiers takes his destiny in his own hands; he takes initiatives, not waiting until the administration says what they have to say, but we have to show initiative.... We give to associations that prepare meals for people who don't have the means, sans-papiers, everyone, and that's something we share with others. *It is the idea behind this initiative, to share with others, even when you don't have a lot of means, you share.*

SPBelgique not only recruited potential members via preparing and distributing food but also by distributing information and assistance to people who were in precarious situations. Admittedly, organizations like Link Meeting also functioned as places where the sans-papiers could freely walk in and get formal advice from professional social workers on how to navigate the various official channels and services available to them throughout the city. No matter how crucial this type of assistance, many sans-papiers readily acknowledged the limits of what social workers could do to support their quest to obtain legal status. Moreover, some sans-papiers actively mistrusted social workers and their tendency to steer the "future orientation" of individual migrants into the direction of "voluntary return" (Cleton and Schweitzer 2021). By comparison, the assistance that SPBelgique provided to newcomers was radically different in nature, as exemplified by the following excerpt from their website:

> You have just arrived in Belgium, either irregularly or with a visa that will soon expire. You are or will soon become a sans-papiers, meaning you will not have authorization to stay legally on Belgian territory. You have two possibilities: either submit an application for asylum and thereby request the protection of the Belgian State, or remain in hiding. *If you decide to remain in hiding, SPBelgique wants to offer you advice, addresses, and possibilities of procedures to be initiated. All the advice you will find here is based on the experience of former sans-papiers who, like you, have been confronted with all the problems you will encounter: where to stay, how to be regularized, how to move around, where to go for help.*

As this example shows, the service provision that SPBelgique provided to undocumented members was deeply rooted in experiential knowledge. During my fieldwork, I overheard people share information about odd jobs, housing conditions in squats across the city, raids at certain metro stops, what to do when you had to go the emergency room, and many more everyday problems. SPBelgique thus provided a space for sans-papiers to share firsthand experience with one another. This was not a trivial accomplishment given the relatively hostile context they were operating in. When a particularly heated argument emerged about the question of whether it would make any difference to organize yet another protest, Abel stood up and reminded everyone how things used to be. "Before, we could not even stand outside for a chat with a couple of people, or we would be chased away or reported to the police by neighbors," he exclaimed in a loud voice. "Here, we can *talk as sans-papiers*. Look around the table. There are at least twenty people here. We should all be grateful that we have a place to meet and discuss the situation in all tranquility now."

Training

SPBelgique not only symbolized a "space for living" in solidarity but also created an activist infrastructure where activists could discuss mobilizing strategies, produce innovative scripts and repertoires, and turn recruits into movement members via training (Karaliotas 2023). Whereas training took place in a very deliberate and structured way in IYJL, it was in a much less formal and somewhat haphazard way at SPBelgique. Discussions on membership mainly revolved around the criteria that should be used to determine whether someone was "worthy" of membership. Presence and "being there" occupied an even more important role in this respect compared with IYJL. With a leadership that was more hierarchically organized and with greater dissent about the general strategy that should be followed within the collective, SPBelgique struggled to achieve a smooth, workable model for training activists. Hence, training tended to occur "on the spot" through a "learning-by-doing" philosophy. As will be apparent in the next section, political actions like protests and marches thus not only served to make activists' claims heard but simultaneously fulfilled recruitment and training purposes.

Above, I discussed how SPBelgique was able to recruit potential members by creating a space of solidarity that helped the sans-papiers navigate the obstacles they face in their everyday lives in the city and escape everyday precarity by fostering conviviality. Nevertheless, SPBelgique aspired to be more than a solidarity space where the sans-papiers could experience a sense of belonging. It also wanted to create a political dynamic that would allow them to break the deadlock and achieve collective regularization for all. This is exemplified by the following internal communication to its membership:

> Our starting point was to have a space for freedom and creation, and our goal was and will always be to get out of this situation of precariousness and illegality. From meeting to meeting, we moved forward with our differences and with our personal miseries. Our quest for papers is not an obsession, because for us, papers are only a pathway to rights.... *It's true: for the moment we haven't changed anything in the sad reality of our situation, but we don't forget all that we have built up till now, and above all, the group that we are building together. Day after day we discover the true meaning of the collective. Despite all the difficulties, we have succeeded in setting up an alternative living space, a space for political work, a space for meeting and opening up.*

Building a "space for political work" also meant that SPBelgique functioned as a one-stop shop for getting information about the latest developments in the political situation and the relative success of various regularization strategies, as well as circulating rumors about pending regularizations. On a personal level, for example, a movement member once testified about what he had to undergo during an interview to determine whether his relationship with a Belgian citizen was real, including the types of questions the government official had asked and how he had prepared for these questions. In a similar vein, I heard testimonies of people who had tried to bribe government officials and paid employers thousands of euros for fake employment contracts to support their regularization dossier. On a collective level, movement leaders often reported back from meetings with labor unions and allied organizations and fed their members updates on discretionary practices at the Office of Alien Affairs. Membership in SPBelgique was thus not only important to receive assistance in overcoming everyday precarity but also to help the sans-papiers fine-tune personal regularization strategies.

The charter that had been drafted by the founding members served as the "official" touchstone detailing rules and norms about membership (see Box 8.1).

BOX 8.1 Articles 5–8 of the SPBelgique Charter

Article 5
The collective is composed of three categories of members: founding members, active members, and adherent members.

Article 6
The founding members are the persons who have contributed to the foundation of the collective.

Article 7
An active member of SPBelgique is any person who accepts to adhere freely to the movement on condition that he *commits himself to respect the provisions of the charter and the internal regulations of the collective and that he takes a share of the responsibilities.*

Article 8
Any person or group of persons who adheres to the ideals and the charter of the collective and who brings contributions in the form of advice, collaboration, or participation in activities and actions is an adherent member.

The multilayered construction of membership at SPBelgique differed from IYJL's distinction between members based on citizenship status. The "founding members" mentioned in Article 6 were the de facto leaders of the collective who called the shots. Citizen allies or *soutiens* largely fell into the third category mentioned in Article 8, in which the Pigment social workers who supported the collective had more influence on the organization than regular *soutiens* who supported the movement because of their political convictions.

Without a doubt, the most contentious category was the second one, comprising "active members." Before I even attended my first meeting, social worker Maud had warned me that there were tensions between founding members and newcomers about the meaning of membership. "Some sans-papiers only come to the meetings to ask for information, without participating in actions. It tires the founding members that there are still sans-papiers out there who do not know their rights," she told me. However, tensions about membership extended beyond lacking awareness about rights. Suspicions were voiced on several occasions that certain sans-papiers opportunistically tried to get themselves on SPBelgique's "membership list" without contributing anything. Later, I learned that this stemmed from earlier rounds of targeted regularizations, when the government had made use of lists of church occupiers (Siméant 1998, 145). This insight became clear to me at a meeting to evaluate a protest that had taken place the week before. There was a general sense of disappointment about the small turnout. "We cannot make political demands if so few people turn up," Mehmed yelled, smashing his hand repeatedly on the table while talking. The room was silent, and nobody dared to speak up for a while. "I have sent 250 text messages by phone, but there is a problem with the people on the list," Ilyas finally said. Next, Adil started sharing his experiences in a squat where he had stayed for the past six months. "I left because the people at the squat were not interested in seeing this as an opportunity to raise awareness and just considered the squat to be a place to sleep. There were also problems with drug dealing and stealing," he said, using this as an example to illustrate the broader problems with the mentality of certain sans-papiers. "The only solution is to make lists of members *to safeguard quality*," Mehmed replied, "lists that we can give to the Office of Alien Affairs with two standards: one including those who *really* participated in the collective and one including those who did not."

The theme of "quality of membership" would continue to dominate SPBelgique's agenda in meetings to come. In the absence of any real political victories for their demands in the first two years of SPBelgique's existence, attention was turned inward to restructuring the organization. During the first restructuring meeting, Abas explained what the goal was. "We need to involve more families," Rashid interrupted him. "You know, cousins, nieces, uncles, parents regardless of their status." "Or maybe we can undertake actions around the local elections?" Mehdi suggested, before being stopped by Abas. "No, we are not here to talk about actions but about the organization and membership," he replied. "It seems like people fail to understand the purpose of the meeting," Anouar said, before translating and repeating what Abas had said into Arabic. When misunderstandings about the purpose of the meeting were finally cleared, a heated debate about membership emerged. "We need to make membership cards, and people have to pay for membership so that we can hire lawyers in case of arrests," Fariss suggested. A fierce discussion on the exact amount that members should be charged took off. "But we do not only need members to pay, we also need to keep attendance to see whether people are *effectively coming* to meetings and actions," Anouar suggested. In the end, the official membership cards and fees would never see the light of day, and the only records kept of members remained the informal registration lists for actions like the Solidarity March (see below). These discussions nevertheless demonstrate the sensitivity of the issue of membership, the recurring frustrations about the lack of commitment of potential members, and the efforts made to come up with new ways to convey organizational expectations to aspiring members.

Many "restructuring" meetings ensued in the months afterward. While these meetings were meant to improve decision-making and divide tasks among "active" members more efficiently, they also sparked fierce internal debates, personal vendettas, and fallouts between people. Several committees had been created that would take charge of mobilization/action, cultural and educational events, media and communication, and juridical aid. At a follow-up meeting with about forty attendees, the assigned leaders of each committee were supposed to report back. Fatima started to become visibly agitated and interrupted the reporting as follows: "I have been in Belgium for four years now, we have already wasted enough time. [starts raising her voice] *We should not sit around here restructuring but need to take action! I propose that we choose a building right now and occupy it!*" The founding members were visibly frustrated by this turn of events, and Anouar tried to explain again why SPBelgique needed to be organized in a more democratic fashion internally to "claim a more dignified life" externally. However, Adil ignored Anouar's intervention, stating that "I definitely do not want to criticize your actions, but I think we are not going to 'win' anything with all these committees, *we don't have to organize just for the sake of organizing.*" When I looked around the room, I saw several members nodding and silently concurring. Adil's statement thus voiced the concerns of members who considered anything other than political action to be a waste of time. "I agree that taking action is necessary," Abas rebutted, "but occupying buildings does not always lead to results. Look at the recent hunger strikes, for example, actions need to be planned well." Ironically, the issue of restructuring the organization would soon fade into the background as SPBelgique became preoccupied with participating in the European March and organizing the Solidarity March. Abas later acknowledged that there was a cyclical character to these internal dynamics:

> At a certain moment you feel the willingness of people who have enough energy to change everything, but at other moments you feel the emptiness. *It almost becomes a cycle. It repeats itself, but the fact that we go forward in spite of that means that it is not a closed cycle, that we can break it from time to time.* Right now, it is really concrete actions that create a dynamic. Sometimes it collapses afterwards, but that is the way it is.

Besides debates about membership, the internal meetings of the collective were dominated by discussions about tactics. There was a clear split between members who figured that mass demonstrations were the key to success and others who remained faithful to the tried and tested formula of "occupations + hunger strikes = regularization." The SPBelgique leadership was convinced that this formula no longer worked. For example, when asked what he thought about hunger strikes, Faisal said, "I am going to tell you one thing. *Doing hunger strikes worked before, now it doesn't work.* When we assess the situation, we see that there are people that have incurable diseases due to hunger strikes…. The last hunger strike of one hundred days did not lead to anything." This assessment was shared by Abas, who stated the following:

> Unfortunately … hunger strikes do not work anymore, they reinforce what is already going on and always lead people to leave the movement.… The problem here in Belgium is that the sans-papiers cannot get it out of their heads, … they believe that it is the only way of struggling that is able to bring people together, and *we have had plenty of discussions within the collective where people accuse us of not being engaged enough because we do not want to organize a hunger strike.*

From an organizational standpoint, the founding members decided that hunger strikes would be excluded from SPBelgique's political repertoire. This is reflected in Article 4 of the Organizational Charter, which only lists "peaceful demonstration, conference-debates, socio-cultural activities, information and awareness campaigns, sit-ins and lobbying" as the "modes of action" of the collective. Mimicking the organizational model of the labor union, SPBelgique's leadership put their faith in "showing their presence on the street" by organizing events and marches throughout the country. In the next section, I will shed light on the question of how "active members" were mobilized to take part in such actions.

Mobilization

SPBelgique recruited potential movement members by creating a solidarity space and trained aspiring activists by immersing them in internal discussions on restructuring the organization and tactics. Participating in these often-contentious discussions made clear to aspiring activists what SPBelgique demanded from "active members," namely: physical presence, commitment to the cause, and a supportive attitude toward decisions made by the leadership. There was no comparable selection process at SPBelgique to the one IYJL relied on to scout potential activists. Anyone who was motivated enough to participate in actions like protests or marches was, in principle, free to join. This relative openness stems from the fact that SPBelgique placed more emphasis on publicly displaying and performing their collectivity, than on highlighting personal activists' stories or episodes of individual risk-taking. Nevertheless, beyond that notable difference, the marches and events that SPBelgique relied on also provided a stage for the sans-papiers to draw public attention to their discursive, embodied, and emotional lived experiences of illegality. As embodied acts, protests and marches primarily aimed to allow the sans-papiers to symbolically step out of the shadows and gain visibility. In the search for ways to gain recognition as political actors, the Belgian labor movement demonstrated to the sans-papiers that mobilizing "the masses" could lead to public legitimacy. SPBelgique member Zouhair expressed this conviction as follows:

> We want to do something to claim rights, but we need to be patient, *we also need a quantity of people.* The only problem in SPBelgique is that there are people who come but they are afraid that there are going to be police controls during demonstrations, they are afraid that they will be arrested. But you should not be afraid.... Struggle is the only way to get rights; we need to carry out demonstrations, and we need to be with many people. *That is the first condition, be with many people.*

SPBelgique activists thus relied heavily on embodied enactment to show themselves, convey their frustrations and anger, and spread their message of solidarity to *soutiens*, the general public, politicians, and the media. The following excerpt from an interview with SPBelgique member Akash demonstrates how "showing yourself" to gain visibility is key:

> *You have to show yourself to the authorities; you have to show that there are lots of people* who are really in danger, in an inhumane situation that no-one can even believe because they work in the black economy, they don't have a place to sleep, they cannot go to school.... The march is a way to show yourself, to show your image, that we are in a big group, that we are united, that we have strength, that we are well organized. So it is very important symbolically.

In Chapter 4, I already explained how struggles over representation unfolded during the organization of the Solidarity March. Here, I would like to shift attention to how the march set in motion processes through which organizational members gradually became transformed into full-blown activists (or "militants," as SPBelgique put it). At the time, the march's organizing committee considered it to be imperative to "begin with a convergence at the very heart of the movement."[2] This emphasis on overcoming differences rather than making concrete demands is illustrated by the marching call:[3]

> We, migrants or settlers, with or without papers, militants, solidarity, and rebellious men and women have decided to march through Belgium for a month in April 2013. A march for dignity.... The "migration policy" today comes down to

a true manhunt at the expense of dignity and freedom. This manhunt is justified by an anti-migration discourse, based on xenophobia, and manifests itself
in repressive safety practices. Just like other people in a precarious situation,
unemployed, homeless, benefit recipients, workers, employees, etc., migrants
and undocumented migrants are designated as scapegoats.... *We cannot just let
this happen, and we want to make visible the violence that affects women, men,
and children in the name of security and the economy.*

Maria, an undocumented Latina member, explained "why we say it is the march
of solidarity with and without papers" as follows:[4]

The primary objective here is to stimulate encounters between undocumented
and documented people.... *But gaining visibility through marching and showing
oneself is not enough, we also need to show an image that is more worthy, more
valorizing, more "real" in the end, of who the sans-papiers are day in, day out
and that our struggle is significant. We are here, we do not leave our heads down,
and we continue.*

Marching is thus a performative way to show the Belgian community that the
sans-papiers are not afraid to show their faces and raise their voices in public
spaces (Swerts 2017). Walking through the streets hand in hand signals that they
are supported by a wide range of sympathizers. The passing by of the marchers
represents a festive display of collective strength and an appropriation of public
space that temporarily "disrupts" everyday life. I witnessed this firsthand at the
start of the march in April 2013. A diverse group of protesters marched side by
side as they passed by "The Little Castle," the refugee reception center in the
heart of Brussels. The protesters carried banners depicting migrants with taped-
up mouths, symbolizing the lack of voice that characterized the situation of the
sans-papiers in Belgium. Spectators who tried to figure out what was going on
found clues in slogans like "*Paroles sans-papiers*" (words without papers), "*Ce
n'est pas mon destin d'etre clandestine*" (it is not my destiny to be clandestine)
and "We are not dangerous, we are in danger." Over the course of the next few
weeks, the marchers walked from city to city to organize encounters with other
sans-papiers and their allies, share stories and experiences, and invite them to
join the movement.

Symbolically, however, the act of marching and the unplanned meetings and
encounters were perhaps even more important than the planned meetings and
encounters. Over the course of the days, a marching community formed with
its own rules and a division of labor where "everyone has their place."[5] At the
beginning of each marching day, roles like timekeeping, translation, note-taking,
mediation, writing in the march diary, newcomer reception, cooking, and so on

were distributed. By getting a "role" in the marching community, sans-papiers could experience what it felt like to be recognized and valued for their contributions to the collective. The embodied act of marching also helped to reinforce feelings of solidarity among participants. For example, on April 9, the marchers embarked on a 15.4-kilometer walk between Willebroek and Mechelen. The following "song" the marchers composed is testament to the sense of community that emerged (Marching Diary, April 10, 2013):

> *Travail au noir,* (informal work,)
> *mariage blanc,* (sham marriage,)
> *Où va ma vie,* (where is my life going,)
> *en attendant?* (while waiting?)
> *Travail au noir,* (informal work,)
> *mariage blanc,* (sham marriage,)
> *en attendant,* (while waiting,)
> *c'est pas marrant....* (it's no fun....)

Although hardly uplifting, the song demonstrates how the march allowed for collective reflection by the sans-papiers on daily routines. In the march's diary entry for that day, the reporter described that "*While walking, the memories come up,* because many of us have traversed several countries by foot in order to arrive in Belgium" (Marching Diary, April 9, 2013). Indeed, fellow marchers shared their migration stories walking side by side. Younes, for example, told me how it took him three attempts to reach Europe. During the first attempt, he was locked up in prison in Greece for six months. The second time, he was detained in Switzerland before being deported. He only reached Belgium after a long drive hidden in the back of a truck via Turkey and Greece. For people like Younes, the march symbolized his migration journey and represented his transition from a regular member to a "militant."

I experienced the mobilizing impact of marching during the journey between Leuven and Brussels. This section was especially important since it was the longest walk, at twenty-seven kilometers. During the march, I had a long conversation with Muhammad. Originally from Algeria, Muhammad had been in Belgium since 2006. He had participated in the church occupations organized by UDEP, but after these occupations ended, he was no longer active in the movement. He lived in a squat in Anderlecht, and when he heard about the march, he immediately knew it was something he wanted to participate in. Muhammad stood out from the rest of the marchers because he was physically disabled. He told me he had a serious health issue that caused his legs to be partly paralyzed. Because of this, we offered to drive him around during difficult parts of the march. When I saw him again that day in Leuven, he proudly told me he had already traveled fifteen kilometers between Mechelen and Sint-Niklaas. He said that he was very tired because they had been sleeping in poor conditions. I had experienced this myself in Ghent, where I spent the night together with the other marchers. Local activists had arranged for us to sleep in a squat, where we had to sleep together in a small room with about twenty people. There was no heating provided, and it was literally freezing that night. The day after, I was physically exhausted. The marchers had been sleeping in these conditions for almost two weeks when we started the final march from Leuven to Brussels. When I asked Muhammad how he felt about the upcoming twenty-seven kilometers, he said: "I want to complete the entire march. I haven't been wearing this T-shirt of the march for nothing." Marching together with about sixty people that day for hours, I experienced firsthand what the march meant to the participants. Participating in it was a step into the unknown for most of the marchers. They revealed themselves as sans-papiers in public, and they experienced the support of the marching community in the process. This is what Muhammad tried to communicate to me during his final kilometers. "I am glad that I have participated in this march," he told me. "The march is like a movie; everyone has their role." Muhammad had been one of the most helpful marchers in terms of cooking, cleaning, and so on. He clearly enjoyed taking responsibilities and being part of a group, and the experience contrasted with his everyday life experience. He told me that he often felt isolated because of his disability. Before he got sick, he could still go out and work, but now he had lost his job. When Muhammad finally arrived in Brussels twenty minutes after the rest of the group, everyone cheered and clapped. This example demonstrates how the embodied act of marching garnered feelings of agency.

Even during the march, however, the solidarity the marchers experienced had already been put to the test on multiple occasions. Earlier disagreements about the meaning of "active membership" and tactics had far from vanished. On the contrary, the following entry from the marching diary illustrates their continued relevance:

> *It seems that some marchers do not yet know the objectives of the march!* Some remind us that we do not participate in the march for tourism but to raise awareness, be heard, exchange, so as to be more creative and come up with new forms of struggle, to have greater visibility, create a national collective, organize national actions and protests.

The discussion about "motivation" would linger on continuously during the three weeks. For example, when I talked to Muhammad, he told me he was "really motivated, in contrast to others." When I subsequently talked to Bashir, a newcomer, he confided in me that "to be honest, I am on holiday here, I am not interested in the march." Similarly, Bacri told me that he had only arrived in Belgium four months beforehand and the march "was a good opportunity to get to know Belgium." Several SPBelgique members also objected to the strategy of the march, arguing that "we need to occupy a church and demand regularization, not talk all day." For these critics, the march lacked the dramatic effect needed to "shake things up." A group of dissenting activists considered the march to be a toothless tiger, and members of the rivaling collective of undocumented Guineans tried to recruit participants for a hunger strike during the march instead. However, the activists who raised this issue were quickly silenced by SPBelgique's leadership. "The organizers are exploiting us, we cannot even talk about hunger strikes while they are getting subsidized over our heads," SPBelgique member Anouar complained to me at a certain point. Abas had accused him and Akash of maintaining a secret list of people who wanted to join a hunger strike after the march. Recurring internal conflicts about membership, worthiness, and tactics thus demonstrate the fragility of precarious agency.

The most pronounced illustration of this fragility was undeniably the "We are all Fariss" campaign, designed to stop his deportation (see Preface). Even though Fariss had participated in the European March and had subsequently turned into a militant who used his experience to "lead by example," this did not prevent him from getting arrested for a minor traffic violation. When I talked to Redouan during a protest in support of Fariss, he told me had been able to briefly talk to him over the phone the day before. "I advised him to start a hunger strike. I know someone who has been released from secure detention when he did so. When you are held in captivity, this falls under the responsibility of the government. Once the doctor decides that Fariss is in danger, he could be released," he claimed. However, when Fariss in effect refused to eat, the immigration officers at the detention center rescheduled his deportation to an earlier date. His physical resistance was thereby rendered null and void. The deportation of Fariss left deep emotional scars among the SPBelgique members he left behind in Brussels. Faisal put it as follows:

> Fariss was a failure for us. A failure because we tried to find solutions with SPBelgique for the deportation. One of the demands of SPBelgique has always been to stop deportations; they are inhumane, so it is really not a good solution. When he was arrested, we showed solidarity with him. *We tried our best, and it was really a failure in the end, we could not prevent the deportation.*

During the first meeting after Fariss's deportation, a sense of defeat and desperation was hanging in the air. "What are we going to do now," I asked Abas. "Nothing, of course," he replied, shrugging his shoulders. "There is nothing we can do." Only eight people showed up that day for SPBelgique's meeting. "People are saying that there is no sense in organizing further after Fariss's deportation,"

Anouar claimed. "Everyone needs time to process things and reevaluate their participation." A prolonged silence ensued. "Maybe we could talk about how everyone feels about what happened as a group," I hesitantly suggested. "No!" Abas replied suddenly and angrily. "Fariss is not the problem; it is the *mentality* of the sans-papiers." Sisokko, a new Guinean member, replied by saying: "It is just that the dynamic of the meetings is bad, we need to know what people really think and communicate better." Afterward, Abas concluded the meeting by saying that Fariss's deportation did not necessarily need to herald the demise of SPBelgique, but it was possible "if we do nothing and let it happen."

Conclusion

In this chapter, I have argued that self-organizations such as SPBelgique function as activist infrastructures that stimulate precarious agency by recruiting potential members, training potential activists, and mobilizing sans-papiers to take action in Brussels. Political hermeneutics plays a crucial role in accounting for the process through which the sans-papiers become "militants." Diverging discursive, embodied, and emotional lived experiences of illegality between the sans-papiers and undocumented youth in part help to explain the subtle—and not so subtle—differences between SPBelgique and IYJL in organizational rituals, practices, and strategies. Shared experiences of criminalization, stigmatization, immobility, fear, and frustration also formed the experiential backbone that sparked the self-organization of the sans-papiers. However, categorical differences within the undocumented community and the lack of institutional receptivity hindered their efforts to flesh out a successful organizing model. SPBelgique's organizing model, rooted in autogestion, solidarity, and presence, tended to overshadow personal stories. Deeply engrained emotions such as frustration and anger were therefore hard to efficiently channel into political action. While stories and emotions were still important drivers for each of the three stages of political subjectivation, they faded into the background in favor of embodied modes of organizing. Physical presence, bodies acting in unison, and collectively "being in motion" instead took center stage when recruiting, training, and mobilizing the sans-papiers at SPBelgique.

First, gathering in cafés over a drink and exchanging stories over communal meals allowed the sans-papiers to experience a sense of community and recognition of their lived experiences. SPBelgique functioned as a solidarity space where people in precarious positions managed themselves, took care of others by providing hot meals, shared tips about housing and work opportunities, and lended an ear to each other's woes and worries. Sans-papiers generally recruited other sans-papiers via word of mouth or personal referrals. Given the extreme precarity that characterizes everyday life in Brussels, being able to reduce dependency via autogestion and enjoy conviviality was often enough to "tie" potential movement members to the organization. Feelings of frustration, compassion, and hope again proved to be the indispensable glue that caused the sans-papiers to stick together under duress.

Second, becoming a member at SPBelgique required recruits to enter the contested terrain of moral obligations and mutual trust and distrust within the collective. Members were expected to have an "active" predisposition and contribute time and energy to the cause, while sidelining their personal worries. "Worthy" SPBelgique members had to adhere to the organizational belief that collective solutions for regularization were preferable to personal solutions. Accusations of "lacking membership quality" were often rooted in suspicions that certain sans-papiers cared more about their name on the participant list than about participating. Active members who aspired to become activists had to prove their solidarity with and commitment to the organization by fulfilling organizational tasks and "voting with their feet," while persistent discussions about tactics were silenced in the name of undermining solidarity.

Third, "active" members transformed into "militants" by participating in the embodied act of marching through the streets. By displaying their capacity to resist mobility restrictions, the sans-papiers aimed to disrupt the status quo. Protests, occupations, sit-ins, border crossings, and marches were performed in public space to gain visibility and claim their right to presence. The experience of revealing themselves as sans-papiers and displaying collective strength was empowering for the activists involved. However, as Fariss's arrest and deportation shows (see Preface), the wall of precarious agency that sans-papiers activists carefully constructed around themselves easily came crumbling down when the state responded forcefully.

The insights from this chapter have wider implications for the sociological literature on the body as well. The sans-papiers' lived experiences of illegality demonstrate how undocumented immigrants' bodies are subjected to the power of the state (see Chapter 6). Yet at the same time, theories of the "disciplined" or "mirroring" body do not adequately capture the agentic qualities of the body. It is precisely because power relations are inscribed upon the body that the body can become a potential site of resistance. Evoking Butler's theory of gender performativity, legal status, and citizenship equally depend on series of repeated performances (Butler 1990). SPBelgique activists showed their collective strength by engaging in bodily acts that ranged from being self-sufficient, occupying buildings, and volunteering to marching and border crossings. The sans-papiers thus gained precarious agency by engaging in bodily acts of resignification that disrupt the series of repeated performances whereby citizenship as we know it is upheld and publicly display their capacity to act upon the world.

Conclusion

The other face of citizenship

Citizenship means to be recognized, I think, but at the same time I don't see citizenship as something that I can get. And so maybe citizenship to me is not necessarily my end goal, like, to become a citizen or to define what citizenship means.… I don't know what it means to be a citizen really.… What we need to make people understand is that to have a Social Security number does not define who we are. It doesn't define how well we work, it doesn't define how well we drive, it doesn't define how good of a student we are, or if we're criminals or not. And I think if we're able to do that, we can redefine citizenship, or change citizenship. (Raquel, IYJL)

We are not recognized. We are not citizens. Yet when you look at the everyday life of a sans-papiers, his integration into society, his social life, even his job, then he lives the life of a citizen. A sans-papiers is a consumer, he pays his food, his rent, his transportation, like a normal citizen. He has friends, a social life, sometimes a love life. He has neighbors, he can get involved in different associations, in different struggles. All this is real but informal. *The citizenship of the undocumented migrant is real but informal.* It is only once regularized, once provided with papers, that a sans-papiers is able to formally acquire this "citizenship" that he or she was already practicing. (Tarik, SPBelgique)

The two quotes above exemplify how IYJL and SPBelgique members Raquel and Tarik understand the meaning of citizenship. As becomes evident from their statements, their relationship with citizenship is a complicated love-hate one. For Raquel and Tarik, citizenship is both a blessing and a curse. From their perspective, citizenship is not an ideal to live up to or a moral standard for how members of society ought to behave. It also does not represent the pinnacle of liberal democracy and human rights that it is made out to be. On the contrary, lived experiences of illegality have caused citizenship to become associated

Citizen X. Thomas Swerts, Oxford University Press. © Thomas Swerts (2026).
DOI: 10.1093/9780197844038.003.0010

with a defective, crumbling institution that upholds the exclusion of, legitimizes state violence against, and produces social injustice for undocumented communities. At the same time, it expresses a personal aspiration to become a "full" member of society and "move on" with their lives. The future inclusion into the realm of citizenship remains something that is out of reach for them; an enigmatic, almost utopian construct that requires a different ordering of society that they may or may not be able to realize. In many ways, as Tarik put it, undocumented migrants already live "the life of a citizen," yet their presence and contributions to society are misrecognized by the outside world. Citizenship tends to be portrayed as a cure-all that would solve most if not all the problems they face in everyday life. However, their struggle over citizenship is not an "end goal" in itself, as it supersedes the question of legal recognition through rights. While citizenship might form the horizon for undocumented activism on both sides of the Atlantic, undocumented activities like Tarik and Raquel are uniquely placed to peek beyond the horizon. That is because the precarious agency that undocumented migrants gain by becoming activists not only encourages them to challenge citizenship as we know it but also, as Raquel put it, to "redefine" and "change" citizenship all together. "Citizen X" thus stands at the epicenter of contemporary struggles over citizenship. This book contends that, at a deeper level, these struggles are *struggles over the meaning of membership of the rapidly changing, globalizing, and essentially migratory world that we inhabit.* Below, I first reiterate why the sociological perspective on precarious agency developed in this book allows us to unravel processes of political subject formation as situated and dynamic, thereby sidestepping the analytical trap of presuming the disruptive capacity of undocumented activists ab initio. Next, I reflect on how undocumented activists mount a hermeneutical challenge to citizenship as we know it that erodes prevailing understandings of citizenship and sets in motion citizenship transformation from below. Finally, I use the experience of doing this transatlantic ethnography to plea for the need to collectively construct a truly global sociology of noncitizenship capable of overcoming methodological nationalism and state centrism.

A situated perspective on precarious agency

Undocumented migrants do not become activists out of thin air. In the introductory chapter, I outlined why undocumented activism is unusual and unexpected from a political and citizenship standpoint. Scholarship informed by post-foundational political philosophy and critical citizenship studies has rightfully identified the undocumented as a group in society that can have a profound impact on the transformation of citizenship and democracy *once they are politicized* (Isin and Nielsen 2008; Rancière 1999, 2010). However, there is a tendency in the critical literature on disruptive politics, acts of citizenship, and immigrant mobilizations to evade the question of politicization by either overemphasizing the constraining power of structure or artificially conflating the disruptive power of agency. In this book, I argue that gaining a better understanding of the processes whereby undocumented migrants become activists first and foremost require us to treat their agency as the *explanans*, rather than the *explanandum*. The situated perspective on precarious agency introduced in this book does just that, since it traces the roots of this agency to lived experiences of precarity that can be transformed collectively into the fuel that fires up mobilization. This process is essentially situated and dynamic, as it takes place under circumstances that are specific to the political contexts wherein undocumented migrants are embedded and it is responsive to changes and developments within those contexts. Furthermore, it puts the spotlight on self-organizations as activist infrastructures where the politicization and transformation of lived experiences of illegality into shared understandings capable of steering political action takes place.

The insights this book contains on precarious agency therefore also speak toward the classical structure-agency debate that has dominated sociology for decades (Sewell 1992). There are three analytical approaches to the traditional chasm between agency and structure: first, to emphasize the power of structure over agency, second, to stress the supremacy of individual agency over social forces, and third, to integrate structure and agency in a single theoretical perspective. Most contemporary authors employ a variation of the third option, implying that structure and agency are two sides of the same coin. However, even within such integrated perspectives, the emphasis on individual agency overshadows the possibility of collective agency. Precarious agency contributes to the further refining of this integrated perspective by demonstrating that precarity can be *collectively* transformed into agency within the confines of activist infrastructures that effectively turn undocumented migrants into fully-fledged activists. The existing empirical literature on undocumented activism roughly falls into two camps that have different interpretations of the possibilities for undocumented migrants to challenge the status quo.

On the one side, "structuralists" tend to regard undocumented activists as constricted agents who are locked into reproducing prevailing understandings of citizenship. This reproduction is understood as an inevitable outcome of actions that take place because they operate in a field that dictates a universe of "political possibles" (Bourdieu 1998, 460). Even when undocumented activists collectively intend to disrupt this field or claim to be motivated by a deeply emotional commitment to change, the power of structure limits what they can say, think, feel, and do. In the camp of "structuralists," we find studies arguing that undocumented activists can only "prove" their moral deservingness by demonstrating how they fit understandings of the "good citizen," the "exemplary student," or the "hard worker" that are culturally dominant in the national context in which they operate (Chauvin and Garcés-Mascareñas 2014). Furthermore, these studies argue that self-organizations are prone to becoming overpowered by well-established CSOs that dominate the field and co-opt their efforts to further their political agenda. Pursuing structural opportunities also risks forcing "less deserving" immigrants even further into the margins (Nicholls 2013). While this perspective contains important insights about the power of social reproduction, it leaves little to no room for marginalized populations such as the undocumented to steer their own boat and sail an independent course toward societal transformation.

On the other side, "autonomists" tend to propagate a romanticized view of undocumented activists as political subjects who can seemingly "break their chains" at will and collectively bring about the downfall of "citizenship as we know it" in a revolutionary endgame. The disruption of prevailing understandings of citizenship is understood as the quasi-automatic outcome of any attempt that undocumented activists make to speak or act up. Scholars in this camp argue that undocumented immigrants' protests are "disruptive" because they "rupture or break the given orders, practices and habitus" (Isin and Nielsen 2008, 36), and announce a different logic of ordering "in the name of equality" (Dikec 2017, 52). Even mundane, day-to-day practices and experiments through which undocumented activists try to lead a "normal" life become interpreted as expressions of prefigurative political imaginaries and "citizenship from below." In the camp of autonomists, instances of mobilization are typically analyzed as standalone cases that "prove" the capacity of undocumented migrants to resist their illegalized status and challenge the status quo, without assessing what preceded and followed these actions. Furthermore, little attention is paid by autonomists to the impact that national and local contexts have on undocumented activists' "acts of citizenship," or to the constraining effects of the fields in which self-organizations operate. Heavily influenced by post-foundational theories of political subjectivation, autonomists thus take the agency of undocumented activists for granted by presupposing the capacity for political disruption.

"Victim" and "hero" tropes in academic scholarship stand in the way of painting a more theoretically and empirically nuanced analysis of the processes through which undocumented migrants become activists. *This book bridges the gap between structuralists and autonomists by uncovering that the processes whereby undocumented migrants gain precarious agency depend on their ability to collectively turn lived-through experiences of vulnerability into strengths.* Precarious agency acknowledges that the structural position of undocumented migrants "in-between" societal inclusion and exclusion provides them with a unique vantage point to understand and act on the world. The partial inclusion and partial exclusion that undocumented migrants experience in interaction with formal institutions allow them to create an intimate understanding of what it means to be accepted into and rejected from the privileged "citizenship club." It also reveals the invisible, symbolic borders and boundaries that are continuously enacted and reproduced in the city by street-level bureaucrats, professionals, employers, citizens, and other inhabitants of the "formal" world. It further allows the undocumented to experience firsthand how these symbolic borders and boundaries can be permeated, transgressed, and crossed in meaningful ways in everyday interactions in the informal world. Their structural in-between position increases their vulnerability at the receiving end of actions and limits the actions they can initiate themselves. Yet it is precisely because of this structural position located in the margins, and their social, physical, and emotional "inhabitance" of institutional cracks, that they can gain precarious agency (Swerts 2017).

The findings of this book illustrate that precarious agency operates as the general principle that connects the individual and collective trajectories of undocumented activists on both sides of the Atlantic. It is thereby able to avoid the analytical fallacy whereby insights steeped in methodological nationalism are reified and extended without warranty. The transatlantic comparison that informs this book makes contextual differences visible and explicit, therefore providing more insight into how undocumented activists strategically navigate, adopt themselves to and respond to diverging political contexts. As the previous chapters have shown, precarious agency penetrates movement dynamics at different scales and levels.

First, gaining and nurturing precarious agency involved struggles over *representation* between organizations in the social movement fields in the United States and Belgium. Focusing on developments within movements at the national scale, I argued that discrepancies in *legal status* led actors with diverging citizenship statuses to interpret the political situation differently. I argued that a distinction had to be made between the types of knowledge and understanding that privileged and underprivileged subjects deploy to make sense of and strategically act in the political environment. The analysis of the history of the undocumented youth and sans-papiers movements revealed that in both cases, well-established CSOs took the lead in politicizing the issue of "migrant illegality" and putting immigrant rights on the political agenda. At the same time, they claimed to represent the undocumented at the negotiation table. In response, conflicts over representation tended to emerge between these CSOs and self-organizations. These conflicts can be explained by the differential political hermeneutics of the actors involved. While underprivileged subjects such as the undocumented form political understandings based on experiential knowledge, privileged subjects do so based on expert knowledge. This created a gap in understanding that calls into question the legitimacy of the latter's claim to representation. It was only when undocumented immigrants established their own organizations that they were able to gain representational autonomy. Both in the United States and Belgium, these self-organizations arose from small, undocumented-led initiatives that found their origin in the margins of the movement. I have described how schools operated as "safe spaces" for undocumented youth, while local community centers and churches fulfilled a similar role for the sans-papiers. When undocumented youth and the sans-papiers alike were able to come up with new ways of political representation that resonated with extra-movement actors, this gave them the strength to take up leadership within the movement itself. These findings thus show that hermeneutic processes affect how struggles over representation unfolded within both movements. However, movement histories in the United States and Belgium also show that the self-representation by undocumented migrants is threatened when states strategically exploit categorical differences to stimulate competition and create divisions between migrants that can overpower calls for solidarity and unified collective action. Furthermore, a complete lack of institutional receptivity combined with targeted repression efforts can sometimes stifle undocumented movements and break activists' determination.

Second, I zoomed in on hermeneutic processes that shape undocumented activist trajectories at the local scale. I first investigated how illegality affects the understandings of undocumented migrants in the city. Comparing the experiences of undocumented youth in Chicago and the sans-papiers in Brussels highlighted the importance of the urban context as a mediator of how legal status is translated into lived experiences. Living life as "an illegal" in the city means different things for the two groups in view of the differential access they have to institutions such as education, work, housing, and public transportation. Yet when closely examining their individual biographies, the stories of IYJL and SPBelgique activists contained similar embodied, discursive, and emotional understandings. Undocumented migrants' mobility came to a virtual standstill when they settled in their city of residence. Experiences of urban immobility reinforced feelings of being "trapped" in their locality. Everyday interactions with street-level bureaucrats, employers, and neighbors in the city fed experiences of stigmatization, illegalization, and criminalization. The precarity of undocumented immigrants' legal status further evoked feelings of self-doubt, fear, anger, and frustration that could lead them to socially isolate and further retreat into the shadows. However, lived experiences of immobility, illegalization, and emotional trauma do not necessarily cripple the ability of undocumented immigrants to act politically. On the contrary, each of these experiences can amount to a "turning point" in the individual trajectories of undocumented migrants that can set them on a path toward becoming an activist. These stories thus contain important lessons on the dialectical relationship between subjection and subjectivation. Furthermore, the unique epistemological vantage point of the undocumented forms a firm basis on which "undocumented activist theories" can be built (Bejarano et al. 2019).

Third, the organizing that goes on within *activist infrastructures* such as IYJL and SPBelgique is highly dependent on the strategic processing of lived experiences of illegality into workable political understandings that can guide collective action. These findings corroborate the work of scholars in social movement studies, gender studies, and citizenship studies stressing the efficacy of storytelling, emotion work, and embodied actions for marginalized populations (Polletta 2006; Jasper 1997; Butler 1990). However, the hermeneutic perspective developed here integrates and synthesizes insights from these fields into a single theory of political action that stresses the fundamental interconnectedness of activist epistemologies and embodied, discursive, and emotional modes of political "knowing" and "acting." Modalities of precarious agency are simultaneously the product of the specific characteristics of undocumented immigrants' everyday experiences, as much as they are shaped by the context in which they are developed and deployed. Without a doubt, existing tropes, scripts, narratives, and repertoires can have a restrictive effect on how undocumented migrants prepare to take the stage (Sati 2020, 354). Yet, the analysis revealed self-organizations as rather unique social milieus that create possibilities for undocumented activists to critically question, experiment with, and rethink established ways of being and acting politically. I have demonstrated that embodiment, narrative, and emotions became politicized in the context of self-organizations to propel recruitment, training, and mobilization forward. The politicization of bodies, stories, and emotions involves a hermeneutic process through which existing understandings are problematized by reinterpreting vulnerabilities as evidence of systemic fallacies and creating a sense of safety, solidarity, and community in the process. Activist infrastructures try to capture the incipient precarious agency that these embodied, discursive, and emotional episodes of collective sense-making evoke, by institutionalizing them in organizational rituals, rules, and norms. However, the analysis also revealed differences in terms of the capacity to do so between the self-organizations under scrutiny. While IYJL's organizational model was highly effective in channeling "raw" lived experiences, the draining effect it had on activists entailed risks of activist fatigue. Furthermore, the failure to unite competing interpretations of the political situation in a single interpretative framework and properly institutionalize norms about membership were in part responsible for the organizational collapse of SPBelgique.

The political hermeneutics of citizenship

On a broader scale, this book argues that political hermeneutics, or the interpretations that actors continuously produce and reproduce about the ordering of society, drive the processes through which irregular migration politics are legitimized and contested. Prevailing understandings of citizenship install a "distribution of the sensible" based on dichotomies between citizen and noncitizen, exclusion and inclusion, inside and outside, worthy and unworthy, and legal and illegal. State institutions have laws, courts, bureaucracies, budgets, technologies, physical borders, and legitimized violence at their disposal to "force" their understandings of citizenship on social reality and legitimize them as political truth (Foucault 1982). Reproducing these understandings in interactions with vulnerable immigrant populations via border spectacles, bureaucratic screening, and physical deportations forms an essential part of the performative strategies through which nation-states hold on to sovereignty in a migratory, globalized world (Schinkel 2009). The grand narrative of liberal democracies revolves around the promise that democratically elected national governments will uphold the rights of their citizens and give them access to protection and a share of the welfare. Prevailing understandings of citizenship increasingly come under pressure when residents who are present on the nation-state's territory are systematically denied rights, protection, and welfare because they lack the proper paperwork. Citizenship then transforms into a way to safeguard the societal privileges of recognized populations while enabling the creation of a vulnerable, exploitable, and deportable "shadow population" (or, expressed differently, undocumented "underclass"). While undocumented migrants participate in and contribute to the social, economic, cultural, and political life of their society of residence, governments deliberately choose to deny this reality. The state's disregard goes hand in hand with tough and dehumanizing talk about the threat that "illegal aliens" supposedly pose to the social order. "Citizen X" thus becomes cast as the ultimate villain who abuses legal loopholes, commits crimes, and profits from welfare and social protection. This illegalization of the figure of the "criminal noncitizen" creates, to evoke De Genova's (2013) terms, a spectacular scene of exclusion that is required to produce, give substance to and uphold the figure of the "good citizen." The Janus-faced nature of citizenship is especially relevant in times when the access of "good citizens" to welfare and social protection is eroding. The meaning of citizenship in times of irregular migration is thus as much defined by how liberal democracies treat noncitizens as it is by how they treat citizens. While the latter is constantly subject to public debate, the former is barely questioned.

Undocumented activism unveils the "other face of citizenship"—an ugly face that all too often remains hidden from public view and that confronts us with the parallel reality of "Citizen X." Compared with the vast amount of material resources that the state apparatus possesses to uphold the status quo, the sparse resources undocumented migrants have at their disposal vanish into thin air. Yet, armed with little more than their stories, bodies, and emotions, undocumented activists engage in an uphill battle against the state over the meaning of citizenship in a globalized world. *This book captures the capacity of undocumented activists to overcome barriers to participation, organize themselves collectively, and challenge citizenship as we know it.* It shows that, under certain circumstances, governing logics *can* be effectively resisted and disrupted by small groups of well-organized, undocumented activists who mount their challenge from the margins. Challenging the status quo and rethinking the meaning of citizenship is at the core of what undocumented activists do. What is at stake in struggles over citizenship is getting fellow immigrants, citizens, allies, the media, and the state to recognize that the undocumented "exist," that they are "human beings," that they constitute an integral part of our society, and that they have to be treated accordingly. The lived-through accounts of the parallel world that undocumented migrants are forced to roam and inhabit tend to strike a chord with supporters and the general public. This recognition does not necessarily revolve around group-specific demands to acknowledge immigrants' ethnic difference or other cultural identities. Instead, it requires politics that address the institutional subordination of noncitizens by redistributing legal status so as to make underprivileged subjects such as undocumented immigrants "full partners in social interaction" (Fraser 2000). Through political action, undocumented activists disidentify themselves with the criminalizing and dehumanizing labels that they are assigned and reidentify themselves as unrecognized residents. From a hermeneutic perspective, disidentification occurs when undocumented activists demonstrate and enact the "institutional cracks" in prevailing understandings of citizenship by juxtaposing official discourses on rights, membership, and safety with lived experiences of rights violations, social isolation, and violence. The other way around, reidentification takes place when undocumented activists demonstrate that they actively participate in and contribute to the social, cultural, economic, and political life of their society of residence. Reidentification does not always have to be disruptive, as strategic considerations can lead undocumented activists on a quest for recognition to reproduce prevailing and exclusionary understandings of deservingness and national identity (Nicholls 2013; Abrego and Negrón-Gonzales 2020). In this respect, as I have argued elsewhere, undocumented activism always requires activists to navigate between the twin logics of disruption and reproduction (Swerts and Nicholls 2021). However, what marries the ethnographic cases of IYJL and SPBelgique with one another across space and time is their ability to function as activist infrastructures where undocumented migrants feel free and capable to question dominant meanings, innovate political understandings, and perform these understandings in public space (Karaliotas 2023). Being able to openly question and think beyond "citizenship as we know it" requires a healthy dose of imagination, creativity, and courage. This capability to conceive of a line of action that may seem impossible is fostered and nurtured in self-organizations, which fulfill an avant-garde role in hermeneutic struggles over citizenship. As the organizational trajectories of IYJL and SPBelgique demonstrated, this involves experimenting with activist strategies that openly defy and resist the power of the nation-state to regulate its external borders and attempt to create more inclusive forms of belonging and membership based on community solidarity and community participation. In its best iterations, it offers a stringent critique of the social injustices that are upheld by citizenship as we know it and prefigures a future world where freedom of movement and full societal membership are treated as fundamental human rights regardless of one's citizenship status.

Toward a global sociology of noncitizenship

The transnational emergence of undocumented activism as a social phenomenon poses a real challenge to sociology. The development of sociology as a discipline was intimately tied to the rise of the nation-state, and this has caused methodological nationalism to be firmly institutionally anchored in the discipline. In this study, I show that it is insufficient to solely focus research efforts on institution-driven transformations of citizenship. It is time for noncitizens themselves to become the primary subjects of investigation, rather than the institutions that try to govern them. However, methodological nationalism and state centrism still hamper sociologists from developing a more general sociology of noncitizenship and its social, cultural, economic, and political implications. For example, ever since the "Marche des beurs," (March for Equality and Against Racism) took place, an entire strand of research in the French-speaking academic world has developed around the question of how undocumented activism relates to traditional concepts of French citizenship (Siméant 1998). Similarly, in the English-speaking academic world, multiple studies have investigated the impact of cultural understandings of American citizenship on undocumented activism (Ramakrishnan and Bloemraad 2008; Voss and Bloemraad 2011). While these emerging strands of literature offer interesting empirical insights into the mobilization of migrants in their society of residence, the theories they generate nevertheless remain too superficial. The case study of the sans-papiers movement in Belgium presented here, which takes place against the backdrop of a multinational and a polyethnic nation-state that lacks a coherent national identity, already calls into question the analytical value of models of national citizenship (Martiniello 2013). It highlights the fact that ideal-typical "models" of citizenship that are essentially intertwined with and rooted in the nation-state are too easily taken for granted as the explicit (or implicit) points of reference. All too often, sociologists examining irregular migration thus let the borders of the nation-state set and dictate the boundaries of their theoretical and empirical work.

I argue that we need to make greater efforts to build a global sociology of noncitizenship that examines illegalizing regimes and contestations of these regimes at a global scale (De Genova and Roy 2020). "Shadow people" are emerging in all immigrant-receiving countries, both in the so-called developed world and in developing countries. If undocumented activists who are severely constrained due to illegalizing regimes can work together to transnationally organize themselves, then there are certainly no excuses left for social scientists failing to do so. I thus take seriously the need for sociology to adopt a global outlook on noncitizenship. Despite its inevitable practical limitations, this book makes a strong case for using a *transatlantic approach* to better grasp how undocumented activists shake up the political game on both sides of the continent.

Studying undocumented activism in the European and North American context has allowed me to distinguish between insights that are theoretically generalizable and can potentially be extended to other marginalized groups in the world and more context-dependent insights. Context-dependent insights have to do with the relative dominance of established understandings pertaining to how groups are *supposed* to express themselves politically in their societies of residence. For example, the transatlantic comparison made apparent that the relative emphasis that was laid on storytelling in the US case versus marching in the Belgian case was reflective of mobilization traditions in both countries. Existing ethnographic studies that examine how undocumented activism unfolds in a single national or local context often fall into the trap of reifying such heavily context-dependent insights. What makes this book rather unique, then, is precisely the transatlantic comparison that allowed for the extraction of deeper-lying processes and mechanisms regarding the processes whereby undocumented migrants become activists. As a result, I argue that the theoretical insights on precarious agency and self-organizations as activist infrastructures contain valuable insights on how to collectively organize and claim rights for illegalized communities in contexts that exceed the ones presented in this book.

Future research on precarious agency could therefore study the political subjectivation of noncitizens beyond the undocumented, such as migrants who are partially recognized, temporary workers, foreign exchange students, unrecognized Indigenous populations, or stateless people. Adopting an intersectional lens can also be a fruitful strategy to get a better grasp on the complex interplay between factors like gender, ethnicity, class, age, sexual orientation, and legal status and how this affects lived experiences of illegality. The hermeneutic perspective that underpins this book can also be used to trace how political understandings travel through time and inform the preservation (and contestation) of collective memory within immigrant rights movements. A global sociological perspective of noncitizenship further requires a systematic comparison of how undocumented activism unfolds at the transnational, national, and local scale (Swerts and Nicholls 2021). Studying how undocumented activism unfolds at the local scale is particularly promising, since cities are gaining in importance as political actors who contest and define the rights and membership of undocumented migrants in a globalized world (Darling and Bauder 2020).

Epilogue
The enduring struggle for immigrant rights

At the time of writing, it is many years after IYJL and SPBelgique ceased to exist, and the last traces of their physical and digital presence seem to have evaporated into thin air. Publishing research that took place multiple years ago arguably has (dis)advantages. The biggest disadvantage, naturally, is the fact that the time lag between data collection and publication prevents this book from making an immediate impact on the public and political debate at the time.[1] However, the ability to trace the ensuing developments within the undocumented youth and sans-papiers movements from a greater distance left me in a better place to evaluate—and appreciate—what makes these self-organizations stand out as ethnographic cases. As a public sociologist (Burawoy 2005), I strongly believe in the capacity of present and future struggles to learn from the past. In this sense, providing an in-depth and detailed account of the rise and fall of two rather exceptional self-organizations contributes to ongoing efforts to record, preserve, and transfer collective memory within immigrant rights movements.

The lessons learned from this transatlantic ethnography of undocumented activism are thus more relevant than ever before. The struggle for undocumented immigrant rights is far from over. Irregular migration is still a top priority on the political agenda in the United States and the European Union. Moreover, nation-states are increasingly trying to get a grasp on irregular migration by restricting mobility and curtailing undocumented immigrants' rights. Given the rise of right-wing populism and the electoral gains made by the far right, the political climate to make demands in the name of undocumented immigrant communities has become less favorable and more hostile. In the United States, for example, the Trump presidency's aggressive efforts to expand and strengthen "the wall" at the Mexico-US border symbolizes the increasingly harsh and dehumanizing stance that nation-states are adopting toward "illegal aliens." In 2018, when President Trump gave his remarks on "the Illegal Immigration Crisis," he stated the following:[2]

> Illegal immigration affects the lives of all Americans.… America is a welcoming country, … but we will not allow our generosity to be abused by those who

Citizen X. Thomas Swerts, Oxford University Press. © Thomas Swerts (2026).
DOI: 10.1093/9780197844038.003.0011

would break our laws, defy our rules, violate our borders, break into our country illegally.... No nation can allow itself to be overwhelmed by uncontrolled masses of people rushing their border.... We got borders. And once that control is set and standardized and made very strong—including the building of the wall ... the illegal aliens will no longer get a free pass into our country by lodging meritless claims in seeking asylum.

The subsequent plans of the Trump administration to build the wall were met with criticism from European leaders, who stressed its costly and ineffective nature. Federica Mogherini, the High Representative of the European Union for Foreign Affairs, harshly criticized Trump's plans, stating that: "In Europe, we have a history that has told that every time one invests in divisions and walls you might end up being in a prison if you build all walls around you. We have a history and a tradition that we celebrate when walls are brought down and bridges are built."[3] Ironically, Trump's efforts to build a wall are only equaled these days by the European Union's recent call to further expand "Fortress Europe" by jointly investing in border enforcement, surveillance technologies, and drones. Observers estimate that more than two thousand kilometers of fences have been installed along European borders in recent years, and stories of illegal pushbacks, denigrating detention practices, and flagrant use of physical violence toward migrants in transit by border patrol officers keep systematically resurfacing. Nevertheless, "borders must be managed," European Commission President Ursula von der Leyen said after a meeting in February 2023, adding that "we will act to strengthen our external borders and prevent irregular migration."[4] The Belgian State Secretary for Asylum and Migration, Nicole de Moor, countered criticism from opposition parties by stating that this would be a wall "with a door." Despite rhetorical wizardry, these examples demonstrate the hypocrisy of the European Union's disdain toward American border politics and the intensification of illegalizing regimes on both sides of the Atlantic.

Irregular migration politics is not a field where "quick wins" or "easy victories" are to be had. In the United States, the seminal political "win" that can be attributed to the undocumented youth movement is probably the DACA policy (see Chapter 4). DACA provided over 825,000 eligible undocumented youth with temporary relief from deportation and work authorization between 2012 and 2021.[5] Many states followed suit by passing additional legislation that helped DACA beneficiaries access benefits like driver's licenses or Medicaid (Gonzales et al. 2020, 62). Academic research on the trajectories of DACA beneficiaries has demonstrated the positive impact of the program on the educational, health, and financial situation of undocumented youth (Abrego 2018; Gonzales et al. 2018; Gonzales et al., 2020). Despite these outcomes, the program became the object of an intense struggle in subsequent years between immigrant rights proponents and Republican politicians, including the Trump presidency, to expand, rescind, and protect DACA.[6] Most notably, the 2017 rescission of the program by the Trump administration put DACA and its recipients in jeopardy. However, in 2020, the US Supreme Court overruled the Trump administration by blocking the termination of the program. On the last legs of his presidency, President Biden's second immigration executive order allowed DACA recipients and other eligible undocumented youth to more quickly receive work visas and offered new measures to protect mixed-status families.[7] Yet, this most recent attempt to protect DACA is anything but an endpoint for undocumented youth. Promising to carry out "the largest deportation operation in history" from day one in office, Donald Trump's second term as President of the United States has been marked by efforts to double down on expanding deportations.[8] Protests that emerged against ICE raids in major cities across the United States have been met with violent crackdowns.[9]

Compared to the US context, there have been little to no "political wins" for the sans-papiers movement in Belgium. The federal government led by Charles Michel between 2014 and 2018 was based on a coalition of right-wing parties that precluded the possibility of a collective regularization campaign and vowed to uphold a "firm yet humane" immigration policy.[10] In practice, State Secretary for Asylum and Migration Theo Francken (N-VA, Flemish Nationalist Party) tried to put this into practice by targeting and stigmatizing undocumented immigrant communities. Talking about the "disgusting" situation of homeless sans-papiers in the Brussels North station, he stated that "If Brussels wants to become a kind of safe haven for illegal transmigrants, then let them do so but not ... at the expense of the federal government. Illegality is still a crime in Belgium."[11] In 2017, when occupiers of the Hotel Astrid in Brussels demanded regularization, the Francken's cabinet officially replied, "No way!"[12] Meanwhile, Franken tried—but failed—to introduce a federal bill that would give the police the right to enter a private residence with judicial permission upon suspicions of undocumented migrants staying there. The federal government led by Alexander De Croo between 2018 and 2024 almost fell when 470 activists of the Union des Sans-Papiers pour la Régularisation (USPR) occupied the Beguinage church once again and performed a two-month hunger strike. In response, Prime Minister De Croo stated that there is "no question of collective regularization for the sans-papiers."[13] Governmental coalitions members of the PS (Walloon Socialist Party) and Ecolo (Walloon Green Party) threatened to leave the coalition if any of the hunger strikers died. State Secretary Sammy Mahdi then struck a "deal" with the hunger strikers, only to then backtrack by later denying its existence.[14]

At the supranational scale of the European Union, prospects for advancing undocumented immigrant rights are equally grim. In theory, the rights of undocumented migrants in the European Union are protected by regulations such as

Article 1 of the European Convention on Human Rights, which states that state parties "shall secure to everyone within their jurisdiction" the civil and political rights set out in the Convention.[15] In practice, however, such rights are undercut by what some commentators choose to call "Fortress Europe," with its emphasis on strict border control and immigration enforcement (Delvino 2020, 73). Besides preventing irregular arrivals, EU policies on irregular migration are "geared to obstruct accommodation in the hosting society, create a 'hostile environment', deny assistance, and ultimately encourage irregular migrants to leave" (Delvino 2020, 74). The response to the so-called European migration crisis and its aftermath is telling in this respect. On April 19, 2015, more than eight hundred people on the move died when a boat on its way from Libya to Italy shipwrecked along the island of Lampedusa. This humanitarian disaster sparked a year of "crisis" on the European continent, where 1.3 million people on the move would arrive on the European continent via the Western Balkan and Mediterranean routes.[16] In response to this unprecedented situation, the renewed EU Agenda on Migration vowed to ramp up external border control and enforcement, tackle irregular migration by targeting smugglers, relocate asylum seekers to spread the "burden," and reintroduce internal border control between member states (Raineri and Strazzari 2021). Furthermore, the striking of the controversial EU-Turkey "Deal," the outsourcing of border control to Libyan authorities, and the conditional use of development aid funds in transit countries like Niger exemplified the European Union's attempts to prevent irregular migrants from reaching the continent all together (Raineri and Strazzari 2020). Meanwhile, the EU Action Plan on return (2015), the Renewed Action Plan on return (2017), and the New Pact on Migration and Asylum (2020) all focus on "making returns more effective and steeping up the return rate throughout the EU."[17] This emphasis on return exacerbates the ability of undocumented migrant communities to exercise their human rights.[18] Such measures are complemented by conscious efforts to criminalize solidarity initiatives and humanitarian assistance to undocumented migrants in Europe.[19]

What is sure and certain, however, is that the struggle for undocumented immigrant rights will endure regardless of the hardening of the political climate. Arguably, the unfavorable political contexts in the United States and Europe have led to shifting strategies on the one hand and movement abeyance on the other hand (see Abrams 2022, 194–95).[20] Given the lack of institutional receptivity at the national and supranational scale, such shifts have entailed a move toward organizing on the local scale while paying more attention to intersectional identities and intercommunity work (see below). This development is intimately intertwined with the global rise of "sanctuary cities" and the urban struggles for undocumented immigrant rights that propel this rise forward (Darling and Bauder 2019). As this book contends, such struggles revolve at their core around the struggle over the *meaning* of citizenship and over who belongs and does not belong in our society. While the world is becoming more migratory, nation-states and supranational entities are desperately doing everything in their power to control and curtail human mobility. What we are witnessing, how-ever, is that irregular migration policies, be it at the national or supranational scale, are failing spectacularly. Costly and spectacular border and deportation policies have no deterrent effect and do little other than make migration jour-neys more dangerous for the immigrants involved (Massey et al. 2016). With new groups and categories of migrants being illegalized on shifting legal and moral grounds by different state entities, the political reproduction of illegal-ity is guaranteed. Cities that experiment with sanctuary policies and practices may offer a way out of this conundrum, as they recognize the local presence of undocumented migrant communities and actively contest national illegaliz-ing policies (Darling and Bauder 2019). However, as I have argued elsewhere, even in favorable local settings, undocumented activism remains as important as ever to pressure municipal actors and established civil society organizations into turning inclusion into reality (Lambert and Swerts 2019). Self-organizations capable of pushing for social change do not emerge anywhere but tend to be concentrated in cities that operate as relational incubators for undocumented organizing (Nicholls 2021). For every self-organization such as IYJL or SPBel-gique that perishes, it is safe to say that there is already a new reincarnation in the making somewhere in the city. In the remainder of this epilogue, I trace how the seeds planted by the undocumented activists on both sides of the Atlantic described in this book flourished into new plants sprouting in charted and uncharted territories.

In Chicago, IYJL leaders took the lead in organizing communities against deportations and fighting for the expansion of existing sanctuary policies to transform the city into a "true" sanctuary where "all residents, regardless of race or citizenship status, must feel safe and have what they need to thrive." Inspired by the previous success of anti-deportation campaigns, former IYJL organizers created Organized Communities Against Deportations (OCAD). It represented a somewhat natural evolution from the organizing that had taken place in IYJL. The "youth" that initiated IYJL became adults, and some activists who qualified for DACA chose to leave the movement. This increased the need for a reorien-tation of organizing efforts. An OCAD organizer reflected upon this shift in an interview:[21]

> One of the things that happened as we were young undocumented people fight-ing deportations was that there was a point at which we had to expand who we fought for particularly to undocumented adults. And that also meant that we had to shift our entire infrastructure and name and way of organizing.... And

it's just really made me realize how there is actually a lack of spaces for adults to organize in and to learn and to talk with each other about stuff. And so I think that's been a really important space for us to have to create in OCAD.

Still undocumented-led, but no longer youth-led, OCAD defines itself as a "a group of undocumented, unapologetic, and unafraid organizers building a resistance movement against deportations and the criminalization of immigrants and people of color in Chicago and surrounding areas."[22] While the immediate objectives had changed and some people who left the struggle had been replaced by others, the hope for a better, brighter, and more equal future remained firmly in place:

We envision a future without displacement and borders; without incarceration and deportations. A future where people can choose to stay or migrate freely. A future where our bodies will not be commodified or exploited to fulfill quotas, fill cages, and used to generate profit. We envision a future where we determine the use of resources to ensure our collective well-being. A future of liberation for indigenous peoples, immigrants, people of color, women, LGBTQI, Black, and all oppressed peoples. A world of dignity and resistance, of transformation, laughter, and love.

Rejecting previous assimilationist strategies, OCAD represents a form of self-organization that takes its cue from past incarnations like IYJL to realize their "revolutionary vision of freedom."[23] Deportation defense campaigns had featured prominently in undocumented youth activism and had also been a staple of IYJL's organizing from the get-go (Kocher and Stuesse 2020). Over the years, room had progressively been made for undocumented parents, queer identities, and youth that did not tick the boxes to be represented. While earlier campaigns tended to reinforce dominant understandings of deservingness to claim the right to stay, the tone and tactics used shifted to more radical terrain with the #Not1More campaign in 2014 and the #AbolishICE campaign in 2018. As a former IYJL organizer explained, these campaigns were essentially "abolitionist" since they fused the call to not deport one more migrant with "a call to shrink mass incarceration systems, … a call to expose the prison industrial complex and directly confront police violence," and "a call to dismantle government agencies that exist solely to bring terror, harm, and violence to communities of color."[24] This abolitionist spirit informed OCAD's mission to take on deportation cases in Illinois. Besides helping arrested undocumented migrants to stop their deportations, OCAD has also contributed to intensifying collaborations and solidarity with Black-led organizations.[25] This shift in tactics stems from the work they started to do in 2017 around the criminalization of brown and

Black communities. This evolved into a campaign to "Erase the gang database" in Chicago, for which a coalition was created with Black-led organizations such as BYP100 and Assatta's Daughters.[26] As an OCAD organizer explained during an interview, this intercommunity work is important to politicize the penalization of brown and Black communities and show support to the Black Lives Matters movement.[27] Compared to the first incarnations of undocumented youth organizing, this type of organizing is also more community-oriented and neighborhood-focused. Besides organizing Know Your Rights workshops in neighborhoods like Little Village, Back of the Yards, and Albany Park, OCAD also helped to organize the first Dyke March in Little Village in 2017.[28] The organization of the Dyke March can be seen in light of the ongoing discussions at the time surrounding President Trump's attempts to withhold funds from sanctuary cities like Chicago. In response, OCAD tried to campaign for expanding sanctuary and eliminating "the carve-outs in the Welcoming City Ordinance of Chicago."[29] As an OCAD organizer explained, "the federal administration has been attacking different communities; immigrant, transgender so, when we talked between OCAD and the [Dyke March] Collective about the march, we wanted to expand the conversation around immigration to include more LGBTQ visibility."[30] Another example of community-oriented organizing took place during the COVID-19 period, when OCAD established a Mutual Aid Fund that provided over eighty thousand dollars to undocumented families in the Chicagoland area.[31] The new forms of self-organizing as exemplified by OCAD show traces from IYJL's legacy while venturing outward in different directions in new and exciting ways. They take an oppositional stance toward the capacity of the state to regulate borders and attempt to create new activist frameworks and practices that are better attuned to the intersectionality of lived experiences of illegality that are out there.

In Brussels, the void left by SPBelgique provided opportunities for intercommunity work and coordination as well with the foundation of the Coordination (Vertongen 2024). From the very start, the Coordination was conceived as an "autonomous network of all collectives of undocumented migrants in Brussels" that aimed to "support actions independent of each group and to organize common actions."[32] Over time, a slew of collectives joined the Coordination, including La Voix des Sans-papiers (VSP), Mobilisation Groupe 2009, the collective Ebola group, Collectif Afghans, Los Latinos por la Regularisacion, the Comité des travailleurs avec et sans papiers, and the Comité des femmes sans-papiers. The membership is as diverse as the names suggest, including undocumented migrants from Senegal, Guinea, Mauritania, Burkina Faso, Morocco, Liberia, Sierra Leone, Syria, Afghanistan, and Latin America. In addition, the members of the Coordination are stratified in terms of their legal status, with some groups claiming regularization through work (mainly Mobilisation

Groupe 2009, Comité des travailleurs avec et sans papiers, and Los Latinos por la Regularisacion) and others claiming regularization as refugees from violent conflict (VSP, Collectif Afghans) or diseases (collective Ebola group). The Coordination thus tried to achieve what SPBelgique had never managed to accomplish: namely, to become a representative organization for all undocumented migrants.[33] Its demands remained firmly centered around collective regularization but also included "the closure of closed centers, prisons for sans-papiers, the freedom of movement, an end to deportations the criminalization of sans-papiers, the respect for fundamental rights such as access to medical care and education and respect for and application of the children's rights."[34] When the so-called refugee crisis hit the European continent in the summer of 2015, the Coordination mobilized its supporters to protest the government's migration policy with the slogan "yesterdays' refugees, sans-papiers of today— for their rights and dignity." Banners stating "the sans-papiers welcome refugees" were prominently displayed at the entrance to the informal refugee camp that emerged in the Maximilian Parc, right across the street from the Office of Alien Affairs. The sans-papiers did not merely symbolically welcome the many refugees that arrived in Brussels that summer but also, quite literally, in practice. It was CollectActif, a handful of former SPBelgique members who united to cook and feed fellow activists with food leftovers, who were among first on the scene. What started off as the relatively improvised distribution of food and water evolved into a highly structured and organized field kitchen (Depraetere and Oosterlynck 2017). The *Cuisine du monde pour tout le monde* (kitchen of the world for the whole world), would eventually prepare more than one thousand meals on a daily basis for over four weeks. They therefore put the idea of "autogestion," or self-management of community resources in direct opposition to the state, into practice. For these undocumented activists, this display of solidarity was a way to continue their civic engagement despite the political setbacks they had experienced in the past with SPBelgique (Swerts and Oosterlynck 2021). During an interview, former SPBelgique member Omar put it like this:

> We were tired of going out into the street and shouting "we are here, we are undocumented, you have to recognize our presence," but *politically, it felt like talking to a wall.* So, with our group, we started to think about ways to just do something about the situation of undocumented migrants.... There was no progress in the political struggle, so we looked for something to maybe change the lives of people.

Ten years later, CollectActif continues to support people in a precarious position regardless of their status via setting up solidarity tables, community meals, food packages, and setting up initiatives in the temporary use of vacant properties (Depraetere and Oosterlynck 2017; Swerts and Oosterlynck 2021). Within the Coordination, la Voix des Sans-Papiers (VSP) replaced SPBelgique as the torchbearers of the "politics of presence" within the movement via a string of occupations in Brussels and Liège.[35] VSP had its roots in the European March of 2012 where SPBelgique represented the Belgian faction (see Preface and Chapter 4) and in the 2014 "March for Freedom," which was organized as a follow-up initiative. The five-hundred-kilometer march whereby undocumented activists crossed borders without authorization and symbolically linked the two European parliaments in Strasbourg and Brussels together took aim at the detrimental effects of exclusionary border policies in "Fortress Europe."[36] They thereby denounced the "racist and prohibitive policies against refugees and migrants" and "the mass drowning in the Mediterranean," demanding freedom instead of Frontex.[37] After this March, VSP was founded by a group of marchers who were determined to reignite the struggle in Brussels. A group of about 260 members coming from twelve different countries, including Senegal, Mauritania, Guinea, Morocco, and Burkina Faso,[38] occupied a former retirement home in Molenbeek. Over ten years, VSP occupied vacant buildings and was evicted twenty-three times. As was the case with SPBelgique, VSP's demands have consistently revolved around the right to regularization for all sans-papiers. However, rooted in their collective experience of evictions, VSP complements this strategy by focusing on the local scale and negotiating their right to presence and housing with municipalities and homeowners. Furthermore, compared to SPBelgique, VSP reaches a more diverse audience in terms of ethnicity, nationality, and gender. In view of the significant number of undocumented women and children among its membership, it also prominently advocates for the rights of undocumented families and children.[39]

As this epilogue shows, Former IYJL and SPBelgique organizers and new generations of undocumented leaders continue to take a leading role in the enduring struggle for undocumented migrant rights on both sides of the Atlantic. Undocumented activists thus remain involved in the the incessant search for effective ways to contest prevailing understandings of citizenship and explore forms of belonging and membership that lie beyond the horizon of citizenship as we know it (Nicholls 2019). As waves of self-organizations come and go, the developments in the immigrant rights movements in the United States and Europe simultaneously demonstrate the relevance of adopting a hermeneutic perspective to preserve collective memory and prevent collective amnesia. It is my sincere hope that the lessons learned by examining the flight and plight of undocumented activism on both sides of the Atlantic, and the deeper insights these lessons contain about precarious agency and citizenship transformation, can serve as a source of inspiration, orientation, courage, and support for activists, policymakers, professionals, scholars, and citizens involved in the enduring struggle to contest practices of illegalization and to promote political inclusion and social justice for immigrant communities.

Methodological and ethical considerations

Undocumented immigrants' stories of hardship, exploitation, perseverance, and achievement have started to surface in recent decades. Journalists have reported the stories of family members separated by deportation. Social scientists have described the stories of unauthorized workers in the urban informal economy, of rejected asylum seekers' struggle to survive, and of undocumented youths' educational experiences. Last but not least, undocumented immigrants themselves have shared their personal stories in public as a way to claim legal rights. When the stories of undocumented immigrants see the light of day, they evoke a broad spectrum of reactions, ranging from calls for immigration reform, social justice, and empowerment to calls for zero-tolerance policies, the closure of borders, and the restriction of citizenship. At the same time, they spark people's interest, because they represent a hidden social reality that they rarely encounter. It is therefore not surprising that these stories have sparked growing interest in sociology. While the sociological urge to "document the undocumented" should be applauded, the methodological and ethical challenges such a venture entails are under-investigated.

From "vulnerability" toward precarious agency

The "do no harm" principle is usually considered the ethical standard for qualitative research on vulnerable groups such as undocumented immigrants. Vulnerable research populations are defined as people who are stigmatized, have low social status, have little power or control over their lives, and live under harmful legal, social, or institutional conditions (Clements et al. 1999, 104). Düvell, Triandafyllidou, and Vollmer translated this principle for studies of irregular migration by arguing that the vulnerability of undocumented migrants should be the focus of an ethical perspective (Düvell et al. 2010). To take this vulnerability into account, researchers must take precautions that permit minimizing the potential risks associated with participation (such as scapegoating, rejection based on community membership, or deportation). In addition to these thematic sensitivities, they also draw attention to cultural sensitivities in gaining access to the community under study or in probing the legal status of respondents. I agree that there is an urgent need to develop an explicit ethical perspective on documenting the undocumented. The overemphasis on vulnerability, however, quickly lapses into victimization, thus disregarding the ability of undocumented people to think and act as moral and political subjects. In this way, I align myself with criticisms of the vulnerability concept, which contend that undocumented participants are "capable, competent, yet vulnerable simultaneously" (Swartz 2011).

I therefore propose to extend the theoretical insights around *precarious agency* outlined in this book to methodological and ethical discussions on how to work with undocumented research participants. A methodological and ethical approach rooted in precarious agency acknowledges the intimate relationship between academic research and power, recognizes existing inequalities in terms of legal status, and requires rethinking the power relationship between privileged researchers and underprivileged respondents. Such an approach requires reflexivity about the privileged positionality of researchers and openness to exploring how this positionality can be used to combat uneven power relations. It also presupposes a commitment to social justice that requires ethnographers to go beyond the position of the bystander who observes from a distance how things unfold.

Privileged and underprivileged epistemologies and positionalities

The implicit starting point here is that unequal distributions of citizenship create fault lines and power differentials between privileged citizen researchers and underprivileged undocumented respondents. I therefore argue that a methodological and ethical approach rooted in precarious agency needs to contribute to the renegotiation of privileged epistemologies, positionalities, and representations.

First, sociological research not only exists on paper but also establishes social relationships between researchers and the undocumented communities under study, including mutual expectations of participation, reciprocity, and integrity that accompany them. Moreover, these relationships are unevenly structured in the sense that there is a power imbalance in favor of—typically—more privileged researchers. Researchers are uniquely placed to legitimize or problematize social phenomena such as the illegalization of immigrant communities. This power stems from what Ackerly and True called the *privileged epistemology* that researchers have, referring to the established rules and beliefs within academia about what is considered to be scientific evidence, convincing argumentation, and proper knowledge (Ackerly and True 2008, 696). As undocumented scholars have rightfully noted, academic epistemology is indeed privileged compared with experiential modes of knowing of underprivileged populations such as the undocumented (Abrego and Negrón-Gonzales 2020, 8). For example, while the lived experiences of undocumented migrants provided the raw data for this book, the translation of these experiences into sociological knowledge was mostly in my domain as a social scientist. The danger that comes with this authority is that if it is (mis)used to reinforce prevailing understandings of citizenship, research inadvertently reproduces power inequalities and reaffirms the status quo. In line with the suggestions of critical migration scholars, I therefore acknowledge the ethical imperative for research to question and destabilize privileged epistemologies. This implies an epistemological shift toward the perspective of the outsider, the marginalized, the illegalized, and the "deviant."

Second, the ethical need to renegotiate power differentials between privileged researchers and underprivileged respondents also pertains to *positionality*. In order to "learn by unlearning," researchers need to be reflexive about their own privilege and how it affects research practice, relations with participants, and research outcomes (Anderson and Loredo 2021, 16–17). Considering positionality therefore requires researchers to be attentive to their own multiple identities; how they are positioned in terms of gender, ethnicity, education, class, legal status, nationality, and cultural membership, as well as how these various positions cause them to think, write, and interact with others in certain ways. Negotiating such power differentials in turn requires researchers to emphasize open communication, enable participation in the research process, and explore the co-creation of knowledge together with research participants.

Third, researchers need to consider the ambiguities involved in representing underprivileged respondents' stories. Given the privileged epistemology and positionality of researchers, they have an ethical responsibility concerning the stories they collect (Pittaway et al. 2010). For Pittaway et al., this implies an ethical perspective that moves beyond "do no harm" principles to a "negotiated reciprocal benefit that challenges researchers to justify their projects with reference to the benefits delivered to the vulnerable groups themselves" (Pittaway et al. 2010, 248). Put differently, researchers need to take into consideration how *representations* of undocumented people's stories are likely to affect and reflect back on the communities under scrutiny. This reflection depends on a continuous process of negotiation between how respondents think their stories should be represented and how researchers aim to use these stories for academic purposes. An ethical approach rooted in precarious agency therefore requires researchers to "give back" to the undocumented respondents by exploring opportunities to change that very situation (Swartz 2011). Below, I illustrate how I negotiated power differentials during the various research phases.

Gaining access to the field as a privileged researcher

Ethnographic research into closed communities such as the undocumented highlights the challenges related to insider-outsider dynamics. Ethnographers are always simultaneously insiders and outsiders. During participant observations, I tried to always keep in mind where I could be situated on various "fault lines," such as legal status, nationality, cultural membership, race, ethnicity, class, and education. As a white, highly educated cis male with a Belgian passport and an American student visa who grew up in a middle-class environment, I was without a doubt a privileged researcher. The relative social position on each of these fault lines influenced how I was perceived by respondents. I actively tried to "play off" certain characteristics to connect more easily with undocumented respondents and build a relationship rooted in mutual trust. This implies that watching from the sidelines would have been both ethically and methodologically impossible. In general, spending an extended period in the field proved to be a productive strategy for gaining access. Building rapport with undocumented activists was a challenging and difficult task, involving tough negotiations, repeated questioning of my intentions, and numerous community "tests." Because my ethnographic fieldwork took place on both sides of the Atlantic, I had to negotiate my status as an insider and outsider in different social settings.

In Chicago, I was perceived to be an outsider in the beginning. Being an immigrant to the United States myself would turn out to be more important than I imagined beforehand. Since I was not a cultural insider, I found it easier to ask "naïve" questions that were useful for my research as a European. Moreover, on numerous occasions I discovered I could gain the trust of my respondents by sharing personal experiences related to migrating to the United States (see Chapter 7). Since the disclosure of one's personal story is an integral part of IYJL's activities, this allowed me to become more of an organizational "insider." I quickly embraced a position in the organization as an "ally." For me to be accepted in IYJL, I had to demonstrate my intentions and earn my place in practice. I used the privileges related to my legal status, including a driver's license, to do so. I drove people around when I could, initially by renting a car and later using my own vehicle. I physically helped build the stage for the "Coming Out of the Shadows" rallies in 2011 and 2012. Since I felt relatively protected due to my student visa, I volunteered to function as a security liaison with the police. I stood beside other activists wearing my "Undocumented

Unafraid" T-shirt at press conferences. I made posters and distributed flyers. I basically tried to do what was expected from other allies in the organization. As one undocumented respondent told me many months later, it had not been until I told her that I was willing to risk being arrested that she started trusting me. That moment, which occurred during the preparations for a potential act of civil disobedience, was several months into my fieldwork.

In Brussels, I was perceived differently from the very start. As a Belgian citizen from Flanders, it was harder for me to adopt the "outsider" role. Although there was a clear distance between the undocumented research participants and myself, I was nevertheless assumed to know the situation in Belgium inside out. Hence, I deliberately tried to emphasize my status as an *outsider* by talking about the fact that I had lived in the United States for the past four years. At the same time, I tried to gain trust by explaining how I had been part of the undocumented youth movement in Chicago. Establishing rapport with research participants in Brussels would prove to be more difficult than it had been in Chicago. As the only white Belgian man in the group, I stood out in an organization where the majority consisted of men of North African descent. This was even more the case because I could not embrace a ready-made role as an "ally" in the organization. The citizen *soutiens* who worked closely with SPBelgique were predominantly white Belgian female social workers. Hence, I felt that the sans-papiers had certain expectations of me in terms of providing help or support for the organization that exceeded the role I wanted to adopt. I thus tried to distance myself from the social workers by incorporating the habits of the sans-papiers and "dressing down" by wearing a leather jacket and hoodie to blend in. By attending the weekly meetings, people eventually started to feel more comfortable around me, to the extent that newcomers assumed I was a sans-papiers from Eastern Europe.

Collecting underprivileged respondents' stories

It is important, if not ethically imperative, to try to maximize undocumented research subjects' participation in the research process. Hence, being open and communicative about the intention of the research from the start, debriefing respondents before and after data collection, allowing for flexibility in the way in which data was collected, and consulting with the research community about the research process at various instances during the fieldwork proved to be fruitful strategies (Lahman et al. 2011). Respecting undocumented research participants' rights is equally important to ensure that data collection is conducted in an ethical way. This requires special attention to procedures concerning informed consent and confidentiality. What should be avoided is the use of pressure or coercion toward undocumented immigrants who do not feel comfortable sharing their stories. Participating in qualitative research often requires undocumented research respondents to relive emotionally painful or traumatic experiences. Stressing the right to withdraw or not answer questions, conveying that pseudonyms will be used instead of real names, and asking indirect and less-threatening questions around legal status were helpful in this respect (Lahman et al. 2011). I also chose to avoid using written consent forms with undocumented respondents because creating such a "paper trail" could entail risks for them and because official-looking forms of this type are often associated with citizenship applications and other forms that can have a negative connotation.

Since the data collection dealt with extremely sensitive information, I made special efforts to be as open and communicative as possible about the research process. At numerous times during the fieldwork, I gave people updates about the things I was working on and thinking about. When conducting interviews, I gave people the opportunity to see the full transcript in case they wanted to clarify things. While this was important for their feelings of safety and confidentiality, in practice nobody asked me to change anything. The measures proposed by the IRB to ensure anonymity were viewed by more seasoned IYJL activists as a denial of their own expertise. Since I was obliged to use pseudonyms, people could not be quoted as "experts" on the matter. Yet some undocumented youth at IYJL had been open about their status in public for a long time. Others, including the majority of SPBelgique members, did not feel comfortable using their real names. Given the IRB's stipulations, I thus made the conscious decision to consistently use pseudonyms for all respondents.

Many of the remarks made earlier about sensitivity also apply to holding interviews with undocumented research participants. Going through undocumented immigrants' life stages, key events, present experiences, and future aspirations was an efficient way to research activist trajectories. Adopting a relatively open interview format where undocumented research participants could tell their stories tended to work better than highly structured, forced-choice interview formats. In general, I found that starting interviews with nonthreatening questions (such as describing their typical day) was a good way to make people feel at ease. I always announced when I would start asking questions about legal status, to obtain people's approval first. I also gave my respondents the opportunity to add anything they liked, by asking whether they wanted to talk about anything else after the last question. When I turned the recorder off, conversations usually continued and sometimes led to interesting insights about things that had not been discussed during the interview.

Asking undocumented respondents to share their stories usually generated interesting data. However, stories of undocumented migrants should always be studied in their social context (Swerts 2015). In Chicago, undocumented youth had perfected the crafting and sharing of life stories as a political tool. The longer they were involved in this type of activity, the more I noticed a tendency to share the "edited" versions of their stories. During interviews, I made special efforts to move beyond these standardized stories. By asking what it felt like to share stories in different social contexts, I learned how emotionally exhausting this can be for undocumented migrants. In Brussels, I also got the feeling from rejected asylum seekers that they had already shared their stories many times. Hence, I tried to ask more-targeted questions based on information I had gathered about the person during the participant observation. I found that many SPBelgique activists were reluctant to be interviewed because they felt they were not "suitable" candidates and would make "mistakes." Therefore, I tried to frame the interviews as informally as possible.

Beyond stories, researchers also have an ethical responsibility to the people they are interacting with. During the data collection phase, researchers examining irregular migration almost inevitably encounter situations or issues where a call for intervention on their part is required or requested (Swartz 2011). Negotiating to what extent you can respond to these situations can be a daunting task. A particularly difficult ethical dilemma occurred in Brussels with an undocumented respondent in need. It was an especially hard winter, and I knew that this person did not have a place of residence at the time. Moreover, he was suffering from personal and mental problems due to his legal status. One time after a meeting, he asked me if he could speak to me outside. I followed him, and he then explained that he wanted to borrow twenty euros. I told him this was not something I could do as a researcher. However, he kept on insisting how important this was in view of his situation. Hence, whereas I had always thought beforehand that I would not do these types of things from an ethical standpoint, in the social situation I decided that my help was warranted. It is thus not always easy to clearly define the appropriate response to demands for ethical intervention beforehand. Other examples included requests for recommendation letters for official purposes. When Akash received a negative decision regarding his application for asylum, he asked me if I could write a letter proving his commitment and good character. As a researcher in a privileged position to do so, to "give back" to respondents, I provided recommendation letters to him and several other SPBelgique members.

Representing stories of precarious agency

Collecting, reconstructing, and representing the life stories of undocumented people requires a specific ethical "responsibility to the story" from privileged researchers (Swartz 2011). What should be avoided is an ethical stopgap solution, in which researchers who work with "vulnerable" groups portray their work as a way of "giving undocumented people a voice." Such claims are problematic, because we need to get rid of the illusion that undocumented people do not have a voice of their own. In fact, in the case of undocumented respondents approached through self-organizations, they have often already found their voice. Instead of speaking "on behalf of" undocumented people, privileged researchers should therefore pay more attention to what undocumented people say, how they say it, what the circumstances are that allow them to speak for themselves, and how what they say is perceived by others.

Privileged researchers also need to think carefully about how representations of underprivileged respondents' stories can reflect back on the community of undocumented immigrants under scrutiny. The use of labels and categories requires special attention in this respect. There is a serious risk of objectification related to categorizing undocumented research participants. For example, terms such as "undocumented immigrants" and "irregular migration" are preferable to "illegal migration" or "illegal aliens." Using the latter terms implies subscribing to processes of "illegalization" that have a dehumanizing and criminalizing effect on undocumented communities. Sociologists thus need to reflect more critically about the potential implications of these representations.

The choices privileged researchers make regarding how to represent undocumented activist stories are not only of methodological and ethical concern but also pertain to the field of theory. My initial interest in the struggles of undocumented migrants was sparked by the theories of political subjectivation advanced in post-foundational political philosophy. As outlined in the introductory chapter, these theories attuned me to the question of how and to what effect marginalized groups like the undocumented can become politically active. However, the more I engaged with undocumented communities over the months and years that ensued, the more I became frustrated with the gap between "highbrow theory" and what Bejarano et al. call "emic" or "native" theories (Bejarano et al. 2019, 11). I tried to bridge this gap by being attentive to undocumented activists' theories and actively debating them in mutual dialogue. The transatlantic nature of my fieldwork presented opportunities to share insights gathered from emic and etic theories floating around between Chicago and Brussels. Confronting sans-papiers activists with videos of IYJL's "Coming out" speeches and American scholarship on storytelling during a popular education seminar, for example, led to a fascinating discussion about the potential effectiveness of such strategies for SPBelgique. Being a European scholar immersed in American academic life also affected attempts at theorizing undocumented activism. The transatlantic academic dialogue that this positionality evoked, heightened my sensitivity for the context specificity of, for example, theoretical concepts that found their origins in the civil rights, gay rights, labour, and squatters' movements. In sum, formulating theoretical insights based on undocumented activist stories requires attention to emic understandings and situatedness.

Making public interventions

There are also "voicing" issues that go beyond the undocumented community's representation in academic texts. In this respect, I had to find out in practice when it was appropriate for me as a researcher to make public interventions and speak about issues concerning the undocumented community. In Chicago, there had been reports of bad experiences with journalists and researchers who either did not respect confidentiality or who misrepresented what their respondents had shared with them. Hence, IYJL activists asked me to write a blog post about best practices with regard to conducting research with undocumented respondents. In response, I wrote a piece that was published on their website, reflecting my own experiences in the field. Since the initial feedback was that the piece had been "too academic," I was urged to include practical tips about what someone can do as a responsible researcher in the field.[1] In Brussels, the situation was different in that there was little to no public debate about the position of undocumented immigrants in Belgian society. Hence, I published several opinion pieces in the media, highlighting their struggles. In the years after my fieldwork was concluded, I also invited SPBelgique members to give lectures and teach classes together with me on several occasions. Instead of acting like gatekeepers who only represent underprivileged respondents' stories to provide ammunition for their academic agendas, privileged researchers can thus act as "gate-openers," who stimulate discussions on power inequalities by giving a platform to undocumented immigrants.

Nonetheless, researchers should remain realistic about the impact they can have by making public interventions on power relations in society. When Fariss got arrested, for example, I could do little more than write him a letter and translate the press releases during the campaign to stop his deportation. However, another opportunity to use my position as a privileged researcher to act as a "gate-opener" proved that it is sometimes worth pursuing the impossible. During a joint lecture in Brussels with SPBelgique activists, a member of the audience stood up and shared his story about being undocumented and wanting to enroll in university. While the university had told him this would not be possible given his status, I used my privilege as an academic to set up a meeting with the university administration and pressure them with legal arguments. In the end, the administration gave in and the student was accepted in the law faculty. In addition, I testified in the media to help raise awareness around this issue. What both examples show is that while researchers themselves may lack the capacity to reconfigure power relations in society, they can nevertheless help to spark change by opening institutional doors for underprivileged subjects.

Lastly, since irregular migration has become a top political priority in the United States and the European Union, it is necessary to be extremely reflexive and careful about the policy implications of sociological research in this field. More specifically, sociologists must ensure that their findings cannot be used to oppress undocumented communities. Researchers are often faced with questions of objectivity and neutrality due to the public nature of the debate surrounding irregular migration. Because of their privileged social position, rare insights into the day-to-day struggles of undocumented people, and the aura of independence that goes together with the social sciences, sociologists are uniquely positioned to take a stand and make public interventions. Such a public sociology can be a powerful tool to *amplify* the voice of undocumented communities, strengthen their claims for recognition, and contribute to more equitable migration policies (Burawoy 2005).

Notes

Prelims

1. All real names were replaced with pseudonyms, as per IRB stipulations.
2. http://schakowsky.house.gov/media/press-releases/schakowsky-thrilled-rigo-padilla-granted-reprieve-calls-immigration-reform-now
3. https://www.chicagotribune.com/news/ct-xpm-2009-12-11-0912100805-story.html
4. See the Methodological appendix.

Introduction

1. https://worldmigrationreport.iom.int/wmr-2022-interactive/
2. https://www.unhcr.org/refugee-statistics/
3. https://missingmigrants.iom.int/data
4. https://www.consilium.europa.eu/en/press/press-releases/2016/03/03/tusk-remarks-tsipras-athens/
5. https://time.com/4475349/donald-trumps-speech-immigration-transcript/
6. http://www.ilo.org/wcmsp5/groups/public/%2D%2D-dgreports/%2D%2D-dcomm/documents/publication/wcms_436343.pdf
7. https://www.pewresearch.org/global/2019/11/13/europes-unauthorized-immigrant-population-peaks-in-2016-then-levels-off/
8. https://www.migrationpolicy.org/research/deportation-and-discretion-reviewing-record-and-options-change
9. http://www.themigrantsfiles.com/
10. https://robparal.com/wp-content/uploads/Illinois-Undocumented-Immigrant-Population.pdf; based on the 2016 US Census.
11. https://www.standaard.be/cnt/dmf20230411_96637282
12. https://www.chicagotribune.com/news/ct-chicago-sanctuary-history-htmlstory.html
13. https://www.chicagotribune.com/2017/04/26/emanuel-hits-trump-on-sanctuary-cities-ruling-tax-plan/
14. https://www.7sur7.be/home/thielemans-moi-je-prends-mesresponsabilites~ab982e4bF/
15. https://www.7sur7.be/belgique/le-projet-gaudi-on-fait-beaucoup-de-musculation-sur-cette-affaire~adc91d0e/
16. https://www.kenniscentrumwwz.be/files/Kennisbank-Items/niet-cahier/onderzoeksrapport-precaire-gezinnen_0.pdf
17. See Chapters 1–4 for past developments and the Epilogue for present and future developments.
18. IYJL website.
19. SPBelgique website.
20. In what follows, I follow Darling's (2014) lead in using the verbs policing/politicizing rather than the nouns police/the political to avoid any possible confusion with the (immigration) police and shift the focus more on processes.
21. Non-citizens can be defined as "a person who has not been recognized by the state as having effective links to the country where (s)he resides" (Office of the United Nations High Commissioner for Human Rights 2006, 5).
22. See Epilogue.

Part 1

1. I deliberately use the term migrant illegality here—and in the remainder of the book—to refer to the outcome of sociopolitical processes of illegalization (De Genova 2002).

Chapter 1

1. https://www.govinfo.gov/content/pkg/CREC-2004-07-22/pdf/CREC-2004-07-22-pt2-PgS8670.pdf
2. MALDEF is a national nonprofit organization that was established in 1968 to protect the rights of Latinos in the United States and that makes use of legal-aid cases to contest rights violations and discrimination against people with an immigrant background.
3. https://www.law.cornell.edu/supremecourt/text/457/202
4. https://www.law.cornell.edu/supremecourt/text/457/202
5. Alameda County. 1985. Tentative Decision, Action No. 588-982-5, California Superior Court.
6. In analogy to ICIRR, the Coalition for Humane Immigrant Rights was founded in 1986 with the help of the Ford Foundation to help educate immigrants about IRCA in Los Angeles.
7. All real names were replaced by pseudonyms as per IRB stipulations.
8. http://www.libertyhill.org/page.aspx?pid=425
9. http://www.youtube.com/watch?v=KBo4dFZdDno
10. http://www.libertyhill.org/page.aspx?pid=425
11. https://www.chicagotribune.com/news/ct-xpm-2006-03-11-0603110130-story.html
12. Although the notion of "safe space" has a long historical lineage that dates to the late twentieth century women's movement (see The Roestone Collective 2014), it is specifically evoked here in the sense of providing a safe environment for undocumented migrants to share lived experiences and organize themselves collectively.
13. https://www.presidency.ucsb.edu/documents/statement-administration-policy-s-2205-development-relief-and-education-for-alien-minors
14. http://www.nytimes.com/2008/02/22/world/americas/22iht-21textdemdebate.10292802.html?pagewanted=9&%2360&%2362&%2359&%2359;!–Undefined+dynamic+function+data_sanitationlib: :sanitize_string:1+called–&%2359
15. http://www.nytimes.com/2008/02/22/world/americas/22iht-21textdemdebate.10292802.html?pagewanted=9&%2360&%2362&%2359&%2359;!–Undefined+dynamic+function+data_sanitationlib: :sanitize_string:1+called–&%2359
16. http://www.washingtonpost.com/wp-dyn/content/article/2009/06/23/AR2009062303406.html

Chapter 2

17. http://www.iyjl.org/how-to-walk-out-of-a-dhs-insecure-communities-hearing/
18. See Chapters 7 and 8.
19. http://www.iyjl.org/national-coming-out-of-the-shadows-day/
20. http://www.iyjl.org/why-this-march-10th-we-will-be-presenting-our-demands-on-a-table/
21. http://www.truth-out.org/archive/item/91877:dream-activists-rejecting-the-passivity-of-the-nonprofit-industrial-complex
22. http://www.iyjl.org/undocumented-students-represent-themselves-in-d-c-court-could-face-deportation/
23. http://www.iyjl.org/how-i-stopped-believing-in-cir-and-learned-to-love-piecemeal-legislation/
24. https://www.americanimmigrationcouncil.org/research/dream-act-creating-economic-opportunities
25. https://www.facebook.com/NationalImmigrantYouthAlliance/info
26. http://www.iyjl.org/our-first-legislative-victory-the-inside-story/
27. http://www.iyjl.org/?p=2758
28. http://abcnews.go.com/blogs/politics/2011/08/obama-administration-halts-deportations-of-non-criminal-immigrants/
29. http://www.solidarity-us.org/site/node/3630
30. http://www.iyjl.org/3-years-of-iyjl-more-to-come/
31. http://m.colorlines.com/archives/2012/06/dreamers_planned_obama_campaign_office_sit-ins_force_deportation_standoff.html
32. http://www.whitehouse.gov/the-press-office/2012/06/15/remarks-president-immigration

Chapter 3

1. All place names are literal translations.
2. Real name used, because a pseudonym was unnecessary here.
3. http://www.ihoes.be/PDF/Sans_papiers_V1.pdf
4. http://www.cncd.be/IMG/pdf/donnons-un-visage-aux-sans-papiers.pdf
5. http://ccle.collectifs.net/
6. libertaire.pagesperso-orange.fr/archive/99/214-fev/sanpap4.htm
7. www.sap-rood.be/
8. Ibid.
9. Unpublished manuscript.
10. http://www.standaard.be/cnt/glojci91
11. http://www.standaard.be/cnt/dmf11052006_049
12. www.ravagedigitaal.org/2006/mei/kerkasiel.htm
13. www.coj.be
14. Unpublished manuscript.
15. UDEP website.
16. Unpublished manuscript.
17. http://www.standaard.be/cnt/3b1p62b3
18. http://www.standaard.be/cnt/6L1RR7LO
19. https://www.knack.be/magazine/acht-jaar-meneer-dat-is-een-tiende-van-een-mensenleven/
20. www.ptb.be
21. http://www.demorgen.be/dm/nl/989/Binnenland/article/detail/420192/2008/09/18/Hongerstakers-Elsene-breken-records.dhtml
22. Unpublished manuscript.
23. http://www.standaard.be/cnt/pm294blr
24. http://www.demorgen.be/dm/nl/989/Binnenland/article/detail/777016/2009/03/18/Duizend-manifestanten-betogen-voor-sans-papiers-in-Brussel.dhtml
25. http://www.brusselnieuws.be/nl/nieuws/bijna-1000-mensen-zonder-papieren-hongerstaking-2

Chapter 4

1. See Chapter 8 for an elaboration of this argument in greater ethnographic detail.
2. Presentations 2010–2012 (internal document).
3. http://www.telebruxelles.net/portail/info/-communale-bruxelloise/ixelles/17586-23-sans-papiers-en-greve-de-la-faim
4. http://www.dewereldmorgen.be/video/2012/03/29/protest-voor-het-leven-een-reportage-over-de-hongerstaking
5. http://www.hln.be/hln/nl/957/Binnenland/article/detail/1415762/2012/03/29/De-Block-heeft-geen-begrip-voor-hongerstakers.dhtml
6. http://www.levif.be/info/actualite/belgique/afghanistan-l-office-des-etrangers-dement-un-projet-d-expulsion-collective/article-4000351041889.htm
7. http://www.nieuwsblad.be/article/detail.aspx?articleid=DMF20130908_00730945
8. http://www.ketnet.be/karrewiet/nieuws/9-september-2013-zonder-papieren

Chapter 5

1. This, in turn, affects emotional lived experiences of illegality.
2. Term referring to "manual laborer."
3. Speech during the 2012 Coming-Out Rally.
4. https://www.chicago.gov/city/en/depts/mayor/press_room/press_releases/2017/february/Chicago_Status_As_Sanctuary_City.html#:~:text=%E2%80%9CChicago%20has%20been%20a%20city,commitment%20to%20inclusion%20will%20not.%22
5. https://robparal.com/wp-content/uploads/Illinois-Undocumented-Immigrant-Population.pdf

6. https://www.washingtonpost.com/immigration/trump-vows-mass-immigration-arrests-removals-of-millions-of-illegal-aliens-starting-next-week/2019/06/17/4e366f5e-916d-11e9-aadb-74e6b2b46f6a_story.html

Chapter 6

1. IOM's Missing Migrants Project, June 8, 2019 (www.iom.int).
2. https://www.ccc-ggc.brussels/sites/default/files/documents/graphics/rapport-pauvrete/rapport-pauvrete-2010/2_rapport_thematique_2010.pdf
3. https://picum.org/wp-content/uploads/2023/08/PICUM_Report_Housing_and_Undocumented_Migrants.pdf

Chapter 7

1. University of Illinois at Chicago.
2. For an outline of how I became accepted as an ally, see the Appendix.
3. IYJL website.
4. This demonstrates that emotions like empathy help to reinforce feelings of membership and community between citizen allies and undocumented activists.
5. Reconstructed from field notes.
6. A program targeting immigrants for criminal prosecution if they had crossed the border without state authorization.

Chapter 8

1. A Moroccan percussion instrument.
2. Preparatory meeting notes.
3. https://marchebelgique.wordpress.com/le-parcours-de-la-marche/appel-de-la-marche/
4. Recorded meetings, March.
5. https://marchebelgique.wordpress.com/charte-de-la-marche-de-solidarite-avec-et-sans-papiers/

Epilogue

1. However, I have continuously intervened in both academic and public debates on undocumented immigrant communities based on this and future research projects. (see Swerts 2015, 2017, 2018, 2021).
2. https://trumpwhitehouse.archives.gov/briefings-statements/remarks-president-trump-illegal-immigration-crisis-border-security/
3. https://www.aa.com.tr/en/europe/europes-own-walls-whitewashed-amid-trump-criticism/750622
4. https://ec.europa.eu/commission/presscorner/detail/en/statement_23_761
5. https://www.britannica.com/topic/DACA
6. https://www.britannica.com/topic/DACA
7. https://www.independent.com/2024/06/18/biden-grants-legal-protections-to-dreamers-and-undocumented-spouses-of-u-s-citizens/
8. https://www.npr.org/2024/07/19/nx-s1-5044582/trump-has-promised-deportations-on-an-unprecedented-scale
9. https://www.nytimes.com/2025/07/05/us/trump-immigration-rights-ice.html
10. https://www.lesoir.be/116203/article/2017-09-26/michel-nous-menons-une-politique-migratoire-ferme-mais-humaine
11. https://www.vrt.be/vrtnws/nl/2018/05/04/francken---geen-opvang-voor-zij-die-procedure-niet-volgen-/
12. https://www.nieuwsblad.be/cnt/dmf20170913_03071449
13. https://www.nieuwsblad.be/cnt/dmf20210701_94892941
14. https://www.vrt.be/vrtnws/nl/2021/07/22/sammy-mahdi-zegt-dat-er-geen-deal-is-met-hongerstakers-ze-zull/

15. https://www.coe.int/en/web/compass/the-european-convention-on-human-rights-and-its-protocols

16. https://www.pewresearch.org/global-migration-and-demography/2016/08/02/number-of-refugees-to-europe-surges-to-record-1-3-million-in-2015/

17. https://www.europarl.europa.eu/legislative-train/carriage/proposal-for-a-recast-of-the-return-directive/report?sid=8201

18. https://picum.org/wp-content/uploads/2021/10/Why-is-the-Commissions-push-to-link-asylum-and-return-procedures-problematic-and-harmful.pdf

19. https://picum.org/wp-content/uploads/2024/04/Cases-of-criminalisation-of-migration-and-solidarity-in-the-EU-in-2023.pdf

20. Whereby more focus is laid on internal movement practices to re-assess and adapt organizing tactics.

21. https://crossroadsfund.org/podcasts/193/

22. https://www.organizedcommunities.org/about

23. https://www.organizedcommunities.org/about

24. https://medium.com/@LaTania/we-fell-in-love-in-a-hopeless-place-a-grassroots-history-from-not1more-to-abolish-ice-23089cf21711

25. https://www.woodsfund.org/news/grantee-spotlight-organized-cummunities-against-deportations-ocad

26. https://www.woodsfund.org/news/grantee-spotlight-organized-cummunities-against-deportations-ocad

27. https://www.woodsfund.org/news/grantee-spotlight-organized-cummunities-against-deportations-ocad

28. https://sixtyinchesfromcenter.org/stories-of-migration-transformation-an-interview-with-ocads-reyna-wences/

29. https://www.organizedcommunities.org/campaigns

30. https://windycitytimes.com/2017/06/18/2017-dyke-march-takes-unity-to-the-streets-of-little-village/

31. https://windycitytimes.com/2017/06/18/2017-dyke-march-takes-unity-to-the-streets-of-little-village/

32. https://sanspapiers.be/wie-zijn-we/?lang=nl

33. https://www.wearebelgiumtoo.be/

34. https://sanspapiers.be/onze-eisen/?lang=nl

35. https://www.ieb.be/La-Voix-des-Sans-Papiers-une-occupation-politique-sociale-et-militante-34334

36. https://freedomnotfrontex.noblogs.org/

37. https://freedomnotfrontex.noblogs.org/

38. https://www.fgtb.be/sites/fgtb/files/actions/pdf_doc/enqute-des-sans-papiers.pdf

39. https://ep.cfsasbl.be/vsp-l-odyssee-des-sans-papiers

Appendix

1. http://www.iyjl.org/documenting-the-undocumented-on-the-intersections-between-ethnography-politics-and-ethics/

References

Abrams, Kathryn. 2022. *Open Hand Closed Fist: Practices of Undocumented Organizing in a Hostile State*. Oakland: University of California Press.

Abrego, Leisy. 2006. "I Can't Go to College Because I Don't Have Papers: Incorporation Patterns of Latino Undocumented Youth." *Latino Studies* 4: 212–31.

Abrego, Leisy. 2008. "Legitimacy, Social Identity, and the Mobilization of Law: The Effects of Assembly Bill 540 on Undocumented Student." *Law & Social Inquiry* 33 (3): 709–34.

Abrego, Leisy. 2011. "Legal Consciousness of Undocumented Latinos: Fear and Stigma as Barriers to Claims-Making for First- and 1.5-Generation Immigrants." *Law & Society Review* 45: 337–70.

Abrego, Leisy. 2018. "Renewed Optimism and Spatial Mobility: Legal Consciousness of Latino Deferred Action for Childhood Arrivals Recipients and Their Families in Los Angeles." *Ethnicities* 18 (2): 192–207.

Abrego, Leisy, and Negron-Gonzales, Genevieve, eds. 2020. *We Are Not Dreamers: Undocumented Scholars Theorize Undocumented Life in the United States*. Durham, NC: Duke University Press.

Ackerly, Brooke, and Jacqui True. 2008. "Reflexivity in Practice: Power and Ethics in Feminist Research on International Relations." *International Studies Review* 10 (4): 693–707.

Adam, Ilke, Nadia B. Mohammed, Bonaventure Kagné, Marco Martiniello, and Andrea Rea. 2002. *Histoires Sans-papiers*. Bruxelles: Vista.

Agamben, Giorgio. 1998. *Homo Sacer: Sovereign Power and Bare Life*. Stanford, CA: Stanford University Press.

Alba, Richard, and Victor Nee. 2003. *Remaking the American Mainstream: Assimilation and Contemporary Immigration*. Cambridge, MA: Harvard University Press.

Amador, Carlos. 2011. "This is Our Country Too: Undocumented Battle for the DREAM Act." *Critical Planning* (summer): 107–14.

Anderson, Nels. 1923. *The Hobo: The Sociology of the Homeless Man*. Chicago: University of Chicago Press.

Anderson, Jill, and Maggie Loredo. 2021. "A Nook That Became a Community." In *Lxs Otrxs Dreamers*, edited by Jill Anderson and Nin Solis, 7–40. Mexico City: Self-published.

Anderson, Jill, and Solis, Nin. 2021. *Lxs Otrxs Dreamers*. Mexico City: Self-published.

Balibar, Étienne. 2004. *We, the People of Europe? Reflections on Transnational Citizenship*. Princeton, NJ: Princeton University Press.

Bartlett, Lesley, and Frances Vavrus. 2016. *Rethinking Case Study Research: A Comparative Approach*. New York: Routledge.

Bejarano, Carolina Alonso, Lucia López Juárez, García Mirian A. Mijangos, and Daniel M. Goldstein. 2019. *Decolonizing Ethnography: Undocumented Immigrants and New Directions in Social Science*. Durham: Duke University Press.

Bloch, Alice, and Sonia McKay. 2017. *Living on the Margins: Undocumented Migrants in a Global City*. Bristol: Policy Press.

Bloemraad, Irene, Kim Voss, and Taeku Lee. 2011. "The Immigration Rallies of 2006: What Were They, How Do We Understand Them, Where Do We Go?" In *Rallying for Immigrant Rights*, edited by Kim Voss and Irene Bloemraad, 2–43. Berkeley, CA: University of California Press.

Bosniak, Linda. 2006. *The Citizen and the Alien: Dilemmas of Contemporary Membership*. Princeton, NJ: Princeton University Press.

Bouchoukh, Abdelwaheb. 2002. "Beaucoup de manipulations ont eu lieu". In *À la Lumière des Sans-Papiers*, edited by Pickels, Antoine, 239–46. Brussels: Editions Complexe.

Bourdieu, Pierre. 1998. *Practical Reason: On the Theory of Action*. Cambridge: Polity Press.

Burawoy, Michael. 1998. "The Extended Case Method." *Sociological Theory* 16: 4–33.

Burawoy, Michael. 2005. "For Public Sociology." *Soziale Welt* 56 (4): 347–74.

Burgers, Jack. 1998. "In the Margin of the Welfare State: Labour Market Position and Housing Conditions of Undocumented Immigrants in Rotterdam." *Urban Studies* 35 (10): 1855–68.

Burgers, Jack, and Godfried Engbersen. 1999. *Illegale vreemdelingen in Rotterdam*. Amsterdam: Boom.

Butler, Judith. 1990. *Gender Trouble: Feminism and the Subversion of Identity*. New York: Routledge.

Butler, Judith, Zeynep Gambetti, and Leticia Sabsay. 2016. *Vulnerability in Resistance*. Durham, NC: Duke University Press.

Calavita, Kitty. 1992. *Inside the State: The Bracero Program, Immigration, and the I.N.S.* New York: Routledge.

Castles, Stephen, Magdalena Cubas, Kim Chulhyo, and Derya Ozkul. 2012. "Irregular Migration: Causes, Patterns, and Strategies." In *Global Perspectives on Migration and Development*, Vol. 1: *Global Migration Issues*, edited by Irena Omelaniuk. Dordrecht: Springer.

Chauvin, Sébastien, and Blanca Garcés-Mascareñas. 2012. "Beyond Informal Citizenship: The New Moral Economy of Migrant Illegality." *International Political Sociology* 6: 241–59.

Chauvin, Sébastien, and Blanca Garcés-Mascareñas. 2014. "Becoming Less Illegal: Deservingness Frames and Undocumented Migrant Incorporation." *Sociology Compass* 8: 422–32.

Chavez, Leo. 1998. *Shadowed Lives: Undocumented Immigrants in American Society*. Fort Worth, TX: Harcourt Brace College Publishers.

Ciré. 2006. *Donnons un visage aux sans-papiers*. Brussels: Ciré.

Clements, John, Mark Rapley, and Robert Cummins. 1999. "On, to, for, with – Vulnerable People and the Practices of the Research Community." *Behavioural and Cognitive Psychotherapy* 27 (2): 103–15.

Cleton, Laura, and Reinhard Schweitzer. 2021. "'Our Aim Is to Assist Migrants in Making a Well-Informed Decision': How Return Counsellors in Austria and the Netherlands Manage the Aspirations of Unwanted Non-Citizens." *Journal of Ethnic and Migration Studies* 47 (17): 3846–63.

Cordero-Guzmán, Hector, Nina Martin, Victoria Quiroz-Becerra, and Nik Theodore. 2008. "Voting with Their Feet: Nonprofit Organizations and Immigrant Mobilization." *American Behavioral Scientist* 52: 598–617.

Corrunker, Laura. 2012. "'Coming Out of the Shadows': DREAM Act Activism in the Context of Global Anti-Deportation Activism." *Indiana Journal of Global Legal Studies* 19 (1): 143–68.

Coutin, Susan. 2000. *Legalizing Moves: Salvadoran Immigrants' Struggle for US Residency*. Ann Arbor: University of Michigan Press.

Darling, Jonathan. 2014. "Asylum and the Post-Political: Domopolitics, Depoliticisation and Acts of Citizenship." *Antipode* 46: 72–91.

Darling, Jonathan. 2017. "Forced Migration and the City: Irregularity, Informality, and the Politics of Presence." *Progress in Human Geography* 41 (2): 178–98.

Darling, Jonathan, and Harald Bauder, eds. 2019. *Sanctuary Cities and Urban Struggles Rescaling Migration, Citizenship, and Rights*. Manchester: Manchester University Press.

De Genova, Nicolas. 2002. "Migrant 'Illegality' and Deportability in Everyday Life." *Annual Review of Anthropology* 31: 419–47.

De Genova, Nicolas. 2005. *Working the Boundaries: Race, Space, and "Illegality" in Mexican Chicago*. Durham, NC: Duke University Press.

De Genova, Nicholas. 2013. "Spectacles of Migrant 'Illegality': The Scene of Exclusion, the Obscene of Inclusion." *Ethnic and Racial Studies* 36 (7): 1180–98.

De Genova, Nicholas, and Nathalie Peutz. 2010. *The Deportation Regime: Sovereignty Space and the Freedom of Movement*. Durham, NC: Duke University Press.

De Genova, Nicolas, and Ananya Roy. 2020. "Practices of Illegalisation." *Antipode* 52: 352–64.

Delvino, Nicola. 2020. "European Union and National Responses to Migrants with Irregular Status: Is the Fortress Slowly Crumbling?" In *Migrants with Irregular Status in Europe*, edited by Sarah Spencer and Anna Triandafyllidou. IMISCOE Research Series. Cham: Springer.

Depraetere, Anika, and Stijn Oosterlynck. 2017. "'I Finally Found My Place': A Political Ethnography of the Maximiliaan Refugee Camp in Brussels." *Citizenship Studies* 21 (6): 693–709.

Dikeç, Mustafa. 2004. "Voices into Noises: Ideological Determination of Unarticulated Justice Movements." *Space and Polity* 8 (2): 191–208.

Dikeç, Mustafa. 2017. "Disruptive Politics." *Urban Studies* 54 (1): 49–54.

Dreby, Joanna. 2015. *Everyday Illegal: When Policies Undermine Immigrant Families*. Oakland: University of California Press.

Düvell, Frank, Anna Triandafyllidou, and Bastian Vollmer. 2010. "Ethical Issues in Irregular Migration Research in Europe." *Population Space Place* 16 (3): 227–39.

Eltis, David, and David Richardson. 2015. *Atlas of the Transatlantic Slave Trade*. New Haven, CT: Yale University Press.

Engbersen, Godfried. 1996. "The Unknown City." *Berkeley Journal of Sociology* 40: 87–112.

Engbersen, Godfried, Marion van San, and Arjen Leerkes. 2006. "A Room with a View: Irregular Immigrants in the Legal Capital of the World." *Ethnography* 7: 209–42.

Escudero, Kevin. 2021. *Organizing While Undocumented: Immigrant Youth's Political Activism Under the Law*. New York: New York University Press.

Fassin, Didier. 2001. "The Biopolitics of Otherness: Undocumented Foreigners and Racial Discrimination in French Public Debate." *Anthropology Today*, 17: 3–7.

Fassin, Didier, and Estelle D'Halluin. 2005. "The Truth from the Body: Medical Certificates as Ultimate Evidence for Asylum Seekers." *American Anthropologist*, New Series 107 (4): 597–608.

Felder, Maxime, Sahar Fneich, and Joan Stavo-Debauge. 2023. "Social Workers and Irregular Migrants in the Assistance Circuit: Making Sense of Paradoxical Inclusion." *Social Inclusion* 11 (3): 116–27.

Flores- Gonzalez, Nilda, and Elena Gutierrez. 2010. "Taking the Public Square: The National Struggle for Immigrant Rights." In *Marcha: Latino Chicago and the Immigrant Rights Movement*, edited by Amalia Pallares and Nilda Flores- Gonzalez, 3–36. Urbana, IL: University of Illinois Press.

Foner, Nancy. 2022. *One Quarter of the Nation: Immigration and the Transformation of America*. Princeton, NJ: Princeton University Press.

Foucault, Michel. 1977. *Discipline and Punish: The Birth of the Prison*. New York: Pantheon.

Foucault, Michel. 1982. "The Subject and Power." *Critical Inquiry* 8 (Summer): 777–95.

Foucault, Michel. 1983. "On the Genealogy of Ethics: An Overview of Work in Progress." In *Michel Foucault: Beyond Structuralism and Hermeneutics*, edited by Hubert Dreyfus and Paul Rabinow, 229–52. Chicago: University of Chicago Press.

Fraser, Nancy. 2000. "Rethinking Recognition." *New Left Review* 3: 107–20.

Galindo, René. 2012. "Undocumented & Unafraid: The Dream Act 5 and the Public Disclosure of Undocumented Status as a Political Act." *The Urban Review*, 44 (5): 589–611.

Garcia Cruz, Gabriela. 2020. "Contesting 'Citizenship': The Testimonies of Undocumented Immigrant Activist Women." In *We Are Not Dreamers: Undocumented Scholars Theorize Undocumented Life in the United States*, edited by Leisy Abrego and Genevieve Negron- Gonzales, 110–127. Durham, NC: Duke University Press.

Gee, Gilbert, Brittany Morey, Katrina Walsemann, Annie Ro, and David Takeuchi. 2016. "Citizenship as Privilege and Social Identity: Implications for Psychological Distress." *American Behavioral Scientist* 60 (5–6): 680–704.

Glaeser, Andreas. 2011. *Political Epistemics: The Secret Police, the Opposition, and the End of East German Socialism*. Chicago: University of Chicago Press.

Goffman, Alice. 2014. *On the Run: Fugitive Life in an American City*. Chicago: University of Chicago Press.

Goffman, Erving. 1959. *The Presentation of Self in Everyday Life*. New York: Doubleday.

Goldring, Luin, and Patricia Landolt, eds. 2013. *Producing and Negotiating Non-Citizenship: Precarious Legal Status in Canada*. Toronto: University of Toronto Press.

Gomberg-Munoz, Ruth. 2010. *Labor and Legality: An Ethnography of a Mexican Immigrant Network*. New York: Oxford University Press.

Gonzales, Roberto. 2011. "Learning to Be Illegal: Undocumented Youth and Shifting Legal Contexts in the Transition to Adulthood." *American Sociological Review* 76 (4): 602–19.

Gonzales, Roberto. 2015. *Lives in Limbo: Undocumented and Coming of Age in America*. Oakland: University of California Press.

Gonzales, Roberto, and Leo Chavez. 2012. "Awakening to a Nightmare: Abjectivity and Illegality in the Lives of Undocumented 1.5 Generation Latino Immigrants in the United States." *Current Anthropology* 53 (3): 255–81.

Gonzales, Roberto, Carola Suárez-Orozco, and Maria Dedios-Sanguineti. 2013. "No Place to Belong: Contextualizing Concepts of Mental Health Among Undocumented Immigrant Youth in the United States." *American Behavioral Scientist* 57 (8): 1174–99.

Gonzales, Roberto, Basia Ellis, Sarah A. Rendón-García, and Kristina Brant. 2018. "(Un)authorized Transitions: Illegality, DACA, and the Life Course." *Research in Human Development*, 15(3–4), 345–59.

Gonzales, Roberto, Kristina Brant, and Benjamin Roth. 2020. "DACAmented in the Age of Deportation: Navigating Spaces of Belonging and Vulnerability in Social and Personal Lives." *Ethnic and Racial Studies* 43 (1): 60–79.

Gould, Deborah. 2009. *Moving Politics: Emotion and Act Up's Fight Against AIDS*. Chicago: University of Chicago Press.

Haas, Hein de, Stephen Castles, and Mark J. Miller. 2020. *The Age of Migration: International Population Movements in the Modern World*, 6th ed. London: Red Globe Press.

Hochschild, Jennifer, and John Mollenkopf, eds. 2009. *Bringing Outsiders In: Transatlantic Perspectives on Immigrant Political Incorporation*. Ithaca, NY: Cornell University Press.

Holston, James. 2021. *Insurgent Citizenship: Disjunctions of Democracy and Modernity in Brazil*. Princeton, NJ: Princeton University Press.

Isin, Engin F. 2002. *Being Political: Genealogies of Citizenship*. Minneapolis: University of Minnesota Press.

Isin, Engin F. 2009. "Citizenship in Flux: The Figure of the Activist Citizen." *Subjectivity* 29: 367–88.

Isin, Engin F., and Greg Nielsen, eds. 2008. *Acts of Citizenship*. London: Zed Books.

Jasper, James. 1997. *The Art of Moral Protest: Culture, Biography, and Creativity in Social Movements*. Chicago: University of Chicago Press.

Kagné, Bonaventure. 2000. *Les Sans-Papiers en Belgique: Trajectoires et Difficultés d'une vie en Marge de la Société*. Liège: Centre d'Études de l'Ethnicité et des Migrations.

Kalubi, Antoine. 2002. "Mais qui accueille la misère du monde?." In *À la Lumière des Sans-Papiers*, edited by Pickels, Antoine, 247–53. Brussels: Editions Complexe.

Karaliotas, Lazaros. 2023. "Infrastructures of Dissensus: Repartitioning the Sensible and Articulating the Political Through the Occupation of Greece's Public Broadcasting Service." *Environment and Planning C: Politics and Space*. 42 (2), 268–86.

Khosravi, Shahram. 2010. *'Illegal' Traveller: An Auto-Ethnography of Borders*. Basingstoke: Palgrave Macmillan.

Kocher, Austin and Angela Stuesse. 2021. "Undocumented Activism and Minor Politics: Inside the Cramped Political Spaces of Deportation Defense Campaigns." *Antipode*, 53: 331–54.

Lahman, Maria, Bernadette Mendoza, Katrina Rodriguez, and Jana Schwartz. 2011. "Undocumented Research Participants: Ethics and Protection in a Time of Fear." *Hispanic Journal of Behavioral Sciences* 33 (3): 304–22.

Lambert, Sébastien, and Thomas Swerts. 2019. "'From Sanctuary to Welcoming Cities': Negotiating the Social Inclusion of Undocumented Migrants in Liège, Belgium." in *Social Inclusion* 7 (4): 90–99.

Lara-Cinisomo, Sandraluz, Yange Xue, and Jeanne Brooks-Gunn. 2013. "Latino Youth's Internalising Behaviours: Links to Immigrant Status and Neighbourhood Characteristics." *Ethn. Health* 18: 315–35.

Laureys, Dawinka. 2013. *Le Mouvement des Sans Papiers et de Soutien aux Sans Papiers à Liège: Plus de Vingt ans de Mobilization.* Seraing: IHOES.

Lefebvre, Henri. 2009. *State, Space, World: Selected Essays.* Edited by Neil Brenner and Stuart Elden. Minneapolis: University of Minnesota Press.

Marcus, George E. 1995. "Ethnography in/of the World System: The Emergence of Multi-Sited Ethnography." *Annual Review of Anthropology* 24: 95–117.

Martinez, Pedro, Claudia Muñoz, Mariela Nuñez-Janes, Stephen Pavey, Fidel Rodriguez, and Marco Saavedra, eds. 2020. *Eclipse of Dreams: The Undocumented-Led Struggle for Freedom.* Chico, CA: AK Press.

Martiniello, Marco. 2003. "Belgium's Immigration Policy." *International Migration Review* 37 (1): 225–32.

Martiniello, Marco. 2006. "Political Participation, Mobilization and Representation of Immigrants and Their Offspring in Europe." In *Migration and Citizenship: Legal Status, Rights and Political Participation*, edited by Rainer Bauböck, 83–102. Amsterdam: Amsterdam University Press.

Martiniello, Marco. 2013. "Immigrant Integration and Multiculturalism in Belgium." In *Challenging Multiculturalism: European Models of Diversity*, edited by R. Taras, 120–38. Edinburgh: Edinburgh University Press.

Massey, Douglas, Jorge Durand, and Karen Pren. 2016. "Why Border Enforcement Backfired." *American Journal of Sociology* 121 (5): 1557–600.

McAdam, Doug. 1986. "Recruitment to High-Risk Activism: The Case of Freedom Summer." *American Journal of Sociology* 92 (1): 64–90.

McAdam, Doug, John McCarthy, and Zald Mayer. 1996. *Comparative Perspectives on Social Movements: Political Opportunities Mobilizing Structures and Cultural Framings.* Cambridge: Cambridge University Press.

McCarthy, John, and Zald Mayer. 1977. "Resource Mobilization and Social Movements: A Partial Theory." *American Journal of Sociology* 82 (6): 1212–41.

McKenzie, April. 2004. "A Nation of Immigrants or a Nation of Suspects? State and Local Enforcement of Immigration Laws Since 9/11." *Alabama Law Review* 55: 1149.

McNevin, Anne. 2011. *Contesting Citizenship: Irregular Migrants and New Frontiers of the Political.* New York: Columbia University Press.

McNevin, Anne. 2013. "Ambivalence and Citizenship: Theorising the Political Claims of Irregular Migrants." *Millennium: Journal of International Studies* 41 (2): 182–200.

Meeus, Bruno, Karel Arnaut, and Bas van Heur. 2019. *Arrival Infrastructures: Migration and Urban Social Mobilities.* New York: Palgrave Macmillan.

Mena Robles, Jorge, and Ruth Gomberg-Muñoz. 2016. "Activism After DACA: Lessons from Chicago's Immigrant Youth Justice League." *North American Dialogue* 19: 46–54.

Menjívar, Cecilia. 2006. "Liminal Legality: Salvadoran and Guatemalan Immigrants' Lives in the United States." *American Journal of Sociology* 111: 999–1037.

Menjívar, Cecilia, and Leisy Abrego. 2012. "Legal Violence: Immigration Law and the Lives of Central American Immigrants." *American Journal of Sociology* 117 (5): 1380–421.

Mollenkopf, John, and Jennifer Hochschild. 2010. "Immigrant Political Incorporation: Comparing Success in the United States and Western Europe." *Ethnic and Racial Studies* 33 (1): 19–38.

Monico, Gabriela. 2020. "American't: Redefining Citizenship in the U.S. Undocumented Immigrant Youth Movement." In *We Are Not Dreamers: Undocumented Scholars Theorize Undocumented Life in the United States*, edited by Leisy Abrego and Genevieve Negron-Gonzales. Durham, NC: Duke University Press: 87–110.

Ngai, Mae. 2004. *Impossible Subjects: Illegal Aliens and the Making of Modern America*. Princeton, NJ: Princeton University Press.

Nicholls, Walter. 2013. *The DREAMers: How the Undocumented Youth Movement Transformed the Immigrant Rights Debate*. Stanford, CA: Stanford University Press.

Nicholls, Walter. 2019. *The Immigrant Rights Movements: The Battle over National Citizenship*. Stanford, CA: Stanford University Press.

Nicholls, Walter. 2021. "The Uneven Geographies of Politicisation: The Case of the Undocumented Immigrant Youth Movement in the United States." *Antipode* 53: 465–85.

Nicholls, Walter, and Justus Uitermark. 2017: *Cities and Social Movements: Immigrant Right Activism in the United States, France, and the Netherlands, 1970–2015*. Chichester: Wiley-Blackwell.

Nowicka, Magdalena, and Steven Vertovec. 2014." Comparing Convivialities: Dreams and Realities of Living-with-Difference." *European Journal of Cultural Studies* 17 (4): 341–56.

Office of the United Nations High Commissioner for Human Rights. 2006. *The Rights of Non-Citizens*, New York: United Nations.

Olivas, Michael. 1984. *Plyler v. Doe, Toll v. Moreno, and Postsecondary Admissions: Undocumented Adults and "Enduring Disability."* Houston: University of Houston.

Oosterlynck, Stijn, Maarten Loopmans, Nick Schuermans, Joke Vandenabeele, and Sami Zemni. 2016. "Putting Flesh to the Bone: Looking for Solidarity in Diversity, Here and Now." *Ethnic and Racial Studies* 39 (5): 764–82.

Pallares, Amalia. 2015. *Family Activism: Immigrant Struggles and the Politics of Noncitizenship*. New Brunswick, NJ: Rutgers University Press.

Pallares, Amalia, and Nilda Flores-González, eds. 2010. ¡*Marcha!: Latino Chicago and the Immigrant Rights Movement*. Champaign: University of Illinois Press.

Patler, Caitlin, and Lauren Appelbaum. 2011. "Reaching the Dream: The Federal DREAM Act, the California Dream Act and Undocumented Student Activism." ULCA Institute for Research on Labor and Employment,*Research & Policy Brief* (10): 1–9.

Patler, Caitlin, and Roberto Gonzales. 2015. "Framing Citizenship: Media Coverage of Anti-Deportation Cases Led by Undocumented Immigrant Youth Organizations." *Journal of Ethnic and Migration Studies* 41 (9): 1453–74.

Pickels, Antoine. 2002. *À la Lumière des Sans-Papiers*, edited by in Pickels, Antoine, 7–19. Brussels: Editions Complexe.

Pila, Daniela. 2016. "'I'm Not Good Enough for Anyone': Legal Status and the Dating Lives of Undocumented Young Adults." *Sociological Forum* 31 (1): 138–58.

Pittaway, Eileen, Linda Bartolomei, and Richard Hugman. 2010. "Stop Stealing Our Stories: The Ethics of Research with Vulnerable Groups." *Journal of Human Rights Practice* 2 (2): 229–51.

Pitts, Victoria. 1998. "Reclaiming the Female Body: Embodied Identity Work, Resistance and the Grotesque." *Body & Society* 4: 67.

Polletta, Francesca. 1999. "Free Spaces in Collective Action." *Theory and Society* 28: 1–38.

Polletta, Francesca. 2006. *It Was Like a Fever: Storytelling in Protest and Politics*. Chicago: University of Chicago Press.

Purcell, Mark. 2013. "To Inhabit Well: Counterhegemonic Movements and the Right to the City." *Urban Geography* 34 (4): 560–74.

Purcell, Mark. 2014. "Possible Worlds: Henri Lefebvre and the Right to the City." *Journal of Urban Affairs* 36 (1): 141–54.

Radburn, Nicholas. 2023. *Traders in Men: Merchants and the Transformation of the Transatlantic Slave Trade*. New Haven, CT: Yale University Press.

Raineri, Luca, and Francesco Strazzari. 2021. "Dissecting the EU Response to the 'Migration Crisis.'" In *The EU and Crisis Response*, edited by Sandra Pogodda, Oliver Richmond, and Roger Mac Ginty, 201–26. Manchester: Manchester University Press.

Ramakrishnan, Karthick, and Irene Bloemraad. 2008. *Civic Hopes and Political Realities: Immigrants, Community Organizations, and Political Engagement*. New York: Russell Sage Foundation Press.

Ramirez, Maria Liliana. 2020. "Beyond Identity: Coming Out as UndocuQueer." In *We Are Not Dreamers: Undocumented Scholars Theorize Undocumented Life in the United States*, edited by Leisy Abrego and Genevieve Negron-Gonzales, 146–68. Durham, NC: Duke University Press.

Rancière, Jacques. 1999. *Disagreement*. Minnesota: University of Minnesota Press.

Rancière, Jacques. 2004. *The Politics of Aesthetics: The Distribution of the Sensible*. London: Continuum.

Rancière, Jacques. 2010. *Dissensus: On Politics and Aesthetics*. London: Continuum.

The Roestone Collective. 2014. "Safe Space: Towards a Reconceptualization." *Antipode* 46: 1346–65.

Sassen, Saskia. 2005. "The Repositioning of Citizenship and Alienage: Emergent Subjects and Spaces for Politics." *Globalizations* 2 (1): 79–94.

Sati, Joel. 2020. ""Other" Borders: The Illegal as Normative Metaphor." In *We Are Not Dreamers: Undocumented Scholars Theorize Undocumented Life in the United States*, edited by Leisy Abrego and Genevieve Negron-Gonzales. Durham, NC: Duke University Press: 23–45.

Schinkel, Willem. 2009. "'Illegal Aliens' and the State, or: Bare Bodies vs the Zombie." *International Sociology* 24 (6): 779–806.

Scott, James. 2008. *Weapons of the Weak: Everyday Forms of Peasant Resistance*. New Haven, CT: Yale University Press.

Seif, Hinda. 2004. "Wise Up!" Undocumented (Im)migrant Youth, Latino Legislators, and the Struggle for Higher Education Access." *Latino Studies* 2 (2): 210–30.

Seif, Hinda. 2011. "'Unapologetic and Unafraid': Immigrant Youth Come Out from the Shadows." *New Directions for Child and Adolescent Development* 134: 59–75.

Sewell, William. 1992. "A Theory of Structure: Duality, Agency, and Transformation." *American Journal of Sociology* 98 (1): 1–29.

Sigona, Nando. 2012. "'I Have Too Much Baggage': The Impacts of Legal Status on the Social Worlds of Irregular Migrants." *Social Anthropology* 20: 50–65.

Siméant, Johanna. 1998. *La Cause des Sans Papiers*. Paris: Presses de Sciences Po.

Simons, Maarten, and Jan Masschelein. 2010. "Governmental, Political and Pedagogic Subjectivation: Foucault with Rancière." *Educational Philosophy and Theory* 42 (5–6): 588–605.

Small, Mario. 2009. "'How Many Cases Do I Need?': On Science and the Logic of Case Selection in Field-Based Research." *Ethnography* 10 (1): 5–38.

Smith, Neil. 1984: *Uneven Development: Nature, Capital and the Production of Space*. Oxford: Basil Blackwell.

Swartz, Sharlene. 2011. "'Going Deep' and 'Giving Back': Strategies for Exceeding Ethical Expectations When Researching Amongst VulnerableYouth." *Qualitative Research* 11(1): 47–68.

Swerts, Thomas. 2015. "Gaining a Voice: Storytelling and Undocumented Youth Activism in Chicago." *Mobilization* 20 (3): 385–402.

Swerts, Thomas. 2017a. "Creating Space for Citizenship: The Liminal Politics of Undocumented Activism." *International Journal of Urban and Regional Research* 41: 379–95.

Swerts, Thomas. 2017b. "Marching Beyond Borders: Non-Citizen Citizenship and Transnational Undocumented Activism in Europe." In *Within and Beyond Citizenship: Borders, Membership and Belonging*, edited by Nando Sigona and Roberto Gonzales, 126–42. Abingdon: Routledge.

Swerts, Thomas. 2018. "'Check Your Privilege': Cross-Status Alliances in the DREAM Movement." In *Relational Poverty Politics: (Un)thinkable Forms, Struggles, Possibilities*, edited by Vicky Lawson and Sarah Elwood, 166–82. Athens: The University of Georgia Press.

Swerts, Thomas. 2021. "Politics Disrupted? Collective Intentionality, Inaugural Performativity, and Institutional Receptivity in Undocumented Migrant Struggles." *Antipode* 53: 355–78.

Swerts, Thomas, and Stijn Oosterlynck. 2021. "In Search of Recognition: The Political Ambiguities of Undocumented Migrants' Active Citizenship." *Journal of Ethnic and Migration Studies* 47 (3): 668–85.

Swerts, Thomas, and Walter Nicholls. 2021. "Undocumented Immigrant Activism and the Political: Disrupting the Order or Reproducing the Status Quo?" *Antipode* 53: 319–30.

Swyngedouw, Erik. 2011. "Interrogating Post-Democracy: Reclaiming Egalitarian Political Spaces." *Political Geography* 30 (7): 370–80.

Ticktin, Miriam. 2011. *Casualties of Care: Immigration and the Politics of Humanitarianism in France*. Berkeley: University of California Press.

Tilly, Charles. 2010. *Regimes and Repertoires*. Chicago: University of Chicago Press.

Uitermark, Justus and Walter Nicholls. 2014. "From Politicization to Policing: The Rise and Decline of New Social Movements in Amsterdam and Paris." *Antipode* 46: 970–91.

Van Hamme, Gilles, Taïs Grippa, and Mathieu Van Criekingen. 2016. "Migratory Movements and Dynamics of Neighbourhoods in Brussels." *Brussels Studies*, Collection générale, n° 97: 1–13.

Van Meeteren, Masha, Godfried Engbersen, and Marion Van San. 2009. "Striving for a Better Position: Aspirations and the Role of Cultural, Economic and Social Capital for Irregular Migrants in Belgium." *International Migration Review* 43 (4): 881–907.

Van Meeteren, Masha, Marion Van San, and Godfried Engbersen. 2007. *Irreguliere Immigranten in België. Inbedding, Uitsluiting en Criminaliteit*. Rotterdam: Erasmus Universiteit Rotterdam.

Varsanyi, Monica, ed. 2010. *Taking Local Control: Immigration Policy Activism in U.S. Cities and States*. Stanford, CA: Stanford University Press.

Vertongen, Youri. 2024. *Papiers Pour Tous. Le cas de la Coordination des sans-papiers de Belgique (2014–2020)*. Louvain-la-Neuve: ACADEMIA-EME.

Voss, Kim, and Irene Bloemraad, eds. 2011. *Rallying for Immigrant Rights*. Berkeley: University of California Press.

Wacquant, Loïc. 2004. *Body & Soul*. Oxford: Oxford University Press.

Wacquant, Loïc. 2008. *Urban Outcasts: A Comparative Sociology of Advanced Marginality*. Cambridge: Polity Press.

Wacquant, Loïc. 2015. "For a Sociology of Flesh and Blood." *Qualitative Sociology* 38: 1–11.

Weber, Max. 1921 (1976). *Wirtschaft und Gesellschaft. Grundriss der Verstehenden Soziologie*. Tübingen: J.C.B. Mohr (Paul Siebeck).

Willen, Sarah. 2007. "Exploring 'Illegal' and 'Irregular' Migrants' Lived Experiences of Law and State Power." *International Migration* 45: 2–7.

Willner-Reid, Matthew. 2015. "Emergence and Decline of a Protest Movement: The Anti-Deportation Campaign for Afghan Asylum Seekers in Belgium." *Journal of Refugee Studies* 28 (4): 505–22.

Wilson, Helen. 2017. "On Geography and Encounter: Bodies, Borders, and Difference." *Progress in Human Geography* 41 (4): 451–71.

Wilson, William. 1987. *The Truly Disadvantaged: The Inner City the Underclass and Public Policy*. Chicago: University of Chicago Press.

Zhou, Min, and Roberto Gonzales. 2019. "Divergent Destinies: Children of Immigrants Growing Up in the United States." *Annual Review of Sociology* 45 (1): 383–99.

Zimmerman, Arely. 2011. "A Dream Detained: Undocumented Latino Youth and the DREAM Movement." In *NACLA Report on the America*, 14–38. New York: North American Congress on Latin America.

Index

For the benefit of digital users, indexed terms that span two pages (e.g., 52–53) may, on occasion, appear on only one of those pages.